THE GREAT TAX ROBBERY

How Britain Became a Tax Haven
for Fat Cats and Big Business

Richard Brooks

ONEWORLD

A Oneworld Book

First published by Oneworld Publications 2013
This paperback edition published in 2014

Copyright © Richard Brooks 2013, 2014

ISBN 978-1-78074-371-4
eBook ISBN 978-1-78074-619-7

Text designed and typeset by Tetragon, London
Printed and bound in Denmark by Nørhaven

Oneworld Publications
10 Bloomsbury Street
London WC1B 3SR
England
www.oneworld-publications.com

For Alex and Joe

Contents

Prologue		7
1	Welcome to Tax Dodge City	10
2	An Unwelcome Guest	34
3	Opportunity Knocks	67
4	Foreign Adventures	93
5	Breaking Up Isn't Hard to Do	124
6	A Rich Man's Kingdom	148
7	Sell-Out	171
8	Hear No Evil, See No Evil	197
9	On Her Majesty's Offshore Service	209
10	Poor Show	223
11	Called to Account	241
Notes		261
Acknowledgements		283
Index		285

List of Illustrations

Figure 1: UK corporate profits and corporation tax (1991–2011)

Figure 2: The proportion of UK corporation tax paid by small companies

Figure 3: Economic growth rates and average tax rates in the UK (1960–2000)

Figure 4: No correlation: the economic growth rates of 22 OECD countries and their overall taxation levels

Figure 5: Barclays buys a gas pipeline (and some tax breaks)

Figure 6: Vodafone Group plc uses Luxembourg and Switzerland to loan Mannesmann AG €42.5bn and avoid billions in UK tax

Figure 7: Behind closed doors: the locked office that is home to Vodafone's Luxembourg companies' multi-billion pound Swiss finance branches (Credit: Richard Brooks)

Figure 8: Pearson US earns a tax break

Figure 9: The business service centre hosting Pearson's Luxembourg companies and branches (Credit: Richard Brooks)

Figure 10: Johnnie Walker goes Dutch

Figure 11: A typical structure used by a London-based hedge fund to minimize tax

Figure 12: Dodgers' charter: Exchequer Secretary David Gauke (seated centre) and HMRC permanent secretary Dave Hartnett (seated right) sign the agreement with Switzerland that effectively de-criminalises tax evasion (Credit: HMRC)

Prologue

Public Accounts Committee chairman, Margaret Hodge MP, looked the country's most senior tax inspector in the eye. 'I am going to start with a rather tough question. It seems to me that you lied when you told the Treasury Select Committee on 12 September that "I do not deal with Goldman's tax affairs."'[1]

Dave Hartnett struggled to reconcile his statement to an earlier committee of MPs with the leaking that morning of an internal memo revealing that he had 'shaken hands' with Goldman Sachs on a deal over a tax avoidance scheme. The normally assured civil servant shifted uneasily in his seat and claimed his response had been taken out of context. In any case, he had met the bank not to settle the tax dispute personally but to resolve a 'difficult relationship issue'.

Goldman's scheme – a plan to avoid millions of pounds in national insurance contributions on bankers' bonuses via offshore companies and trusts – had crumbled under legal scrutiny and other companies deploying it had long since coughed up. The famously belligerent US investment bank, by contrast, 'resisted for five more years', recorded the leaked memo. Yet when its resistance was eventually defeated by a tax tribunal and it came to agreeing the bill, Goldman was excused an interest charge of around £20m that was almost as much as the national insurance they had tried to avoid. Even the top taxman confessed this was a 'mistake'.

The giveaway might indeed have been excused as a slip-up had it not slotted into a pattern of big business winning tax deals that would never be given to anybody else. While taxpayers out in the recession-hit real world were feeling the heat of increasingly impatient tax demands, the MPs were also grappling with another, far larger, 'sweetheart' deal for a large corporation.

Just a few weeks before the Goldman Sachs settlement, the same taxman, Dave Hartnett, had sat down with the finance director of Vodafone and reached an agreement over an offshore scheme through which Britain's third biggest company finances its world-wide businesses. The arrangement had saved the company several billions of pounds in tax over a decade but potentially fell foul of British anti-tax avoidance laws. Vodafone itself had set aside over £3bn to cover the tax and interest costs for just half these years but after meeting Mr Hartnett walked away with a £1.25bn bill for the whole lot, plus a raft of other concessions. Flush with his negotiating success, Vodafone's finance director told stock market analysts the following day that his deal with the taxman was 'very good' and 'preserves the very significant benefits of our efficient group tax structure, which we have benefited from for many years'.

The deal was far from good for every other taxpayer in the country. Within weeks of it being exposed it had sparked a protest movement and enquiries from two parliamentary committees. Their questions were stonewalled by ministers and mandarins who repeatedly claimed that confidentiality laws barred any discussion. In fact, the MPs established, HM Revenue and Customs could choose whether to divulge details of its settlements to parliament. But the discretion was vested in Mr Hartnett, who, it so happened, had also approved the deals that he had negotiated and was now being asked to account for. 'My problem with this,' thundered Hodge, 'is that you are the guy who does the deals, you are the guy who sits on the board that vets the deals, you are the Commissioner who vets the deals and you are the guy who decides what comes into the public domain,' adding (for anybody left in doubt): 'It is an outrageous, unprecedented situation.'

With little seasonal goodwill, five days before Christmas 2011 Hodge's committee published what she called a 'damning indictment of HMRC and the way its senior officials handle tax disputes with large corporations'. Amid the litany of 'governance' and 'process' failings, the most powerful criticism was also the simplest. 'The department [HMRC] is not being even-handed in its treatment of taxpayers,' concluded the MPs.

Parliament had often lamented the complexity and occasional incompetence of British tax collection. This time it scored a direct hit on something much more serious.

When a tax system favours an elite over the majority it is fatally undermined. The veracity of senior officials was not the point. Nothing less than the integrity of British taxation was at stake.

1
Welcome to
Tax Dodge City

'*I like paying taxes. With them I buy civilization.*'
American Supreme Court Judge Oliver Wendell Holmes, Jr, 1927

'*I'm mortified to have to pay 50%. I use the NHS [but] I can't use public transport any more. Trains are always late, most state schools are shit, and I've gotta give you, like, four million quid – are you having a laugh? When I got my tax bill in . . . I was ready to go and buy a gun and randomly open fire.*'
Pop star Adele, 2011

As I contemplated the dazzlingly remunerative possibility of writing a book on tax avoidance, one slightly deflating factor in the calculations was the prospect of handing over 40% of the income to the taxman.

But a quick check of what I get in return lifts the gloom. For every pound I earn I will pay around 7 pence for immediate access to professional healthcare for my family, 5 pence for my children's education, 2 pence for living in relative security, around the same to have the country I live in defended and 11 pence for pensions and social security for my compatriots and my future self. I even contribute half a pence to aid the developing world and, less heart-warmingly, 3 pence in interest to the various institutions from which we have collectively borrowed in order to spend more on these things than we have paid in so far. I might have plenty of quibbles with how the government to which I hand over a large chunk of my income spends it, but I can't doubt the overall value I get for my money. Despite all the waste in the system – the misguided ventures, the mismanagement, the disastrous IT contracts, the consultants' fees, the overpriced private finance deals – as a provider of the things we need most of all the state remains fantastically efficient compared to any feasible alternative.

It cost HMRC just £3.5bn to gather £446bn in taxes in 2010/11, a collection fee of 0.8%. Even if the costs incurred by businesses in playing their part in the process were added to this figure, it would still be far lower than that for other revenue-raising organizations; a typical charity spends between 15 and 25% of its income on fundraising.[1] Spending the money is relatively cost-effective; the Department for International Development, for example, spends 3% of its budget on running costs, whereas Britain's largest (and apparently well run) charity in the same sort of field, Oxfam, lays out 10% on support costs.[2] The collective provision of healthcare through the National Health Service is far more efficient than private systems elsewhere in the world. An authoritative study into healthcare systems over twenty-five years published in the *British Medical Journal* in 2011 concluded: 'In cost-effective terms, i.e. economic input versus clinical output, the USA healthcare system was one of the least cost-effective in reducing mortality rates whereas the UK was one of the most cost-effective over the period.'[3] The central distinction between the systems is that one is privately funded, the other paid for by tax.

If this were a club only a fool would not join. In fact nobody does opt out, but plenty happily enjoy the benefits of membership without paying their subs. These include tax evaders, who in principle at least can be hauled before the club committee and given a good ticking off and a demand for arrears or – in the more serious cases – expulsion from the club for a short spell at Her Majesty's pleasure. They undermine it not just by depleting its funds, but by weakening their stake in it. Just as the best-run clubs comprise members paying their dues and demanding they're properly spent, so honouring tax obligations strengthens a country's democracy.

Tax evasion is simple enough: it's the cash-in-hand plumbing job or piano lesson that doesn't make it onto a tax return, the offshore income that remains hidden from the taxman, or the more sophisticated fraud involving multiple business accounts and dodgy invoices. It is strictly criminal, although in almost all cases it is punished only with civil penalties. Prosecutions for evasion of direct taxes (like income tax) run at just thirty per year even though the offence is estimated by HMRC to cost around £5.5bn annually (a similar amount is charitably assigned to taxpayers'error' and 'failure to take reasonable care').[4] Other observers argue credibly that the figure is in fact far higher, perhaps over £40bn, since the Revenue somehow manages to overlook large swathes of the black economy it should be pinning down.[5] Evasion of indirect taxes (VAT and customs levies like tobacco duty) officially costs about £7bn annually and generates around 350 prosecutions.[6] Tax credit fraud amounting to around £400m a year generates 60 or so prosecutions.[7] Benefit frauds, which cost £1bn a year, were prosecuted 9000 times in 2009/10.[8] This table shows the hierarchy of tolerance towards cheating the public purse:

Tax/benefit	Prosecutions per £1bn of fraud [a]
Direct taxes (e.g. income tax)	5
Indirect taxes (e.g. Customs duties)	50
Tax credits (child and working family)	140
Benefits (e.g. unemployment, disability)	9000

So theft by the poor warrants the full force of the law and evading duties on booze and fags is pretty serious too. A dim view has been taken of the former ever since the birth of the welfare state, the noble intentions of which were not to be undermined by the dishonest. Now it's the stuff of eye-catching tabloid stories and makes a politically unmissable target. Customs and excise frauds have older and more piratical origins and for hundreds of years have faced the stern law-enforcement traditions of Customs officers.

But evasion of direct taxes meets with more understanding, perhaps reflecting the historical reluctance of the income tax authorities to question a person's honesty when incomes were not always meticulously recorded, nor expected to be. Income tax evasion, usually a crime of omission, can also be harder to prosecute, as the Revenue was famously reminded in 1989 with the acquittal of Ken Dodd by a hometown jury, even though there was no dispute he had taken a fortune in cash and omitted it from his tax return. And income left off a tax return might turn out not to be taxable in the first place, as a 2012 jury found to be the case with the thousands of pounds deposited in football manager Harry Redknapp's Monaco bank account by his chairman Milan Mandaric.

There is plenty of prejudice behind the inconsistencies, too. Less well represented, the poor make easier targets than the rich. Claiming from the state a benefit to which one is not entitled is viewed less sympathetically than evading a payment that should be made. The former is theft, the latter a bit of ducking and diving. But in truth the intention is similar in both cases. Indeed, tax evasion is likely to involve greater sums and be driven by greed alone with no element of need (a tax evader, by definition, has the means to pay his dues). Yet wealthy 'tax scroungers' face no meaningful deterrent in the way that benefit fraudsters do; prosecutions for the thousands of rich individuals secretly stashing millions in offshore tax havens, for example, are forsaken in favour of generous 'amnesties' and inter-governmental agreements that effectively decriminalize the richest form of tax evasion.

Mind the gap

This apparent indifference to certain forms of tax dodging can turn to the most remarkable defensiveness. In May 2005 I asked for information on a concept that the Revenue had been working on for some years: the 'Tax Gap'. This is the difference between what the tax authorities collect and what they would do if everyone played by the letter and spirit of the rules. After putting up a series of risible arguments against disclosing this information – it would 'embolden' people to dodge tax and even hit the stock market (which would *never* do) – the Revenue was told to hand over the data by the Information Commissioner. He made the obvious point that 'if the public realized the extent to which tax evasion is a drain on the economy it could create an atmosphere in which evasion and avoidance would be less socially acceptable'. Only after wasting tens of thousands of pounds setting up a tribunal hearing that it refused to go through with did the Revenue finally, three years after first being asked, reveal the Tax Gap.

What emerged was a measure not just of widespread tax evasion but of a far trickier form of tax dodging: tax *avoidance*. The term has long been understood to cover the legal reduction of tax bills by exploiting loopholes in tax law and can be traced back to the 1900s, when shifting income offshore was first described in parliament as 'legal avoidance' in contrast to 'evasion by omission'.[9] This longstanding offshore dodge was closed down, in principle at least, in 1914 when most British residents became taxable on all their worldwide income. It was the start of a routine in which tax avoidance schemes would be legislated against by successive governments operating on the principle that income tax should be levied on real incomes, not those reduced by steps taken to get round the laws.

Tax avoiders would then find a smarter trick to subvert the new law. So, for example, post-1914 the better-advised tax avoider would put income into offshore trusts that ensured the income *really* remained his but was not treated as belonging to him by the new tax law. And when tax law and administration adapted to counter these structures, there would be further tricks to get round these changes. By 1937, the pattern prompted the then chancellor to describe tax avoidance as 'the adoption of ingenious methods for reducing liability which are within the law but which none the less defeat the intention on which the law is founded'.[10] Fifty years later, renowned tax judge Lord Templeman expressed the concept in terms of the financial result: 'The taxpayer engaged in tax avoidance does not reduce his income or suffer a loss or incur expenditure but nevertheless obtains a reduction in his liability to tax as if he had.'[11]

HM Revenue and Customs today defines avoidance in a way the pre-war chancellor would recognize, as involving transactions with tax consequences that are 'unintended and unexpected [by legislators]'.[12] In other words, engineering lower tax bills in accordance with the letter of the law, but not in its spirit. When more recently, for example, a millionaire City headhunter called Philippa D'Arcy entered into a convoluted series of transactions involving the short-term sale and repurchase of government securities ('gilts') to generate tax-deductible 'manufactured interest' payments offset by a non-taxable gain (if you're confused, don't worry, you're supposed to be) she didn't part with a penny in anything apart from fees but created a £600,000 tax break.[13] This was clearly tax avoidance, on any definition. As it was when one of Britain's biggest multinational companies, Prudential, executed a financial derivative transaction known as a currency swap at a manipulated price purely to generate a similarly lopsided result that knocked £30m off its tax bill.[14] The arcane laws they were relying on were not intended to be used in these ways and the taxpayers reduced their tax bills without incurring any real cost.

After much legal toing and froing to establish whether these ruses really did squeeze through the loopholes their creators had targeted, the City millionaire kept her tax break, the insurance company didn't. But in the tax avoidance lottery it's impossible to lose more than the lawyers' and accountants' fees that are a fraction of the winnings on offer. And if you can afford it, your chances are good; official figures show that an individual with a tax avoidance scheme, if investigated, has a 50/50 chance of keeping the tax break, while a big company has around a 60/40 chance.[15] What's more, if he loses he's no worse off (beyond his advisers' fees) than if he hadn't taken the bet. With such sporting odds, and the taxman acting like a deranged bookie giving losing punters their stakes back, it's not surprising that an entire tax avoidance industry quietly operates from hundreds of offices across Britain. The millionaire and the insurance company did not stumble across their loopholes; the schemes were sold to them by experts in their field, men and women whose lives are dedicated to prospecting for tax wheezes. It's a gold rush that makes some spectacularly rich but takes a heavy toll on everybody else. HMRC puts the cost of such 'artificial' tax avoidance at around £7.5bn annually, though it admits even this is an underestimate since it covers only the schemes it identifies and, despite rules demanding disclosure of tax avoidance, not all is spotted.[16]

This chicanery has long provoked strong reactions. In 1914 Liberal chancellor Lloyd George described tax avoidance techniques as 'malignant, mischievous, pernicious, poisonous methods for tempting honest people to defraud the revenue', though he declined to tackle them since decent people had better things to do. 'There is no doubt at all if a man sets his mind, and has nothing else to do, he can devise all sorts of schemes for the purposes of avoiding the revenue. But if he is busy it will be otherwise. It is the old story, Satan finds some mischief for idle hands to do.'[17] What Lloyd George reckoned without was the thousands of advisers that would devise the schemes for the busy. When nearly a century later comic Jimmy Carr bought one of their more dubious products – sending most of his £3m earnings into an offshore trust before borrowing them back indefinitely so he could continue to enjoy his income but effectively pay tax at around 1% – Prime Minister David Cameron echoed Lloyd George's sentiment in describing the ruse as 'morally wrong'.

Cameron's intervention marked quite a progression for the right-of-centre political establishment, in rhetoric at least. As chancellor in the 1920s, Winston Churchill asserted the right of a man 'so to arrange his affairs as not to attract taxes enforced by the Crown so far as he can legitimately do so within the law'.[18] Carr's immediate tweeted self-justification after being exposed by *The Times* – 'I pay what I have to and not a penny more' – reflected this view, though he rapidly recanted in the face of universal ridicule and potential career death. Fellow comedian Frankie Boyle better caught the public mood when he counter-tweeted that tax avoiders should 'look at it as a children's hospital buying you a pool table'.

Churchill was, however, right; it's a truism that the law must set the boundary for taxation. But the law never perfectly matches the right thing to do and certainly has never kept up with the schemers. Avoidance might be legal but, in passing the burden onto everybody else, it is essentially a selfish act. It could even be thought more distasteful than straightforwardly dishonest evasion. A tax avoider's efforts in pursuit of self-enrichment at the expense of others tend to be far more concerted, contrived and calculated. Even the big tax avoiders recognize the moral bankruptcy if it suits them: when Tesco sued the *Guardian* in 2008 over (in this instance mistaken) allegations of large-scale tax avoidance, the company's lawyers claimed the reports amounted to 'a devastating attack on its integrity and ethics'.[19]

When it involves using laws in ways that were not intended by legislators and would not have been tolerated had they been foreseen, tax avoidance is at heart an anti-democratic business. Tax policy-makers define tax avoidance by reference to the underlying purpose of the tax laws they put on the statute book. And as long as they frame laws that tax real economic results, this is a sound approach. So when in 2011 George Osborne told parliament that 'we are doing more today to clamp down on tax avoidance than in any Budget in recent years',[20] we were reassured he was getting to grips with the wealthy dodging their contributions to Britain's depleted finances. But should we have been?

Relief on the Riviera

With her bling and perma-tan, Philip Green's wife Tina certainly looks at home in Monte Carlo. And maybe the Riviera sunshine does appeal more to the native South African than dreary old London. But why live on this particular overcrowded 2km stretch of the Mediterranean coast?

Free from income tax in Monaco, Tina Green is the ultimate owner, through a series of offshore companies and trusts, of the Arcadia business empire run by her husband Philip and comprising some of the British high street's biggest names such as Topshop and Dorothy Perkins. It is a set up that in 2005 famously enabled the Greens to take a £1.2bn dividend from Arcadia tax free, saving them the £300m tax that would have been due if it had been paid to a UK tax resident.

When protesters took to the streets in the autumn of 2010 to target Britain's biggest tax avoiders, they made Green's business one of their main targets. But were they right to dub him 'Britain's most notorious serial tax avoider'? As Green pointed out, he pays income tax here and his companies pay corporation tax. His wife really lives in Monaco, just like many sports stars including Paula Radcliffe and businessmen such as Sir Stelios Haji-Ioannou.

Look again at the Revenue's definition of tax avoidance. There is nothing 'unintended' in a Monaco resident not paying UK income tax on dividends from a British business. By ensuring the Arcadia group has long been in his wife's hands, Philip Green exploits not an overlooked wrinkle in British tax law, but a well-known fault line in the world financial system. On at least six separate occasions before the tax scandal broke, Philip Green used the expression 'I bought Arcadia' to describe his acquisition of the company in 2002.[21] But legally *Mrs* Green bought it. So on the official view of tax avoidance, the man whose business empire is in the hands of his tax haven-based wife is still *not* a tax avoider. Of course on any plain understanding of the term, tax avoiding is clearly what Green is doing. He is going out of his way to escape, dodge, avert, circumvent – *avoid* – a tax bill. He and his wife can cruise on their £20m Benetti yacht, the *Lionheart*, courtesy of a British business empire that thrives on taxpayer-funded infrastructure and a work-force educated at public expense, while contributing a far smaller share of their income towards these things than even their lower-paid customers and staff. But officially they are *not* avoiding tax.

The more realistic public understanding of tax avoidance explains why Arcadia became one of the early targets of UK Uncut, the protest movement that erupted on Britain's high streets at the end of 2010. As it did for another well-known retailer, Boots. Following its takeover by a private equity group in 2007, the company's tax payments halved as the new owners loaded the company up with the billions of pounds of debt on which it now makes tax-deductible interest payments. As a result, out of operating profits of over £1bn in 2010/11, the now Swiss-controlled group paid just £59m in tax.[22] Tax reduction was central, as it is to most private equity buyouts, but again this structure would not meet the official definition of tax avoidance. Nor would the corporate contortions of the British multinationals that break up their businesses and shunt different parts around the world for fiscal rather than commercial reasons. When a company such as drinks giant Diageo saves tens of millions of pounds a year in tax by setting up a Dutch company to own proudly Scottish brands like Johnnie Walker purely for tax breaks, leaving its Kilmarnock distillers with marginal profits and paying minimal taxes, again this is officially *not* tax avoidance.[23]

One bizarre episode best illustrates the gap between the technocratic view of tax avoidance and the real world. In 2002 the chairman of the Inland Revenue repeatedly told a Parliamentary Select Committee that the sale of 650 tax offices to a Bermuda-resident company, Mapeley Steps Ltd, did not involve tax avoidance. But when the MPs came to question Mapeley's chief executive some weeks later, he admitted the company had 'structured its tax affairs to minimise exposure to capital gains tax'. The committee declined to enter the make-believe world in which going offshore to 'minimise exposure' to tax was not avoiding tax: 'Tax avoidance was clearly one of Mapeley's objectives in the way the deal was structured,' it concluded.[24] What independent MPs thought was clearly tax avoidance was, officially, nothing of the sort.

Now you see it, now you don't

The MPs were more in tune with public opinion than the mandarins. Few would disagree that a British company that 'structured its tax affairs to minimise' its tax bill on British income by using an offshore tax haven had avoided tax. In June 2011 when a BBC survey asked whether 'the government should crack down on tax avoidance by business operating in the UK' it defined tax avoidance as 'where people or businesses arrange their financial affairs to minimise the amount of tax they pay while remaining within the law'. Eighty-four percent of people agreed with the proposal.[25]

But since the kind of 'structuring' favoured by Philip Green, Boots, Diageo and Mapeley does not meet the official test of tax avoidance, none of their schemes – which five out of six people would evidently like to see stopped – enter calculations of the 'Tax Gap'. HMRC's estimate of corporation tax avoided by companies is just £3.6bn,[26] a figure reached by looking at what it calls 'artificial avoidance' schemes of the sort that meet its limited definition of tax avoidance. The scale of what could be called the 'real world' tax avoidance favoured by the Greens and Diageos, as opposed to the technocrat's narrow legalistic version, is not officially measured but is undoubtedly far higher. A report for the Trades Union Congress by tax campaigner Richard Murphy in 2008 took a broader view and came to a figure of around £12bn for tax avoided by companies, and £13bn for individuals.[27] Across the 770 largest multinationals dealt with by the Revenue's Large Business Service in 2011, £25.5bn of tax was at stake on enquiries,[28] around half of which relates to the real world tax avoidance of structuring businesses to reduce tax.[29] And many times this amount again is likely to be lost to offshore arrangements that the Revenue either fails to notice or chooses not to contest. Tax investigators can in any case only nibble at the edges of these arrangements, merely checking they haven't been mis-priced and leaving untouched several tens of billions of pounds every year of real world tax avoidance. Which represents a sizeable proportion of the cuts demanded by the government's deficit reduction programme, set in its 2010 spending review at £42bn in 2012/13, rising to £83bn in 2014/15, but certain to be substantially more after a couple of years of economic stagnation.[30]

It is only against the limited band of 'artificial avoidance' that the government makes any meaningful move, but this is enough to sustain the Great Illusion at the heart of recent governments' tax policies. Like any decent table magician, successive chancellors direct the audience's attention to what they want it to see while away from the punters' gaze the trick is played. Artificial avoidance meeting the official definition is very publicly tackled, while more quietly the opportunities for some, especially the biggest companies, to 'structure' their way out of a tax bill are expanded. As a result, the biggest corporate tax avoiders no longer need to design their own schemes; the government does it for them.

State-sponsored tax dodging

Of course companies and rich individuals still *choose* to exploit the rules to their limits, and their choices make them legitimate targets of protests. But the critics who say the demonstrators should be waving placards outside the Treasury have a point, too. The central issue in British tax avoidance today *is* a political one; it is nothing less than the legal sanctioning of real world tax avoidance. So what the government regards as tax avoidance diverges ever further from what everybody else does – broadly transactions designed simply to reduce a tax bill below real income at the relevant headline rate – and from Lord Templeman's similarly plain view of the practice.

The gap widens in two ways. First, clear flaws in tax law are not corrected when they give undue tax advantages to business. The limitless tax deductibility of interest payments used by Boots to slash its tax bill is the archetypal example, damaging enough that just six weeks before the May 2010 election, a then shadow Conservative tax minister David Gauke promised to get tough on this excess. But by the time he was in a position to do something about it as a real minister, his tune had changed. The rules would not be altered, he announced in November 2010, because they 'are considered by businesses as a competitive advantage'.[31]

The richest individuals benefit similarly from the government's reluctance to confiscate their sweeties. Although blatantly artificial income tax avoidance schemes rarely survive long after their discovery, structural advantages that facilitate real world tax avoidance linger on the statute books. Perhaps the most iniquitous tax break is the uniquely British exemption for income kept offshore by 'non-domiciled' individuals who, usually through some quirk of inheritance, can claim allegiance to another country despite being full UK residents. Entrenched by successive governments, the status enables the *Daily Mail*'s English-born-and-bred proprietor Lord Rothermere, for example, to save tax by channelling income from his media empire through a network of offshore companies and family trusts.[32]

Second, the rules of the game are relaxed to render real world tax avoidance increasingly irresistible to the rich and large corporations. In the late 1990s the last Labour government removed the tax on dividends that had ensured companies at least had to cough up some tax on profits if they wanted to pay them out to their owners, and would have presented the Arcadia group with a £300m bill on Mrs Green's dividend. In 2000, Chancellor Gordon Brown responded to the demands of his new friends in the world of private equity by reducing capital gains tax from 40% to 10%. The income that with some basic financial engineering they transformed into capital gains would famously be taxed at lower rates than their cleaners were paying.[33] Then, as one of its final measures, New Labour began dismantling the rules that guarded against industrial-scale tax avoidance by British multinationals, exempting from tax profits returned to the UK from overseas subsidiary companies and in the process creating a substantial new impetus to send income offshore. All were measures enabling the privileged, with the right advice, to take their tax bills way below their real incomes multiplied by the prevailing income tax rates. But again, none would be avoiding tax.

The coalition government swiftly followed up with tax exemptions for companies' tax haven branches and for profits parked in tax haven subsidiary companies in the most contrived manner. At the same time, the Treasury persists with allowing tax breaks for the costs of funding these offshore set-ups from the UK. In other words, income can be moved to tax havens and costs kept in the

UK: a deliciously simple recipe for real world tax avoidance. Even a senior tax partner in one of Britain's 'Big 4' accountancy firms earning handsome fees from these new opportunities shook his head when I discussed the changes with him: 'What they've ended up with is the worst of all worlds.'[34] But exploiting the new rules will, of course, *not* be tax avoidance.

The result of the sustained retreat from taxing the biggest companies is tax contributions that lag behind corporate profits. Between 1999 and 2011 British companies' profits increased by 58%, while corporation tax payments went up by less than 5% (a gap only marginally accounted for by a cut in official corporation tax rates from 30% to 28% in 2008). If 2007 – before the financial crisis began – is considered instead, the figures become 54% and 29% respectively[35] (see figure 1). Other studies have looked at trends in effective corporation tax rates for Britain's largest companies

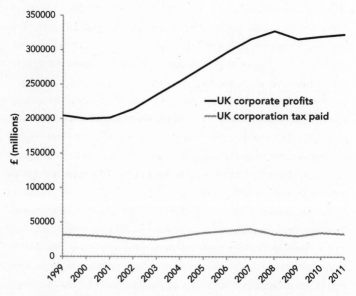

Fig. 1 UK corporate profits and corporation tax (1991-2011)[36]

and found them to be around 5% below their officially declared rates, much of which is attributable to structures adopted for tax purposes.[37]

This pervasive, expanding tax avoidance does more than just short-change government finances. Available almost exclusively to wealthy companies and individuals, it widens inequality. It also distorts the democratic process. A mega-rich 'non-dom' lured to the UK with the promise of keeping his offshore fortunes tax free as a favour from the government is disproportionately likely to become a major donor to a political party with privileged access to some powerful people and influence in matters beyond taxation. Most famously of all, the benefits of non-dom status have helped Lord (Michael) Ashcroft to make huge donations to the Conservative Party and become close to its leading fig-ures, notably William Hague. Much the same can be said for Sir Ronald Cohen and his relationship with Labour's Gordon Brown, although his versatility makes him popular with the coalition too and he is now a leading light in David Cameron's plans for the Big Society.

Tax avoidance exacerbates business inequality, too: a corner shop can't afford the VAT schemes and offshore structures that Tesco has used to reduce its financing costs and eventually its prices at the till. Small companies' share of the corporation tax bill rises as that of large companies falls (see figure 2), while their share of the economy remains fairly steady.[38]

Tax dodging becomes yet one more force in the homogeniza-tion of British business. Providing extra returns on high-margin, high-risk business, it can also promote more unsavoury business practices with no long-term economic benefits: it's no coincidence that widely mis-sold 'payment protection' insurance policies on loans and dubious 'extended warranties' on electrical products were run from tax havens by the likes of Barclays and Dixons. It creates risks for companies' shareholders, employees and society at large, as

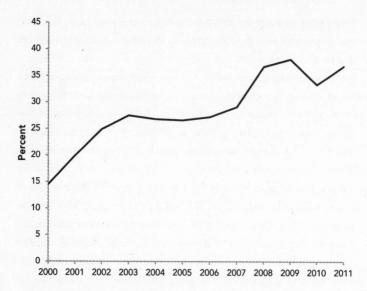

Fig. 2 The proportion of corporation tax paid by small companies ('small company' defined as one not required to make quarterly corporation tax instalment payments, the threshold for which is annual profits of £1.5m)[39]

amply demonstrated by the tax-incentivized 'gearing up' of private equity-owned businesses such as Boots, by filling them with debt for the tax breaks. The resulting drain on the companies' funds has left thousands out of work, and businesses, such as chains of care homes, unable to cope with economic downturns.

Tax avoidance even destabilizes economies. A 2009 presentation from the Organization for Economic Cooperation and Development (OECD) on the causes of the greatest financial crisis since the 1930s listed several 'tax policies as exacerbating factors'. Top of the list was 'tax arbitrage linked to tax treatment of debt'; then there was 'deduction for interest expense (not equity)'; 'exemption/deferral of tax on foreign profits'; 'tax haven affiliates (conduits)'; 'hybrid instruments' and 'tax bias encouraging growth of bank profits (over asset protection/management)' caused by 'favourable capital gains tax treatment of stock options, corporate tax deduction on exercise of stock options'.[40] Cut through the jargon and these are the weapons of real world tax avoidance in Britain today. In the wake of a crisis that nearly collapsed the world economy, they're still attacking tax revenues and distorting economies. They give tax advantages to economy-swamping levels of debt and bankers' bonuses based on illusory profits that conceal sometimes cataclysmic risks. What's more, they're being sharpened by the British government.

At the same time, the enforcement of tax laws for the privileged is blunted. An easy tax ride has become part of selling Britain abroad as the tax authorities take their role beyond tax administration into promoting 'inward investment', traditionally the realm of the business department and the Foreign Office. The Treasury minister responsible for tax administration in Britain, David Gauke, spelt this out in a 2010 speech at tax consultants Deloitte. 'A competitive tax system is not just about lower headline rates, it's also about the way you tax, and the relationship you have with business,' he explained.[41] Britain's senior tax official – who also gave Vodafone its deal – told a conference in India in 2010: 'We are committed to handling disputes in a non-confrontational way and collaborating with customers wherever possible.'[42] One senior official privately put it more bluntly: 'We used to have a priority to collect tax, now we have a priority to have a good relationship.'[43] Which is about as permissive an atmosphere as the real world tax avoiders could hope for.

HM Treasury plc

As well as facing less than zealous policing of existing laws, big business can increasingly set its own new ones. The most infuriating aspect of this to those of us who like to report the furtive capture of the machinery of government by powerful vested interests is that there's no secret about it. The Treasury's mission is unashamedly to adjust the framework of tax legislation to suit large business. Thus 'working groups' set up to revise laws governing profits shifted into tax havens are run by the companies, such as Vodafone and Tesco, that seek to save fortunes by doing precisely this. Consultation processes descend quite openly into simply agreeing laws requested by big business. Where the government had initially proposed, for example, exempting from tax companies' foreign branches only if they were in countries with normal tax rates, business said it wanted its tax haven branches exempted too. So in 2011 that was precisely what it got.[44] This is not so much the well-documented phenomenon of 'regulatory capture', whereby those being regulated determine the government's approach to them; it's the white flag of abject regulatory surrender.

Business lobbying for lower taxes is nothing new. When formal income tax was first introduced by William Pitt at the end of the eighteenth century his Whig opponents claimed the tax, then at no more than 10% and reserved for the very wealthy of the day, 'would strike with peculiar force at industry and the fruits of industry'. The other main objection, voiced by a landed Scottish MP, was that the tax 'would encourage a spirit of migration'. The City of London was characteristically helpful, calling it a 'galling, oppressive and hateful inquisition'.[45] There is no evidence to bear out the naysayers' prophecies, which have wearying echoes of today's empty threats from industry bodies that companies will 'quit the UK' at the slightest tax rise (or even failure to reduce tax). The main difference is that, over 200 years on, governments either cynically or cravenly capitulate.[46]

History would in fact go on to show that relatively high tax levels have coincided with better economic performance, possibly because tax cuts for the wealthy translate not into greater investment, as neo-liberal economic theory would have it, but

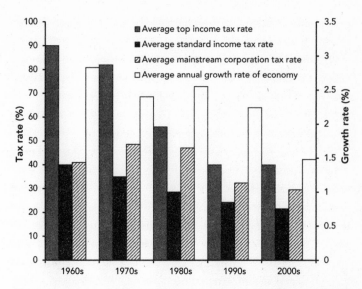

Fig. 3 Economic growth rates and average tax rates in the UK (1960–2000)[47]

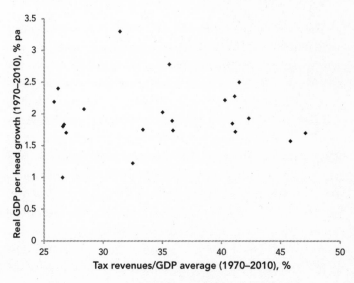

Fig. 4 No correlation: the economic growth rates of 22 OECD countries and their overall taxation levels.[48]

lower public investment, greater inequality and lower productivity (see figure 3).

Current international comparisons also suggest that relatively high-tax countries fare no worse in terms of economic growth than low-tax ones, while their citizens benefit from better public services (see figure 4). In short, demanding reasonable tax contributions is nothing for a country such as Britain to fear.

But today's corporate anti-tax lobby has hit upon the evidently winning formula of headline-grabbing threats to emigrate and more sophisticated, pseudo-intellectual efforts to undermine the whole notion of taxing capital (profits and gains), as well as labour (employees' earnings). At its heart is the proposition that capital can do as it pleases, it can go where it likes and must therefore be taxed very lightly if at all. It cleverly reverses the traditional view that 'unearned' income derived from capital is less deserved than a wage from an honest day's work and ought to be taxed at least as severely. And the theory behind it is bunk.

The most influential intellectualizing on tax in Britain takes place at the Oxford Centre for Business Taxation, which is almost permanently plugged into the Treasury. Part of Oxford University's Saïd Business School, set up by Monaco-based businessman Wafic Said, it is funded by a group of FTSE100 companies including Vodafone and Tesco and boasts a Barclays Bank Lecturer in Taxation (with optional Post-Irony Studies).[49] Among its questionable conclusions is that corporation tax, although directly a cost to the shareholders of a company, is not really paid by companies but is passed on primarily to their employees. If the workers don't pay the company's tax bill through lower wages, goes the theory, the shareholders will take their money to a rival economy that will appreciate them more and tax them less. This is hotly disputed by more independent organizations, which conclude that since capital and markets are not quite as mobile as the neo-liberals suggest, the bill ends up primarily where it should with the shareholders.

It is a tax on capital.[50] Which explains why all those campaigning for lower corporate tax – the CBI, the Institute of Directors and others – represent capital; why would they bother arguing against corporate taxes if they could just pass the bills onto their staff? And when corporate tax stories routinely hit share prices, it's clear shareholders don't think 'never mind, we'll just take it off the poor suckers working for us'. The point was most eloquently made in the US in 2011 by satirists Yes Men, who put out a spoof story that General Electric had seen the error of its tax avoiding ways and was going to make a large voluntary tax payment, prompting a collapse in its share price.

The corporate level is also an eminently reasonable one at which to levy a tax, since it is the point where capital comes together, acquires a distinct legal character and enjoys privileges such as the limited liability that passes risks from its activities onto others. The companies formed then make profits using public infrastructure and services such as the healthcare and education provided to their employees.[51] Some business leaders understand this. 'The company wouldn't exist without the work of British people, without the contribution of British universities, without the support of the British government,' conceded GlaxoSmithKline chief executive Andrew Witty (who might, incidentally, want to pass the message on to his company's tax department). But in uniting as a limited company to exploit public goods, the capital holders also relinquish much of the responsibility they might individually have felt to pay for them. The company directors acting as their agents do so under a broad remit that some have argued demands slashing tax bills as far as possible since this is in the financial interests of the shareholders that they must serve.

Yet when it comes to taxing these shareholders on their dividends the law assumes that the company has been taxed fully on its profits in the first place. As HMRC explains: 'Companies pay you dividends out of profits on which they have already paid – or are due to pay – tax.'[52] Pension funds receiving dividends are not taxed again and 'credit' is given to individuals receiving dividends for the tax deemed to have been paid by the company on the profits forming the dividend. So basic rate taxpayers pay no further tax on dividend income, while higher rate taxpayers pay only the extra required to ensure that overall the profits distributed are taxed at whatever their income tax rate is for that year. And when a company avoids tax – even to the point of paying no tax at all – its dividends are treated no less generously in the hands of the recipients. So corporate tax avoidance subverts the entire principle of ensuring that capital, as well as labour, pays a share of taxation.

Tax haven Britain

The current government nonetheless insists that 'the consensus, among economists at least, is that it's predominantly the employee who foots the bill', and uses the misconception of a few academics funded by big corporations to justify ultra-low corporate tax rates and the introduction of a whole new world of tax avoidance opportunity. By 2014, it boasts, Britain will have 'the lowest [corporate tax] rate [21%] of any major western economy, one of the most competitive rates in the G20, and the lowest rate this country has ever seen'.[53] And by sending profits into the world's tax havens with the government's encouragement, British multinationals will shave further billions off already modest tax bills. Even giving some credence to the overblown notion of 'tax competition' among nations, quite why the world's seventh largest economy should sell itself so cheaply looks like a mystery (but is in fact explained simply by the corporate capture of tax lawmaking).

The cost of this capitulation will of course be passed on to other taxpayers, both individuals and the small businesses that can't afford the lawyers and accountants to run offshore outposts. By massively reducing their tax bills, large companies will win yet another competitive advantage over the smaller enterprises that ought to be the engine of economic recovery. Meanwhile, billions of pounds will be poured into the unregulated, secretive and financially volatile territories that, in the wake of the 2008 financial crisis, the G20 London summit of leading nations promised to all but shut down.

At the same time, current tax minister David Gauke complains about 'campaigners choosing to stoke the fires of public opinion' when 'legitimate behaviour by taxpayers, consistent with both the letter and spirit of the law, is being classified as avoidance'.[54] The schemes of Arcadia, Boots and all the others are not tax avoidance but 'legitimate behaviour'.

They could of course constitute legitimate behaviour only in a country where the richest corporations are not just permitted to dodge their fair contributions but are positively encouraged to do so, leaving everybody else to pick up the tab. Such a nation might be called a tax haven. Or it might be called Britain.

2
An Unwelcome Guest

A short history of income tax and those who dodge it

'It is a vile, Jacobin, jumped up Jack-in-Office piece of impertinence – is a true Briton to have no privacy? Are the fruits of his labour and toil to be picked over, farthing by farthing, by the pimply minions of bureaucracy?'

> From *Man Midwife. The further experiences of John Knyveton, MD, late surgeon in the British Fleet during the years 1763–1809*, by Ernest A. Gray.[1]

In an altogether different age, when Britain was struggling with 'wars abroad' and lumbering under huge budget deficits, Prime Minister and Chancellor of the Exchequer William Pitt the Younger first imposed 'certain duties upon income'. The new tax would compensate for declining customs and excise duties as battles against the French hampered trade and depleted the nation's coffers. But even though it would pay for a war of national survival, the first formal income tax of 1799 – levied at a maximum 10% on incomes over £200 – was a regretful innovation. Brought in as a last resort only after other taxes had failed to yield sufficient funds, it was by its architect's own admission 'repugnant to the customs and manners of the nation' and would be repealed as soon as possible.

Pitt's successor, Henry Addington, honoured the promise as soon as the ink was dry on a 'definitive treaty of peace' with France three years later, only to reimpose the tax after fourteen months when the truce proved little more than the prelude to twelve years of Napoleonic war. The 'temporary' income tax this time hung around until Wellington's 1815 triumph at Waterloo allowed it once again, after heavy petitioning, to be withdrawn from service, accompanied by a celebratory pulping of all parliamentary papers associated with the despised duties.

A generation later, however, government finances were struggling to cope with a recession and the loss of a tax that had produced a useful £12m a year for the government, a good quarter of its revenue. By 1841 Tory leader Robert Peel was mocking the Whig chancellor Francis Baring (of the banking family):'Can there be a more lamentable picture than that of the Chancellor of the Exchequer seated on an empty chest – by the pool of bottomless deficiency – fishing for a budget?' Just one year later, and by now prime minister for the second time, Peel – once an opponent of the tax – squeezed a new version through parliament both to deal with the crisis and to compensate for a series of reforms under which duties were reduced and tariffs on hundreds of goods scrapped as part of a free trade policy that within a few years would culminate in his repeal of the Corn Laws. Although Peel accompanied the income tax, yet again, with a politician's promise to repeal it within five years, he had firmly entrenched its importance to government finance.

Economic necessity did not bring popularity for the tax. But repeated commitments to scrap it over the following decades, notably from great rivals Gladstone and Disraeli, became increasingly less realistic. By the early 1860s income tax accounted for over one seventh of government revenues and had proved crucial in funding the Crimean War, even at no more than 1s 4d in the pound, or 6.5%. When Gladstone failed in his 1860 budget to deliver the repeal he had promised in his first budget of 1853, Disraeli opportunistically assailed him as 'the hero of a popular delusion for seven years'. Few now doubted that income tax was here to stay.

Nineteenth-century political knockabout over any sort of tax – whether on income or anything else – was possible only because 200 years earlier parliament had wrested tax-raising powers from the monarch. Charles I's 'ship money', levied on coastal towns to pay for naval defences without parliamentary consent, had been at the root of the English Civil War. Among the priorities of Cromwell's ensuing Protectorate was to establish control over the collection and expenditure of state funds (although royal prerogative over taxation was not formally abolished until the 1689 Bill of Rights). For this it created a new machinery for tax administration made up of local commissioners, surveyors and collectors who would be occupied for a century and a half with a haphazard collection of direct taxes on people (as opposed to indirect taxes on goods such as excise duties). The most important was the 1692 Land Tax that lasted until 1963, its longevity explained by the immobility and visibility of land and consequent difficulty of dodging it (which, incidentally, explains why in today's new age of tax avoidance it is thought by many overdue for reintroduction). Expedience and the personal prejudices of lawmakers dictated that in various eras land tax would be supplemented by levies on scores of possessions including carriages, pleasure horses, racehorses, silver plates and (pandering, some say, to Pitt's misogyny) female servants, as assessed by the new officialdom.

Delegated to local worthies, tax administration was far from uniform, fair or efficient but it did establish a legal framework within which income tax would eventually operate. Today's tax inspectors' powers, for example, owe much to invasive eighteenth-century measures to detect the dodging of window tax, a levy introduced in the late seventeenth century as a less intrusive way of a gauging a person's means than asking for details of his income.

To counter the widespread abuse the new 'surveyors', today's tax inspectors, were granted 'full power to pass through any house or houses, in order to go into any court, yard, or backside thereunto belonging'. Disgruntled taxpayers, on the other hand, could by then have their day in court by taking a disputed tax assessment to the King's Bench, as could surveyors if they disagreed with local tax commissioners. One window tax dodger, whose conversion of two windows into one with a connecting pane of glass had been deemed tax effective by his local commissioners, was disappointed when a judge decided 'this is a manifest evasion of the Act'.[2] As a contrived but transparently honest attempt to escape a tax bill, today's tax semanticians would characterize the ruse as 'avoidance', not evasion. Before the professionalization of tax dodging, however, there were no such niceties.

Victorian spongers

Even at the rates typically levied in Victorian Britain – never venturing above two shillings in the pound (10%) for the highest incomes – income tax evasion was commonplace. The first report from the Board of Inland Revenue, established under Gladstone's chancellorship in 1853, recorded four years later that 'the amount of evasion of the duty . . . must be very considerable'. By 1872 the Board published its first estimate of the losses, putting it at £1.5m, or around 40% of the total income tax due (compared to somewhere between 3% and 30% today, depending on whose figures you believe).

The Revenue Board also made its first comments on *legal* income tax avoidance, which took the form of transferring bonds abroad so that dividends on them would be paid outside Britain and the tax net at the time. Individuals in Paris, recorded the commissioners, were receiving tens of thousands of pounds in interest on British bonds. There, they noted with heavy irony, 'the first of these millionaires was a clerk in a money changer's office, and that he resided in an apartment at a rental of £16 per annum, while his wife at the same place conducted a small dressmaker's business.'[3] (A century and half later, something not too dissimilar can be found at the letter-box tax haven addresses of many a multinational company, but now the sums run to billions.)

Such tax avoidance arrangements were still rare, perhaps because there was as yet no sophisticated 'offshore' system to facilitate schemes on any scale and – as the level of tax evasion demonstrated – there was the far easier option of simply omitting income from a return with little threat of detection, or perhaps the tacit approval of a friendly local surveyor or commissioner. And rates of tax typically below 5% probably weren't enough to justify the reorganization of a person's financial and business affairs that would be required.

Tax avoidance would become a serious pursuit only once income tax itself had become, over a century after its introduction, what Edwardian chancellor Herbert Asquith could call 'an integral and permanent part of our financial system'. 'Gladstonian Finance', under which income tax was to be a stopgap until government debt was paid off, had had its day, and persistent spending on the military, not least for an expensive Boer War, was being added to by growing bills for relieving poverty. Income tax, efficient to collect and more evenly distributed than the duties previously relied upon, would become the primary means of funding the growing commitments. By 1906 direct taxes such as income tax and land tax had overtaken indirect taxes as the primary source of government revenues.[4] 'If we are to have social reform we must be ready to pay for it,' explained Asquith in one of his 1907 budgets, 'and when I say we, I mean the whole nation, the working and consuming classes as well as the wealthier class of direct taxpayers.' We were all in it together.

Two years later, in a riposte to opponents who argued that income tax should only ever be a war tax, Asquith's successor Lloyd George insisted that what became famous as his 'People's Budget' *was* a 'war budget'. 'It is for raising money to wage implacable warfare against poverty and squalidness,' he declared. The welfare his government was beginning to provide – such as old-age pensions and free school meals – was to be paid for not just by a new land tax but also a 'supertax' on income, taking the top rate to 7.5% and breaking the taboo on what among Victorian thinkers had been the iniquitous notion of 'progressive' tax rates that rose with higher incomes.

A healthy economy nevertheless kept even the new supertax in single digits until the Great War stretched out beyond both the generals' and the Treasury's expectations and demanded some quick funds. By 1918 standard income tax reached 30% and the additional surtax for the highest earners hit 22.5%. From 1915 any business prospering from the war also faced a hefty 'excess profits duty' that rose to 80% of what it earned above its pre-war profits.

This complex extra tax – imposing a large bill but full of loopholes – presented the first wholesale tax avoidance opportunity for businesses rather than the individuals controlling them. Using techniques such as shifting expenses and stocks around and inflating their own wages, taxes on profits could be dramatically – and lawfully – reduced. The schemes prompted the first explicit anti-tax avoidance law, designed to protect excess profits duty by enabling tax surveyors to ignore arrangements set up to get round it. In 1920 a group of MPs recommended replicating the measure for all income tax, giving the Revenue the 'power of ignoring, for the purposes of assessment, any fictitious or artificial transaction entered into for the purpose of evading or avoiding income tax'.[5] To the disappointment of an increasingly professional body of tax officials – whose Association of Tax-Surveying Officers estimated that £100m had been lost to tax avoidance 'during the last few years' – the MPs were rebuffed by the coalition government's Conservative chancellor Austen Chamberlain.

Serious tax avoidance wasn't confined to the spivvy world of war profiteering, though. Higher income tax rates enticed many of the wealthy to look offshore for some relief. By 1926 future Labour chancellor Hugh Dalton was spluttering that 'the rich are not only getting richer . . . some of them are going to Jersey', where they would become 'non-residents' beyond the taxman's reach. But they did at least have to live on the rocky outcrop off the French coast, and Channel Island life in the inter-war years wasn't the ball that it is now. So two British businessmen went one better, adding a new layer of sophistication to tax avoidance in order to procure the fiscal benefits of 'abroad' without the inconvenience of actually staying there.

A question of trust

One of the tawdriest episodes in the annals of British tax avoidance originated in Lloyd George's quietly radical 1914 budget. By imposing tax on a Briton's income wherever it arose in the world, regardless of whether it was repatriated, the then chancellor presented a potentially huge tax bill to two Liverpudlian brothers, William and Edmund Vestey. Born into one of the city's oldest family trading firms, by the outbreak of the First World War the Vesteys had built a successful shipping business and established near-monopoly control of South American meat production, the substantial income from which would be caught in Lloyd George's big net.

When the brothers' intensive lobbying efforts against the new legislation failed and they had tired of moving around Europe dodging tax bills, they turned to something cleverer. They would now stay at home in England but divert income from their business into a 'trust' that was no more than a legal arrangement among themselves and a couple of Parisian lawyers. By exploiting a medieval legal construct originally used by knights to guard their belongings while they were away crusading, the Vesteys distanced themselves enough from their income, they hoped, to shake off an income tax charge. The trustees could then simply lend money to a British company controlled by the brothers, from which they in turn borrowed money, enabling them to enjoy the fruits of their business empire, plus their British homes, without a corresponding tax bill. (The scheme, incidentally, would find an echo in the Jersey trust-based scheme infamously deployed by British comedian Jimmy Carr nearly a century later.) And to top it all, in 1922 William Vestey bought a peerage from the people's chancellor, now prime minister, Lloyd George.[6]

These offshore manoeuvres provoked a rash of anti-tax avoidance laws through the 1930s, as the Revenue sought to tax income from assets moved offshore and income that the wealthy continued to 'enjoy' even when sheltered in a trust. But the secrecy of trusts, for which no public records are required, made them hard to find in the first place – it had taken the Inland Revenue inspectors many years to discover the Vesteys' – so the taxman was always several steps behind the latest move. And when one form of trust-based avoidance was outlawed, another would immediately form to do its silent work for a few years before it too could be neutered.

The Vesteys' refusal to pay their dues to the country they were proud to call home, while a million of their compatriots paid for their loyalty with their lives, proved the allure of tax avoidance even in times of dire national need. So emergency tax rises in the late 1930s to pay for rearmament ahead of a likely second world war – the value of financing a war effort early enough having now been learned – were accompanied by more laws to counter avoidance of income tax, which for the highest earners could be 98%, and a new 'excess profits' tax that in 1940 was levied at 100%.

Post-war, a large national debt and the costs of building a new welfare state left no room for major tax cuts. Although there were some repayments of the tougher tax bills used to fund the war, such as the 100% excess profits tax, Clement Attlee's austere chancellor Sir Stafford Cripps was adamant there would be 'no tax remission spree'. And it was in this spirit that his successor Hugh Gaitskell soon shored up Britain's business tax base against the tax avoidance possibilities created by expanding peacetime international trade. Most importantly, new laws tackled the practice of underpricing sales to, or overpricing imports from, overseas affiliates. This so-called 'transfer pricing' abuse, which often involved inserting a tax haven company in the middle of legitimate transactions, could seriously reduce or eliminate tax bills. A British company importing £1000 worth of widgets, for example, might pay £1200 to a company based in a tax haven but within the same corporate group, which would pay the £1000 to the company selling the widgets. The result, which the new rules ought to negate, was simply to move £200 of the group's profits from the UK to the tax haven. Together with an important law banning companies from moving their tax residence abroad without the Treasury's approval (rarely given and on pain of imprisonment for directors if ignored) Gaitskell's laws erected a defensive wall round Britain's corporate tax base.

Offshore explosion

The Attlee government's protective stance would not be notice-ably relaxed by the Tory governments of the fifties even as they presided over economic recovery. By the end of the decade, there were over twice as many companies – almost 400,000 – operating in Britain as there were before the war, generating significantly greater profits.[7] Business wealth was spread far beyond the Vesteys of this world, dramatically broadening the population for whom income tax avoidance might pay. And if the expanding business and share-owning population were the new tax avoidance customers, their suppliers were to be found among the legal profession and a resurgent merchant banking sector.

For the right fee the banks would set up trusts, companies and partnerships to mitigate top income tax rates that soared above 80% by the early 1960s. Alongside British businessmen, the blossoming world of entertainment provided a new generation of high earners eager to sign up for a service chronicled in journalist Nigel Tutt's 1989 study, *The History of Tax Avoidance*.[8] When a fourteen-year-old Hayley Mills, for example, was given a $30,000-a-year Hollywood deal in 1960 her earnings from films such as *Pollyanna* were paid into an offshore company that paid the bulk of the income to an offshore trust in the hope that it would escape tax, while the young Hayley survived on a less heavily taxed £400 annual 'salary'.

The leading tax accountants to the stars, a Cavendish Square outfit called Kimble & Jones, had a client list that read like the guest list for a West End awards night, featuring Albert Finney, Tommy Steel, Christopher Plummer and others who felt the taxman was unreasonably plundering the spoils of their success. Among their more sophisticated schemes was a plan for screen siren Julie Christie, fresh from *Doctor Zhivago* success, to shelter $100,000 from an effective tax rate of over 90% in 1965. The idea was to convert the cash into a tax-free capital gain, income from which would be released in smaller amounts over a period of years to incur lower tax bills. It required a web of companies, trusts and thirty-five separate transactions, all signed off in a single sitting at the Grosvenor House Hotel, Park Lane, three days before Christmas 1965.

For many big earners, as the Beatles would sing a few months after Julie Christie signed on thirty-five dotted lines, the 'Taxman' was allowing 'one for you, nineteen for me' and there were few stars with international earnings who weren't flocking to the lawyers and bankers who could keep their money out of the taxman's clutches. When, for example, David Frost made it in the US he converted his income from across the Atlantic into an investment in a Bahamian partnership between himself and his local company, Leander Productions. Frequent stopovers in Nassau on returning from the States for the Leander board meetings – which were essential to keep the company, and the whole scheme, out of the British tax net – appear not to have been too onerous for the *That Was the Week That Was* star.

Frost was just one of many among the jet set exploiting a parallel development in the world's financial structure: the post-war tax haven boom, led by Britain's 'overseas territories' such as the Cayman Islands, Bermuda and the British Virgin Islands. Operating in a constitutional limbo between colonialism and independence, these relics of Empire combined secrecy, absence of tax and minimal regulation with the protection and lingering prestige of the mother country. Closer to home, the Crown Dependencies of the Channel Islands and the Isle of Man were building on centuries of harbouring financial and political fugitives by similarly expanding their offshore financial services through banks and trust companies. Before long most of these eighteen territories would become mere shop fronts for tax dodging, tailoring their laws at the behest of the financial interests controlling them so that they could offer precisely the vehicles required by Britons and others looking to escape their bills back home.

Secrecy surrounding individuals' and companies' tax affairs, which was pierced only very occasionally, meant that the harm to the British economy was insidious. Even in government, there was only muted official concern outside the Revenue itself. The Foreign Office believed that financial services offered the best economic hope for the territories' long-term independence and, like a teenager's parents, didn't want to know exactly what they got up to along the way. In the days of exchange controls and currency crises it was largely left to the Bank of England to watch the islands' financial activities and ensure they didn't leak valuable sterling. And it was, at best, indifferent to tax dodging. As late as

1975 an appalled taxpayer reported to Chancellor Denis Healey that while his government was clamping down on tax dodging, at a tax conference in Jersey a Bank of England official 'was giving advice on how to avoid tax. I wonder if this is really part of the Bank of England's duties?'[9]

Strip show

For companies, liable at the time both to income tax and a further tax on profits with origins in a wartime levy, the tax reduction ploy of choice became 'dividend stripping', a device to engineer the repayment of these tax bills. The thousands of new private companies in the expanding post-war economy – some making profits, others losses, often under the same ownership – formed an ideal market for the scheme. The loss-makers would buy shares about to pay a dividend and claim relief for their business losses against the dividend income, generating an instant repayment of the tax originally paid by the company that paid the dividend. The shares were then returned to their original owner at a price that gave it a slice of the tax avoidance spoils. When the Inland Revenue took one of these schemes on a long battle through the courts all the way to the House of Lords in the early 1960s, the outspoken Lord Denning – who a few months later would famously report on the Profumo scandal – captured the nature of the transactions by depicting 'prospectors digging for wealth in the subterranean passages of the Revenue, searching for tax repayments'.[10] But in seeking to strike out the tax benefits he was in the minority among his peers who were deciding tax cases according to legal precedents set decades earlier by judges for whom income tax had still been an intrusion into a gentleman's affairs.

In 1929 Scottish judge and sometime Conservative politician Lord Clyde had ruled in favour of an Ayrshire bus firm that had been put in the hands of its founder's children in order to duck a £10,000 tax bill, with the words: 'No man in this country is under the smallest obligation, moral or other, so to arrange his legal relations to his business or property as to enable the Inland Revenue to put the largest possible shovel in his stores.'[11] Around the same time, Britain's richest man, the Duke of Westminster, was saving a few pounds by paying tradesmen and servants not in wages but through what were then tax-deductible 'annuities' (continuous annual payments transferring income to another person). These arrangements also defeated the Inland Revenue's attempts to impose tax on their 'substance' rather than their strict legal form, with English judge Lord Tomlin echoing Clyde: 'Every man is entitled if he can to order his affairs so that the tax attaching under the appropriate [law] is less than it otherwise would be.'[12] These two men's views – at the same time liberal and legalistic in asserting the right to exploit the letter of the law – were to dominate the courts' view of tax avoidance for almost half a century and provided a conducive backdrop to the growing industry in tax scheming.

By the early 1960s the business was seriously vexing those on the left. Debating a statutory clampdown on the dividend-stripping ruse in parliament in 1960, Harold Wilson, then in opposition, likened 'the parasites' indulging in it to 'smugglers of old'. The difference was that 'they are far less romantic and glamorous and they rob the Exchequer on a far vaster scale than all the smugglers who ever sailed the High Seas'. His ire turned into action after his 1964 general election victory. In came a brand new tax replacing income tax for companies, which finally eliminated the dividend-stripping trick: corporation tax. Another new tax, capital gains tax, would – so it was planned – stop a staple of tax avoidance, the conversion of streams of taxable income into previously non-taxable capital gains. But there would also be eye-watering tax rates of over 95% on some personal incomes (and over 40% on average earnings) that certainly weren't going to endear income tax to the British people.

In fact, whatever else they achieved, extreme tax rates took their toll on the tax system itself. Surveying a black economy estimated to be costing Britain £2bn a year and legal avoidance thought to have hit half a billion pounds annually by the end of the seventies, one of the few journalists to report tax dodging critically, *Private Eye*'s Michael Gillard, remarked on 'the erosion in public honesty and moral values which had taken place in a country previously thought of as more honest than most when it came to paying tax'.[13] Britain's best-loved TV comedy series, *Only Fools and Horses*, revolved around cash-in-hand trader Del Boy and announced proudly in its signature tune: 'No income tax, no VAT'. The programme's creator John Sullivan would acknowledge that the lead character was rooted not in the Thatcher years in which it was broadcast but in the sixties and seventies London of his own upbringing, when tax dodging became a socially acceptable act of rebellion.

If Del Boy personified popular sentiment towards illegal income tax evasion, a scion of the Vestey dynasty did much the same for legal tax dodging when the family's ongoing avoidance schemes were reported in the late 1970s. 'Let's face it, nobody pays more tax than they have to,' he shrugged. 'We're all tax-dodgers, aren't we?'[14] His comments chimed with the judgments of law lords like Clyde and Tomlin: it was everybody's right to minimize tax using the legal devices, such as trusts and annuities, now readily available. Those on the right could accept this while those on the left could denounce it and, when elected, legislate against techniques of which they disapproved. But as Wilson's late-sixties government did precisely this in Westminster, a new front in the tax-avoidance war was opening up just a mile away in Mayfair. The enemy was more calculating than anything the taxman had encountered before and would take tax avoidance to a level of artifice that eventually proved too much even for a judiciary determined to safeguard the individual's rights against the taxman.

A bad smell

Tax avoidance advisers like Kimble & Jones operated with clear consciences. They sheltered their clients' income from what were by any standard bracing tax rates, especially for people whose income might be high in one particular year but otherwise sporadic or earned over a short career. Even those running the 'dividend stripping' schemes maintained – less convincingly – that they were merely generating compensation by way of tax relief for genuine business losses. What none of these advisers would admit to was the blatant manufacture of tax breaks. Which was why Bernard Kimble, for one, steered clear of schemes invented by what would become Britain's most notorious tax avoidance 'factory'. 'I do not like the smell of it,' he said.[15]

The Rossminster affair has a special place in tax folklore as the genesis of artificial tax avoidance, in which tax laws are contorted beyond all recognition to produce results entirely at odds with their purpose. It warranted not one but two books[16] in the 1980s and is of such importance to this tale that it merits a brief retelling. Rossminster undermined the whole basis of taxation: that people and companies would be taxed on their real incomes and gains and that their personal and commercial dealings would determine what those were. In Rossminster's world this reality was replaced with one in which tax liabilities vanished with the wave of a tax planner's wand.

Roy Tucker and Ron Plummer met in 1968 in the London office of an American accountancy firm that was beginning to establish itself as a leading player in the growing British bean-counting market, Arthur Andersen. Plummer, twenty-eight, and Tucker, thirty-two, were both ambitious tax managers, helping US expatriates and others 'manage' their British tax bills. Although the academic Tucker and the more practical Plummer worked well together, the latter soon chose to further his career at a second-tier

London bank, Slater Walker, set up by accountant Jim Slater and leading Tory MP Peter Walker in 1964, and with an edgy reputation for asset-stripping some of Britain's sleepier businesses. Far from being the end of Tucker and Plummer's relationship, however, this early separation was the key to a partnership that transformed British taxation.

The long-haired Tucker, described by journalist Michael Gillard as looking 'like the schoolboy genius who might just blow up the chemistry lab' and 'a walking compendium of the taxes acts', was also less than content at Arthur Andersen. His fertile imagination was not satisfied by the firm's stock-in-trade plans for UK-based American clients looking to exploit the joys of non-domiciled status and the flexible concept of tax residence. He began to contemplate techniques with wider appeal.

Tucker's first brainwave came in 1970 with the 'capital income plan', under which a tax avoider would pay a tax-deductible annuity in return for a lump sum taxed at a lower rate or, if other breaks could be engineered, not taxed at all. The scheme would of course work only if the recipient of the annuity was not taxed on it. So Tucker established a tax-exempt charity, Home and Overseas Voluntary Aid Services, which would play the tax avoider's stooge by paying out the lump sum and receiving the annuity payments. While millions flowed through the scheme, donations to the charity barely exceeded £100, and all Tucker could claim in the way of good works was: 'We put in a bit of money ourselves to finance the odd children's outing.' The polished 'corporate social responsibility' PR machines used by today's tax avoiders were some years off.

Wheezes like this were too hot to handle even for Andersens, a firm that thirty years before it collapsed in the Enron scandal was already at the racier end of the accountancy business. Tucker had overstepped a certain professional mark; rather than merely advising clients on what tax 'opportunities' there might be out there, he was 'marketing' tax avoidance schemes to as many takers as possible.

Not only did the big firms doubt whether some of Tucker's more artificial tax schemes would survive the courts' scrutiny, they also feared for their reputations (punctiliousness that was not destined to last). Launching raids on the Exchequer was unseemly for well-connected firms and presented a prohibitive conflict of interest when they were also performing objective audit work for the same clients (again, not a qualm that would survive).

By August 1972 Roy Tucker & Co was open for business just round the corner from Slater Walker in North Audley Street, Mayfair. Staffed by former Andersen colleagues and a couple of ex-employees from the tax avoider's favourite recruiting ground, the Inland Revenue, Tucker's tax avoidance production line was quickly primed for action. His contacts in the accountancy and insurance worlds would provide the sales outlets but he also needed to get the raw material – money – from somewhere. Which was where his old colleague Plummer, making a name for himself round the corner at the Vogue House, Hanover Square offices of Slater Walker, came in. Plummer's employer already had an appetite for the more unorthodox business that larger banks shunned (once more, scrupulousness that forty years on looks rather quaint).

Among the early joint efforts was the 'exempt debt scheme', a complicated arrangement for those facing bills under the relatively new capital gains tax laws. The idea was to manufacture a capital *loss* that could be set against a customer's real gain and eliminate the tax bill. Using money borrowed from Slater Walker, the customer would make a pair of long-term loans to a specially created company that he also owned. The loans would be adjusted so that, on one of them, Tucker's customer was repaid far more than he had lent the company. But this would empty the company of funds, so when it was liquidated its shareholder, namely the customer, lost money on his shares. Which left him with a matching gain on a loan and loss on his shares. The tax magic lay in the exemption from tax of gains on loans under tax laws governing debts at the time, while losses on shares could be set against genuine, completely unrelated, taxable gains. The 'exempt debt scheme' customer would thus emerge with an artificially created tax loss with which to eliminate the gain on which he wanted to avoid tax. Up to thirty Tucker clients bought the scheme, paying hundreds of thousands of pounds in fees to the new masters of tax avoidance, most of it destined for the offshore trusts that Tucker, Plummer and colleagues had set up for themselves and their families.

This tax avoidance marketing success owed a great deal to another lasting innovation in the art of tax avoidance: the heavyweight legal opinion to bolster the sales campaign for a tax scheme. A respected tax barrister would be recruited to give a scheme the legal thumbs up, so that it could be pitched to would-be tax avoiders with a silky seal of approval. They could then complete their tax returns assuming they would benefit from the scheme and keep their fingers crossed that the Revenue would not question them. Only the small print would reveal that such opinions were no guarantee of success should the taxman object, but even then the avoider would be spared the most penal consequences of a tax investigation since he could confidently claim to have acted in good faith on the best legal advice. This was, and remains, a lucrative sideline for many a barrister and no bar to higher judicial office. One of those signing off Tucker's exempt debt scheme, Andrew Park, would become a High Court judge who decided the fate of many later tax avoidance schemes before being brought out of retirement in 2012 to review some of the tax authorities' more controversial tax settlements (see chapter 11).

Despite this kind of legal cover, after a couple of years funding Tucker's schemes Jim Slater went cold on the business. He didn't entirely understand it, his banking margins were relatively small and he'd grown wary of a business that was beginning to take political flak. He was out of the tax scheming business and Plummer was at a career crossroads.

The scheme of things to come

The 33-year-old accountant could either ease himself into a life of humdrum commercial tax planning for the bank or pursue his adventure elsewhere. Convinced that funding tax avoidance had far from run its course, in July 1973 Plummer took what for someone who had left school at sixteen with no O levels was quite a step: he set up a bank. It would be called Rossminster, an aptly hybrid name conveying flinty Scottishness with its first syllable and snobby respectability with the second. Appointing a high-profile tax QC in Desmond Miller as its chairman and poaching tax accountants and bankers from Slater Walker, plus former Guards officer and future Tory MP Tom Benyon (and, later, future Defence Secretary Sir John Knott as a consultant), Plummer assembled a team with expertise and connections. Round the corner from his St George's Street, Mayfair offices, meanwhile, sat Roy Tucker, fizzing with ideas for the new bank. Consolidating marketing, financing and legal execution under one roof, Rossminster would transform these tax wheezes into choice financial products for the wealthy. The Tucker and Plummer show was still very much on.

The pair's most successful schemes exploited a tax break that remains at the root of tax avoidance today: the deduction against taxable income available for payments of interest. The beauty of interest is that, unlike other expenses, it can be generated without any real business but simply by moving money around, a job Rossminster could do as effectively as any logistics firm transporting real goods from A to B. So a very simple scheme, for example, involved funding clients' purchases of government bonds, or gilts, interest income from which was tax exempt. The client could set the interest costs of his borrowings against his other income, while the corresponding interest received on the gilts was not taxable. Again, there was little change in income or wealth for the client, but an ongoing tax break as long as the loan and gilts were held.

A quicker tax avoidance hit came from Rossminster's 'non-deposit scheme', whose surreal name matched its mechanics. A client would take a loan from Rossminster and pay all the interest on it up front, generating instant tax relief. At the same time another Rossminster company would take the debt off his hands in return for less than its face value. Clients and bankers would sign sheaves of paperwork in one sitting and money would go round in a circle more or less instantly. The client was no better or worse off; he may, to illustrate, have borrowed £100,000, paid £10,000 interest up front and then paid £90,000 to have what had become an interest-free loan taken off his hands. In tax terms he had paid a large sum of interest (£10,000) and made a corresponding gain on a loan (£10,000). The former was tax-deductible, the latter not taxable. Once more, a big tax break for no real financial outlay.

This scheme alone was taken up by around 230 people in 1973/74 and as the business grew and the schemes multiplied Tucker's offices often resembled a passport office during the holiday period. Dozens of meetings would take place in a single day to sign off the deals, with punters including the same sprinkling of stars that had long graced London's tax avoidance salons. John Lennon, Roger Moore and Englebert Humperdinck were all visitors to Tucker's Audley Street offices. They were there to snaffle up not just the annuity and 'non-deposit interest' schemes, but myriad other ruses including the 'commodity carry', the 'one year high income', the 'trust takeover loss', the 'deferred purchase capital loss', the 'gross annuity' and many other schemes understood only within a few walls in Mayfair.

Spirits soared and Rossminster's Christmas party sing-song made full use of the rhyming potential of Tucker's surname (not to mention, in later verses, that of its role as banker). To the tune of 'Men of Harlech', they chorused:

> *We sell tax schemes for Roy Tucker,*
> *Sell them just to any old sucker,*
> *This client's good, and that's a fucker*
> *Make the buggers sign.*[17]

Healey raises an eyebrow

If tax avoidance was in rude health the economy was in anything but, as a world oil crisis plunged Britain into a recession that would see the arrival of the International Monetary Fund in 1976. With the Inland Revenue chairman and experienced tax inspector Sir Norman Price complaining that tax avoidance was now a 'national habit', and finding a sympathetic ear in the incoming Labour chancellor Denis Healey in 1974, a stern response was inevitable. (As were stiff tax rates: Healey immediately increased the top rate of income tax from 75% to 83%, which just enhanced the allure of Rossminster's services to an expanding clientele that included wealthy peers from a Conservative Party to whose coffers Rossminster made regular contributions.)

In each of his annual finance bills the chancellor who famously remarked that the difference between tax evasion and tax avoidance was 'the thickness of a prison wall' would bring in a raft of anti-tax avoidance laws. He would outlaw both older schemes of the sort employed by the likes of David Frost and, crucially, the new Rossminster ones that depended on the elixir of tax avoidance – interest payments that could be created with the stroke of a banker's pen. By the time he had finished, tax relief for interest was available only on personal mortgages. But Healey's fire was directed just at rich individuals, not companies. Corporate Britain continued to enjoy generous tax relief for interest payments, a privilege that over the following decades would enable them to indulge in Rossminster-style money-go-round schemes on a scale that would have made Tucker and Plummer blush.

Every time Healey took the axe to tax avoidance, however, the hydra grew new heads, until in his 1978 budget he took an unprecedented step. It came when he closed down Tucker's 'commodity carry' scheme, an ingenious plan involving mirror 'forward' contracts to buy and sell commodities such as coffee and sugar at some future point. As time passed and the price of the commodities moved, it would be clear which contracts were losing money and which were gaining. And by running the contracts through a partnership, in which the client would be a partner, the tax trick became possible. Any change in a partnership's ownership terminates the 'accounting period' for which its results are measured for tax purposes and thus crystallizes whatever profits or losses have been realized at that point. So in the 'commodity carry' scheme the partnership would sell the contracts that had fallen in value, realizing a loss, immediately following which its accounting period would be brought to an end by Rossminster's client transferring its interest in the partnership to an offshore Rossminster company. This would generate instant tax losses for relief against the client's completely unrelated income in a particular tax year. The gains on the profitable contracts, by contrast, would not be cashed in until some later date and would by then accrue to the offshore company and not be taxable. Thus, a broadly neutral set of transactions was carved up into loss-making ones that were kept within the British tax net and profit-making ones that escaped it. Healey decided to stamp on this trick *retrospectively*, rendering 'commodity carry' schemes executed up to two years beforehand ineffective.

The move stepped over a bright constitutional line: that the law existing at the time of a person's actions, and only that law, should govern them. But what Healey's junior minister Joel Barnett called 'one's abhorrence of retrospective legislation' was trumped by 'one's abhorrence of people literally taking hundreds of millions of pounds away from every other taxpayer who is having tax deducted from them'. This demonstration that henceforth tax schemes would be shut down and tax reclaimed well after their execution placed a sword of Damocles over the tax avoidance industry. 'It was vital,' explained Barnett, 'to kill the mass marketing of tax schemes once and for all.'[18]

But the threat wouldn't last much longer than the year his own party remained in office. More significant for the long-term future of tax avoidance was what Healey had *not* done. He had rejected another widely mooted and more permanent measure that the Tories would have struggled to remove from the statute book (and which Tucker and Plummer had fully expected): a blanket anti-avoidance law that would allow a court to strike out a scheme if it were designed to avoid tax. This was to prove a costly missed opportunity in the war on tax avoidance, as subsequent governments failed for another generation to follow Healey's lead on retrospective legislation, emboldening avoiders who learned that if they could find a loophole they were in the clear.

It wasn't just laws that were changed to deal with Rossminster; so was the Inland Revenue's hitherto somnolent response. In 1975 a senior tax inspector who had cut his teeth on tax evasion at the tougher end of Britain's black economy was charged with tackling tax avoidance. The handful of cerebral tax inspectors sitting in their cardigans in the Revenue's draughty Somerset House headquarters mulling over what was termed, with a hint of resignation, 'legal avoidance' became a new Special Investigations Section (SIS) staffed by some of the Revenue's sharpest minds. Armed with new powers to demand information and a widening network of intelligence on tax schemes, the complexities of which had long confounded tax inspectors' abilities even to notice them in the first place, the taxman took the fight to Rossminster. Rather than meekly accept what it was told about a scheme, SIS demanded proof of the transactions involved, hoping to find flaws in the carefully choreographed arrangements. If you were going to avoid tax, went the thinking (now regrettably unfashionable), then you would at least have a long and expensive fight with the taxman on your hands.

The Revenue's new zeal enjoyed both political backing and a spot of welcome publicity when the *Sunday Times* started to expose some of the bigger schemes and report potential losses to the Exchequer running into the hundreds of millions of pounds. Tax avoidance even forced its way onto the TV screens for the first time with London Weekend Television pitting Labour MP and fierce Rossminster critic, Jeff Rooker, against Peter Rees, a QC and Tory frontbencher who had advised the firm on schemes and would go on to become a Treasury minister in Mrs Thatcher's government with direct responsibility for the Inland Revenue. Rooker put the cost of tax avoidance at £1bn and proposed radical action. The furore forced an admission from Tucker: 'I am not arguing taxation is not necessary. Spending on behalf of the state is not only necessary, but good. If my schemes became too successful, it would be an intolerable situation and have to be changed.'[19]

Away from the limelight the Revenue tax sleuths increasingly believed that Rossminster's schemes, executed in conditions of utmost secrecy and obscured from the authorities' view as far as possible, had passed beyond clever loophole-exploitation into something more dubious still. Subscribing to Samuel Johnson's maxim that 'where secrecy or mystery begins, vice or roguery is not far off', SIS investigators were beginning to ask whether Tucker and Plummer had breached Healey's 'prison wall'. They were also provoked, many believed, by the appearance of some big corporate names on the Rossminster client list, including builders Wimpey and stock market darling of the day National Car Parks. The enterprise *had* become 'an intolerable situation', and it needed not just to be changed but pulled apart.

Mayfair raid

As it happened, Tucker and Rossminster, alarmed by Healey's 1978 retrospective legislation, were already winding down the tax avoidance operation that had by now spawned 1200 separate companies. But SIS was not letting them slip away from the party without paying for the damage. Perhaps not too surprisingly the tax investigators detected a discrepancy between the success of the men behind Rossminster and the figures on their tax returns. Somewhere in the maze of offshore trusts and companies behind the operation, was there lurking a huge tax liability that the Revenue should be picking up? The investigators' big break came when a Rossminster staffer responsible for the offshore structures, fearing a messy demise to the business, called the Revenue and offered to spill the beans. He eventually laid out just how Tucker's and Plummer's earnings had made their way to offshore trusts in a manner that still left the pair with access to them. If true, surmised SIS, much more income should have appeared on their tax returns and this might no longer be legal avoidance, but fraud.

At dawn on 13 July 1979 seventy tax inspectors and twenty-eight police officers raided Rossminster's Mayfair offices and its leading lights' homes across the south-east. Operation Wimbledon foreshadowed a long and acrimonious battle involving a decade of enormous tax assessments, bankruptcy cases and unsuccessful claims for damages against the Revenue. There were, however, no convictions beyond a £1000 contempt of court fine for Tucker for refusing to explain the convenient disappearance of some desk diaries. The taxmen believed these diaries would have proved that certain transactions and meetings essential to a number of schemes had not actually taken place. For Rossminster's clients the agony was also prolonged. Obfuscation and delay had been the preferred response to Revenue enquiries, and it took years for the slow process of litigation even to begin. By the time Rossminster closed its doors to new business at the end of the 1970s, ninety-six of its cases were lined up before the courts, with hundreds more in the queue behind and the Revenue questioning all in the minutest detail.

The taxmen's victory was sealed on 12 March 1981, when the House of Lords passed judgment on a Tucker 'exempt debt' scheme that predated Rossminster itself (such is the glacial pace of tax justice). Eight years earlier a company owned by farmer William Ramsay had sold the family farm in Lincolnshire and leased it back to raise some cash for his family to invest in other businesses. But the Ramsays also wanted to avoid paying corporation tax – then at 40% – on the gain, and turned to Tucker's scheme to create an offsetting capital loss of around £175,000. By the time the law lords came to consider the arrangement, however, they were not quite the protectors of a man's right to dodge his dues that they had been fifty years earlier. Leading their unanimous defeat of the scheme, Lord Wilberforce – a great-great-grandson of renowned slavery abolitionist William Wilberforce – concluded that a series of steps set up to create a tax benefit, such as an 'exempt debt' scheme, could be looked at together rather than transaction-by-transaction. He cut through the thicket of contrived transactions intended to generate a non-taxable gain and a corresponding tax-deductible loss. 'The true view regarding the scheme as a whole,' he decided, 'was to find that there was neither gain nor loss.'[20] (He would also, later, speak disparagingly of fellow barristers who proffered helpful opinions on tax avoidance schemes to the likes of Tucker, or 'those who retail opinions' as he icily dismissed them.)[21]

Literal interpretation of tax law appeared to be on its way out with flares and kipper ties, as a succession of courtroom battles over tax avoidance developed and refined what became the 'Ramsay doctrine' of ignoring transactions executed entirely for tax avoidance. Almost all Rossminster's several hundred clients capitulated in their battles with the Revenue and never wanted to hear the words 'exempt debt', 'company purchase' and 'reverse annuity' ever again. Rossminster had, however, changed tax avoidance forever. Like pioneering scientists, engineers or responsible business leaders, Tucker and Plummer had innovated and taken their industry to a new level of sophistication. But their true legacy was not a technical one; it was to have made artificial tax avoidance a marketable service. Tucker himself provided a fitting epitaph for Rossminster: 'I think people may now have got into the habit and will find it difficult to change.'[22]

At least the courts now stood in the way, and the Inland Revenue had high hopes that they could be trusted to strike out transactions clearly designed for tax avoidance. But tax lawyers and accountants were not about to be put out of work and, as Tucker foretold, would not kick the habit. They just diverted their attention to bigger and better opportunities on offer in an even richer league.

A new lease of life

The weird and wonderful scheming of Rossminster's clients had been inherently uncommercial. What would a Lincolnshire farmer want with an 'exempt debt' scheme, if not to avoid tax? But for large companies, especially banks whose trade was to move money around, the question was less clear cut. Complex transactions might appear sufficiently commercial to get past judges who had evidently taken against entirely contrived tax avoidance. And lurking within the tax laws were some juicy tax breaks, designed to encourage investment but eminently exploitable for this more subtle form of tax avoidance.

Most lucrative were 'capital allowances', which until 1983 allowed a business to set 100% of the cost of buying 'plant and machinery' against its income immediately (far outpacing the equipment's real depreciation). The idea was to improve industrial productivity by encouraging investment, but from the late 1970s this single measure generated a tax industry all of its own. Instead of buying their equipment, companies that might not have instant use for a big tax break would lease the equipment from a banking group that legally bought the equipment and had plenty of profits to soak up the tax allowances. When this involved new investment there were few complaints, and the 'finance leasing' business it spawned became an integral arm of British business banking. But increasingly the system was exploited purely for tax benefits. Profitable companies with potentially large tax bills ('tax capacity' in the argot of avoidance) that could be reduced by gobbling up such allowances included Midland Bank's merchant banking arm, which was at least a recognized financing business and, more improbably, Marks & Spencer. The nation's favourite underwear retailer in fact had its own business, St Michael Finance, which thrived on tax breaks.

Even public bodies like transport authorities and local councils got in on the act, transferring ownership of vehicles, fittings in council houses and much else to banks that could pick up a tax break. Companies could sell their existing plant to a bank, which would claim the allowances, only to rent it back immediately using the money generated from the sale. No real change, just a quick extra tax break. Or a completely unrelated company with 'tax capacity' but no real interest in the plant – introduced by matchmaking accountants now alive to their audit clients' 'tax profiles' – could buy it with money borrowed from a bank, then lease it to the same bank for eventual onward leasing to the company that was going to use it. The company buying the plant would have matching income (from the lease) and expenses (the costs of interest and repaying the loan), so no economic profit or loss, and would never go near the equipment in question but would pick up the tax allowance.

Definitions could be stretched helpfully wide. The costs of making feature films, for example, qualified for the allowances since the 'master negative' was 'plant' in the business. So tax relief could be claimed for production costs immediately rather than when the income from the film arrived much later (if at all). Schemes to multiply tax relief for investors way beyond their real input by borrowing through special partnerships proliferated, and films were made as much for the tax breaks that could be leveraged from them as for their cinematic value. Some pushed their luck too far, such as when the tax industry inflicted the 1981 turkey *Escape to Victory* on an unsuspecting public. British investors put up 25% of the costs but claimed 100% as tax allowances. The footballing prisoners of war led by Sylvester Stallone might have broken free at the end of their 4–4 draw with the Germans, but eleven years later the law lords gave the investors a 5–0 drubbing and struck out most of the tax allowances the film supposedly generated.[23] (Over the following thirty years, while tax breaks for industrial investment were reduced, persuasive lobbying from the film industry would see its generous reliefs persist, and the 'film partnership' became a standard invest- ment vehicle for the wealthy seeking to cut their tax bills. Many schemes were considered by the authorities to have overstepped the line into tax avoidance, essentially claiming too much tax relief for too little real investment. In 2012 the partnership behind the highest-grossing film of all time, *Avatar*, was being challenged by the taxman, potentially presenting investors including Wayne Rooney, Andrew Flintoff and Andrew Lloyd Webber with large tax bills.[24])

These schemes might have appeared almost as contrived as the Rossminster ruses that the Revenue defeated that fine spring morning in 1981, but there was a crucial difference: the leasing schemes looked to have at least some commercial purpose. Even the apparently circular ones, where a company sold its own equipment to a bank only to lease it back, in effect amounted to the company borrowing money using its assets as security. Wasn't that what finance companies were there for? The flavour of commerciality meant that for the SIS investigators who had raided Rossminster, success against these new schemes depended on showing that they did not meet the arcane legal requirements for the tax reliefs, such as whether companies had properly 'incurred' their costs, or whether plant was actually being used in a trade. It was the kind of attritional war that Britain's bankers and accountants could fight while claiming they had not veered into anything 'artificial'. But that was exactly where, within a few years, they would end up.

Offshore plc

While the exploitation of industrial tax breaks was taking serious avoidance from Mayfair to the City, outside the tax advisers' and inspectors' offices the era of late-twentieth century economic liberalization was dawning. From 1979 Margaret Thatcher's government began implementing the monetarism and financial deregulation advocated by the 'Chicago school' of economic theory and championed here by the new prime minister's favoured think tanks such as the Institute for Economic Affairs. Her first and perhaps most significant move was the abolition of exchange controls, the system of currency regulation designed to prevent destabilizing inward and outward flows of finance. Soon followed by the removal of credit controls and the 'Big Bang' deregulation of the City, the reforms opened up the British economy in more than just the intended sense. They created a perfect freebooting environment for tax avoidance at a level to dwarf anything seen thus far.

By limiting offshore movements of funds, exchange controls had prevented companies simply moving large amounts of capital into the world's tax havens where it could turn a quick tax-free buck. With large offshore financial flows restricted to payments for goods, services and genuine investment, cross-border tax avoidance had been restricted to 'transfer pricing' schemes. These involved the manipulation of prices of transactions between companies in different countries and against which laws, albeit imperfect ones, had existed for thirty years. But with the shackles removed from international finance, a simple trick became easier and, for many companies, irresistible. Money could be placed in a tax haven sub-sidiary company in return for share capital in that company, and then either invested or even lent back to the British company from which it came in the first place. The high interest rates employed in the battle against inflation at the time meant a quick accumulation of tax-free profits offshore, matched by a corresponding reduction in taxable profits back home.

One of the first multinational companies to cash in was Pearson, the owner of Penguin books and the *Financial Times*, which in 1979 placed £20m surplus cash in a Jersey-registered company for deployment in several high-yielding schemes made possible by the currency relaxations. It doubled its money in five years, free of UK tax. But in order to get out of both the UK's and Jersey's taxes, the company needed to ensure it was not 'managed and controlled' – a trigger for tax residence – in either place. Its direc-tors toured Europe's tax havens, holding thirty board meetings in Paris, Amsterdam, Brussels, Luxembourg, Geneva, Monaco and elsewhere to ensure the peripatetic company remained stateless for tax purposes.

A new International Division was set up in the Inland Revenue to take on the growing threat of cross-border tax avoidance by multinational companies, just as the Special Investigations Section had been created to deal with Rossminster. It naturally took a dim view and argued that, since Pearson's UK-based directors really controlled the Jersey-registered company, it remained tax resident in the UK. When a tax tribunal disagreed, it was clear that if big companies got their paperwork right they could save serious money through an offshore corporate 'money box', and within a couple of years the Revenue's new international investigators had discovered hundreds of them being filled with cash from blue-chip Britain.

Confronted with the evidence of thousands of offshore companies controlled from the UK, in 1984 Thatcher's second chancellor, Nigel Lawson, belatedly agreed to plug the growing hole in his bucket. In came 'controlled foreign companies' laws stipulating that corporate profits diverted to tax haven subsidiaries would still be taxed in the UK. But with a raft of exemptions and let-outs, the voluminous laws were full of loopholes requiring remedial action in almost every subsequent finance bill. And just as tax havens like Jersey would tailor trust laws for wealthy individual tax avoiders, so they were only too pleased to help companies dodge Lawson's new laws.

City breaks

At the same time, economic conditions were tilting British business further towards tax avoidance. Monetarism and soaring interest rates eventually brought inflation under control, but an overvalued pound was ruining exporters' competitiveness and ushering in a reliance on the City's banking industry to sustain the balance of trade.[25] And for the financial services which became disproportionately important to the economy – especially after the 'Big Bang' deregulatory reforms of 1986 – tax avoidance and facilitating customers' tax evasion were increasingly key business lines. Duff loans from around the world, notably those associated with that era's sovereign debt crisis, could be 'parked' in the London operations of the world's banks in order to pick up some UK tax relief. The big British banks, meanwhile, all set up 'offshore deposit-takers' in Britain's Crown Dependency tax havens for customers preferring to receive income without tax being withheld, naturally advising them to put the income on their tax returns – as they would of course do.

But, as the jewel in Britain's commercial crown, by the 1990s the City was in a strong position to press for changes in an archaic tax system. The more esoteric financial products in which it was now dealing were taxed under laws dating back nearly two centuries following abstruse legal precedents. Tax legislation made no provision for the newfangled instruments like derivatives and securitizations on which London's renewed pre-eminence in the global markets was based.

This amounted to a reasonable case for change and translated under mid-nineties chancellors Norman Lamont and Kenneth Clarke into four consecutive years of legislative upheaval to the corporate tax system. The outcome was a hugely complex patchwork of overlapping tax regimes covering loans, foreign exchange and derivatives transactions, over which the same tax lawyers and accountants who, twenty-five years before, had eschewed the grubby business of tax avoidance would soon be salivating.

These lawyers and accountants' clients would come from the multinationals whose shareholders' returns could be greatly enhanced by reducing a tax bill that officially accounted for over 30% of profits. At the same time, the companies' directors were increasingly being paid through bonuses and share awards determined by these returns, under the prevailing economic orthodoxy that said executives could only be trusted to act in their shareholders' interests if they had the right financial incentives. Tax avoidance would thus feed straight into the ever-fattening pay packets being handed out in the boardrooms where decisions over tax scheming, and how much of it to indulge in, were being made.

The rewards on offer from tax avoidance, as well as the opportunities to indulge in it, were multiplying and the perfect tax avoidance storm was about to break.

3
Opportunity Knocks

The great corporate tax loophole industry undermines the British economy

As an opening setting for a tale, an insurance company's tax department won't set many readers' pulses racing (although I do, sadly, know one or two whose it will). Especially when the *dramatis personae* are chartered accountants. But a meeting in February 2002 between bean counters from British insurance company Prudential and the firm widely regarded at the time as Britain's most active tax avoidance consultant, Ernst & Young, was eventually to transform the government's approach to tax scheming.

The visiting tax consultants didn't hang about before unveiling their wares, presenting what they would delicately describe to the men and women from the Pru as a 'tax enhanced method for a UK company to hedge a foreign currency exposure'. Since Prudential had borrowed €500m on the euro markets the month before, they knew the insurance company had just such an 'exposure'. And for a company that reports its results in one currency but has debts or assets in another, 'hedging' is a routine safeguard against market movements hitting profits; in Prudential's case, if the euro strengthened against the pound, its debt would cost more in sterling to repay. By striking an agreement with a bank to 'swap' certain amounts of currency at a fixed exchange rate when the debt is up for repayment, and in the meantime to swap amounts representing what the differing interest payments would be on euro and sterling debt, this risk can be removed. The foreign currency debt legally remains, but the 'currency swap' removes exposure to the currency and money markets.

All pretty standard, but not yet 'tax enhanced'. Under the tax laws brought in by the mid-nineties' Tory government, currency swaps would be taxed under two sets of rules, one covering foreign exchange, another 'financial instruments' such as interest rate swaps. Although the laws were complex, the principle was simple: the tax outcome should follow the economic result, so that if a hedge produced an overall profit it would be taxed and if it made a loss this could be deducted from a company's other taxable profits. But intricate, overlapping tax laws make perfect playthings for a tax consultant, and the Ernst & Young advisers had certainly had their fun before their visit to the Pru. In one eureka moment, they had found an 'asymmetry between the foreign exchange and financial instruments regimes' that could be translated into what they called 'the opportunity' for Prudential. Under a currency swap with Royal Bank of Scotland, Prudential would agree that, when its euro loan was due for repayment, it would buy euros from the bank. So far, so standard. The rates it agreed for these exchanges were not, however, genuine market ones but more generous 'off-market' rates. And for being on the wrong end of the 'off-market' price, the bankers would be compensated with up-front premiums. The tax magic of this was that the premiums thus paid by Prudential would be deductible in computing taxable profits under the 'financial instruments' laws while its subsequent, broadly corresponding, gain on the later exchange of currencies – at those favourable 'off-market' rates – would not be taxable under the 'foreign exchange' tax rules. Hey presto! Instant tax avoidance from the snappily named 'tax-efficient off-market swaps' ('TOMS').

Or so the advisers thought. As did Prudential's attentive 'Director of Group Financial Reporting and Tax' Ms Nikki Maynard. Within days, the smart former Arthur Andersen accountant had persuaded Prudential's chief treasurer John Foley to sign up, and by 7 March 2002, a fortnight after Ernst & Young folded up its flip chart, the main currency swap contract was signed. Its most crucial clause, on which seven years' litigation would hang, stipulated that 'Prudential plc shall pay GBP £65,000,000 to the Royal Bank of Scotland plc on 12 March 2002 *in consideration of* the Royal Bank of Scotland plc *entering into this transaction*' [emphasis added]. Identical wording was attached to a £40m payment to Goldman Sachs under a similar scheme five months later.

To qualify for tax relief under the financial instruments tax laws, these amounts needed to be payments for entering the swaps, not part of the swaps themselves; hence the precise wording in the contract. Unfortunately for the company, five years after the deal a tax tribunal saw through the facade. The description, it found, 'seems to us to have been chosen to suit the Ernst & Young Opportunity. But as a statement of what really happened it was a misnomer, a deliberate mislabelling.'[1]

This was about as humiliating a verdict as the measured tribunal chairman Stephen Oliver QC could have delivered, but the company and its advisers still pursued appeals against it through the courts. For the company there was £30m tax at stake; for Ernst & Young there was a £300,000 success fee riding on it (the £200,000 signing-up down payment was safe). That figure, however, was far from the full size of the accountants' dog in this particular fight. The Revenue had already revealed that the scheme had been 'marketed pretty narrowly and in conditions of even more secrecy [than other schemes] to about 30 multinational or other large corporate enterprises',[2] at a potential cost to the public finances of £1bn – or at least half a dozen of the major acute hospitals that New Labour was struggling to fund at the time. Ernst & Young's interest in the outcome could be estimated at around £10m. But they were not to collect, as the higher courts endorsed Oliver's contemptuous dismissal of the machinations of some of Britain's best-paid professionals.

Similarly less than full and frank accounting for tax avoidance was seen when another Prudential wheeze, this time designed by accountants PricewaterhouseCoopers, was considered by a tax tribunal. The dispute concerned not the scheme itself, which involved Luxembourg and Gibraltar companies within the Prudential group, but the disclosure of tax advice on it. Although the details were not disclosed, the payment of a dividend was clearly a crucial element, but Pru emails stressed: 'Please do NOT include reference to the dividend in the approvals note as that would give it an inevitability' (emphasis in original). Another described the dividend as 'a point to gloss over'. This was a clear attempt to imbue the scheme with a commercial uncertainty that it didn't really have but which was known to be essential since, back in 1981 in the Ramsay case, Lord Wilberforce had decided that schemes where money went round in a circle in preordained steps would be struck out. The tribunal and higher courts concluded that the accountancy advice had no legal privilege and the Pru should hand its papers over.[3]

Despite such successes in the tax tribunals and courts, the Revenue was litigating a vanishingly small fraction of large corporate tax cases. But even these showed the lengths to which a leading British company and its advisers were prepared to act at the turn of the twenty-first century in pursuit of a tax break. They were quite willing to 'mislabel' payments and mislead investigators by omitting from paperwork key elements of highly contrived schemes. The spirit of Rossminster had been revived at the pinnacle of British business.

That the man from the Pru had come so far from knocking on doors in his raincoat and trilby collecting insurance premiums was explained by the potential of tax avoidance to transform a struggling company's finances. Wholesale changes in the pensions business in the 1980s had thrust Prudential into the 'personal pensions' market from which, as one of the most serious 'mis-sellers', it was to emerge with a tarnished reputation and, in 1998, a £1bn bill for its misdemeanours. It was not the best time for a company to have its wings clipped and, when the stock market slumped as the dot.com bubble burst, maintaining financial returns was a tall order. The company was already looking east to China but that was for the long term; nowhere in the outside world was going to generate the extra profits it needed. But there was somewhere inside the company itself that might produce the goods: the tax department. In 2001 and 2002 Prudential's corporate tax charges were £21m and £44m,[4] so £30m would be a big saving and add almost 10% to the earnings per share that stock market analysts keep their eyes on.

Prudential typified the transformation of many a staid British multinational into exotic tax avoider, as strains on corporate earnings fuelled demand for tax reduction across business. Happily for them, both the financial markets and tax systems had developed in ways that maximized the opportunities for the likes of Ernst & Young to peddle exactly this service. After two decades of financial deregulation a multinational company could borrow hundreds of millions of pounds' worth of foreign currency with a single phone call. Scores of companies could all do so at the same time and the multi-trillion dollar foreign exchange markets would register barely a flicker. And the cash was available equally for real business or speculation. The €500m debt at the heart of the Pru's scheme was itself no more than a punt on exchange rates, the tax tribunal noting: 'Between the date of issue ... in December 2001 and 2011 when redemption was possible, Prudential anticipated ... no need for euros.' If a company needed a 'foreign currency exposure' for a tax scheme, it could conjure one up without too much trouble. And by 2002 tailored derivative contracts were readily available from banks encouraged by regulators who believed – disastrously, it would transpire – that they reduced risk in the financial system and the more there were, the safer the system.[5] The investment banking arms of RBS and Goldman Sachs could knock out a TOMS to order as easily as the sandwich shop next door would rustle up a BLT, and there was every fiscal incentive for corporate Britain to gobble them up.

Act of folly

Labour's first chancellor since Denis Healey was just as outspoken as his predecessor had been on tax dodging. 'A Government committed to the proper funding of public services will not tolerate the avoidance of taxation,' vowed Gordon Brown in July 1997, 'and will be relentless in its war against tax avoidance.' To prove his intent, he claimed he had 'already identified a series of significant tax abuses' that he would block in order to 'bring in a cumulative total of £1.7 billion over four years', while the Inland Revenue would give serious thought to the 'general anti-avoidance rule' from which Healey had shied away.

This turned out to be what Brown observers soon recognized as the usual budget bluster. The £400m or so per year was the fairly standard haul from closing the loopholes waiting to be dealt with that year. The anti-avoidance rule would not happen in thirteen years of his government, mainly because mandarins and special advisers all fell for the exaggerated complaint that it would be nightmarish to administer. In fact the most significant announcement for the future of tax avoidance in that 1997 budget was one that officially at least had nothing to do with the subject: the scrapping of tax credit payments to pension funds on the dividends they received. It foreshadowed the ending in 1999 of a system under which, since the 1970s, corporation tax had been charged when a company paid out a dividend. This charge, known as 'advance corporation tax' or ACT, was set at around 20% of the dividend being paid and, once handed over to the Revenue, could be set against a company's final corporation tax bill.

For big publicly listed companies paying dividends, ACT was all but impossible to avoid. So if a company paid out all its post-tax profits, it had already paid a minimum 20% tax. With corporate tax rates officially at 30% (but in effect slightly lower after legitimate allowances), this set some kind of limit on the incentive to avoid tax, since only a limited proportion of profits could possibly be 'sheltered' from tax. For many firms, in fact, there was no incentive to reduce UK taxable profits because the 20% ACT bill arose on dividends from profits earned all over the world, whereas their corporation tax bills were largely based on UK profits which even at 30% were often far lower.

With the abolition of ACT *every* large UK company had the incentive to avoid tax; a pound off the corporation tax bill was a pound added to the bottom line profit. As tax accounted for 30% of that profit, halving the tax bill with a scheme or two could boost post-tax profits by market-impressing margins. And these would by now feed straight through into the bonuses of the executives responsible for a company's tax strategy. What was more, since the markets were comparing the company with competitors that might already be using the latest wheeze, and needed to be satisfied not just yearly but quarterly, companies would keep coming back for more of the tax avoidance pushers' addictive products.

Return to Rossminster

So it was that by the early 2000s, an era littered with corporate scandals from Enron in the US to Equitable Life in Britain, outwardly respectable companies and their professional advisers had been propelled into the kind of scheming last seen by the tax inspectors who raided Rossminster's offices over twenty years before. Neo-liberal ideology and a couple of extra noughts on the end of deals had seen off any lingering scruples.

Indeed the difference between Rossminster in 1979 and early twenty-first-century corporate tax avoidance was simply value; no single Rossminster scheme came anywhere near the £1bn that TOMS might have cost. But the big money at stake meant that tax avoidance was now practised not by a couple of maverick accountants who were rubbing the authorities up the wrong way but by firms who were hand in glove with the government. While Prudential, for example, was using TOMS and other schemes, it was also at the heart of the government's plans for its new 'stakeholder pensions'; Ernst & Young was acting as administrator for Railtrack and PwC was busy as the government's adviser on the London Underground public-private partnership. They were also half of a Big 4 cartel (following Arthur Andersen's demise) on which Gordon Brown was dependent for the delivery of his cherished private finance initiative. At the same time the increasingly omnipotent accountants-cum-consultants were routinely wining and dining senior officials, not to mention supporting the main political parties by providing staff for research and offering handy retirement jobs for old officials (including senior Inland Revenue staff). They were never going to get the 6 a.m. 'knock' that Rossminster did.

Not that the situation wasn't vexing the Revenue. 'Those who are peddling very contrived, very artificial schemes,' the Inland Revenue's tax policy boss Dave Hartnett told an interviewer, 'should question the ethics of what they are doing.' It was one early example of a well-crafted public intervention by the civil servant who professed an interest in Roman orator Cicero (as well as 'food, wine') in his *Who's Who* entry and who, with his tousled hair and florid features, would dominate the tax avoidance debate for a decade. Harnett also, tellingly, differentiated 'aggressive' tax avoidance from other sorts, a distinction that would ultimately legitimize techniques that cost the Exchequer far more than the 'aggressive' schemes he was condemning. Arrogant tax avoidance professionals shrugged off Hartnett's comments. 'They are trying to raise the moral standard, but that is all very well if you are Mother Teresa,' sniffed PwC's Mother Superior John Whiting (now Treasury adviser on 'tax simplification'). 'We in this country operate on the basis that you pay your taxes according to what the law says . . . There are some schemes that are beyond the pale. But to suggest that all taxpayers should stop trying to reduce bills – I'm sorry, that's not how things operate.'[6]

Indeed it wasn't how things operated in a world where salaries for Big 4 accountancy firm tax partners were now hitting the high hundreds of thousands on the back of tax avoidance. No area of the tax code was safe from the accountants' loophole-detectors. So it was no surprise when the same firms that were picking apart corporate tax laws spotted the booming bonus culture as another fat meal ticket.

Rich pickings

Just as with corporate taxation in the 1990s, employment tax laws had been put at the service of free market capitalism. Successive governments from the 1980s had introduced, and then repeatedly enhanced, an array of tax breaks to 'incentivize' the payment of wages in the form of shares. In broad terms, they operated by allowing a company a deduction against its taxable profits for payments to fund employee share schemes even though the employee would not be taxed on the receipt of shares until some time later. The idea was that workers with an interest in their employer's share price would work harder in the corporate interest and thereby improve the country's economic performance. Once again, however, benign if hopelessly naive intentions turned into tools for the subversion of the tax system.

By the late 1990s a rash of tax avoidance schemes had broken out, as billions of pounds' worth of bonuses were channelled into shares in offshore companies and trusts. From there they would quickly be paid to deserving bankers, management consultants and other masters of the millennial universe, not as taxable income but as more favourably taxed loans, dividends or even the proceeds of selling options. In short, the banker would get his cash without paying full tax and national insurance on it, while the company would get its share scheme tax break when it had in fact paid instant bonuses never intended to be eligible for a tax concession. Not for the first time, however, the advisers overreached themselves and handed the Revenue – far keener to take on the avoidance of income tax than corporation tax – a series of courtroom victories.

Test cases against Deutsche Bank (involving a Caymans-based scheme designed by Deloitte), UBS (a Jersey escape from tax set up by Ernst & Young for 426 bankers with bonuses worth £100m) and management consultants PA Consulting (another Jersey scheme dreamt up Ernst & Young for a fee of £355,000 just for the first year of the scheme), would all eventually end in wins for the taxman. Roughly a decade after the schemes were used, judges led by the Court of Appeal's Sir Alan Moses – who had acted as junior counsel for the Inland Revenue in the late 1980s – had reversed the courts' turn-of-the century lurch towards tolerating avoidance and had turned seriously against contrived schemes. However cleverly dressed up as something else, the bonuses were taxable as part of the recipient's wages.[7] Other schemes folded before they reached the courtroom steps. Twenty-one companies employing an offshore bonus scheme sold by PwC coughed up, while only one of its users, Goldman Sachs, continued to argue (unsuccessfully) for a few more years, before settling on terms that would reverberate through the tax system several years later. Happily for

Goldman's accountants, such reverses arrived long after they had trousered their up-front fees.

While Ernst & Young, PwC and Deloitte had cornered the market for City bonuses, KPMG's febrile tax-planning brains were specializing in ways for the world's wealthy to avoid inconvenient tax bills on personal windfalls. At the same time as their colleagues in the States were selling schemes that the head of the Internal Revenue Service said passed 'from clever accounting and lawyering to theft from the people'[8] and picking up a $426m fine for their troubles, KPMG's British partners were punting out schemes like the 'round the world' plan to avoid capital gains tax. In 2000 one of its customers, the former chairman of FirstGroup, Trevor Smallwood, used the scheme to sell his shares in the company that had grown from the purchase of Aberdeen's public bus service, via the acquisition of privatized rail businesses, into one of the UK's largest travel companies. He did so through a trust that, claimed the accountants, moved from Jersey to Mauritius – from where it was said to have sold the shares – and back to the UK in the same tax year to exploit a loophole and escape a £2.7m tax bill. The courts concluded that the trust in fact never left KPMG's Bristol office and the scheme failed.[9]

Soon afterwards KPMG put dot.com entrepreneur Jason Drummond – who according to one newspaper at the time was 'richer than the Spice Girls put together and is about to get even richer' – into a fantastically contrived scheme to shelter a multi-million-pound gain on a share sale. The founder of Virtual Internet would buy other people's life insurance policies before surrendering them, creating artificial tax losses that would wipe out Drummond's otherwise taxable gains. The ruse became 'a preferred strategy for KPMG's clients', said a tribunal before dismissing it as having 'no purpose ... other than the facilitation of the tax avoidance strategy', in which the financiers were 'acting out a charade'.[10] And it wasn't long before KMPG was caught out again, flogging an immensely complex scheme involving loans to offshore trusts which were then traded at losses to offset the taxable incomes, totalling £156m, of sixty-four clients led by Graham Edwards, now chief executive of Telereal Trillium, the property company that owns the country's jobcentres under a PFI scheme. A tax tribunal concluded: 'The scheme is entirely artificial and the appellants had no commercial purposes in entering into it other than generating an artificial loss to set against taxable income.'[11]

Amid all these shenanigans, however, KPMG and the other firms never once breached the 'prison wall' between avoidance and evasion on this side of the Atlantic. 'Advisers in America became dishonest,' Dave Hartnett later observed. 'I haven't seen that to anything like the same extent in the UK.'[12] Unlike in the States, he might have added, no investigations into exactly how the schemes were devised and sold were ever conducted.

Open sesame

What Hartnett and officials over at the Treasury *had* seen was an alarming fall in corporation tax receipts from a high of £34.3bn in 1999/2000 to £28.1bn in 2003/04, discomfiting Treasury economists and prompting awkward questions from Gordon Brown as his second term spending splurge turned into stubborn budget deficits.[13] The reasons for the shortfall clearly included corporation tax avoidance and leakage from another source upon which the chancellor was increasingly reliant: income tax from bumper City bonuses. The latter loss was especially galling for a chancellor who defended big City bonuses in the face of public anger, but was not collecting the 50% in tax and national insurance he expected as the price of his principles.

Schemes enabling big business to avoid VAT payments were flying off the tax advisers' shelves, too. Ernst & Young, described by

Hartnett as 'probably the most aggressive, creative, abusive provider' of schemes, had devised a ruse in which shoppers using plastic would pay 97.5% of their bills to the shop for their purchases and 2.5% to another company for 'card handling services' that were exempt from VAT. Bills were instantly carved up at the electronic till into the proportions required to produce the 2.5% VAT-free fee within the same total and most customers had no idea they were being corralled into tax avoidance. Although Ernst & Young pioneered the scheme with Tesco, and other shops including W.H. Smith, Marks & Spencer, Boots and Sainsbury were all enthusiastic users, it was Debenhams who ended up, unsuccessfully, in court over their version, which they codenamed PITA, or 'pain-in-the-arse'.[14] It certainly was for other, smaller, shops being undercut by tax avoidance. Not to mention Gordon Brown, glumly staring at reddening public finances.

So when in the weeks before the 2004 budget the chancellor's officials called the Revenue for some tax-raising ideas, the taxmen were ready with plans they had been mulling – in the face of studious Treasury indifference – for years. One idea was to overhaul the tax authorities' pedestrian response to tax avoidance, with inspectors only identifying schemes two or more years after the event, by which time they had been flogged to death. Instead, the government would demand that the hawkers of new wheezes come clean up front under a new 'disclosure' regime.

This was not before time. Similar rules had long been operating productively in the United States, but progress here had been prevented by an ill-timed move from the Inland Revenue in the opposite direction of 'customer service'. And the biggest companies were the most favoured customers even though their tax avoidance was going through the roof. A 2004 Revenue survey of one hundred of the largest companies – prompted by the drop in corporation tax receipts – found that the tax inspectors dealing with them considered 16% to be 'serial avoiders', 39% 'opportunistic avoiders' and

45% 'non-avoiders'.[15] The figures tallied with a survey that Deloitte had prepared privately, showing that 52% of multinationals used 'novel tax planning ideas which they would expect the Revenue to challenge and/or test in the courts'.[16]

There was indeed plenty for the new disclosure system to flush out. In August that year, tax avoidance 'promoters' reported selling 259 separate tax avoidance schemes in the first two months of the new regime: 161 'financial' schemes of which the Pru's TOMS would be an example, and 98 'employment' schemes that usually ensured big bonuses went untaxed. Most would have been sold to dozens of customers who had to reveal on their tax returns the type of scheme they were using. This was a massive information dump, and galvanized the response to tax avoidance. The system was far from perfect – many tax scheme 'promoters' couldn't resist hunting out loopholes in the disclosure rules themselves and others brazenly ignored them – but before long it had proved the most effective single anti-tax avoidance measure on record. The Revenue could analyse and either investigate or outlaw schemes within weeks rather than years. In the first five years of the scheme, estimated HMRC, sixty-two different schemes were legislated against, blocking an estimated £12.5bn in tax avoidance.[17]

The power of early intelligence also taught the Treasury minister responsible for tax, Dawn Primarolo, a one-time firebrand nicknamed 'Red' Dawn who had slipped quietly into a life of junior ministerial loyalty, that 'we are not always able to anticipate the ingenuity and inventiveness of the avoidance industry'. Henceforth, she announced in December 2004, share-based schemes to avoid income tax and national insurance on bonuses worth an anticipated £2bn that year would be shut down retrospectively. Even if a tax avoider found an effective loophole, once it was picked up under the new rules it would be shut down and a back-tax bill handed to the avoider. It was the first time such a measure had been used since Denis Healey moved against Rossminster's 'commodity carry' scheme in 1978.[18] As then, righteous indignation from tax advisers turned amateur constitutionalists was not long in coming. Guardian of the inalienable British right to avoid tax, PwC's John Whiting, reliably pronounced: 'We don't do retrospective taxation here. You are taxed on what it says in the law when you do the thing, not what someone decides later.'[19] The move worked nonetheless and share schemes rapidly subsided with no more revolutionary consequence than a few bankers paying the right amount of tax.

What worked for income tax avoidance would not, however, be extended to equally expensive corporate tax dodging. A year later Dawn Primarolo was in the House again, announcing the closure of a complex 'dividend strips' scheme through which banks were buying the rights to dividends on shares (so-called 'strips') without owning those shares. They would then sell those rights and claim that a loophole in tax laws meant that the proceeds were not taxable while the costs of buying the strips would be deductible in calculating their profits. Overall, it was estimated that the scheme would have cost around £4bn and, in Hartnett's words, 'wiped out, substantially, the tax liability of banks and other financial institutions using it'.[20] Yet neither this nor a string of later corporate tax schemes would be closed retrospectively, allowing those deals already signed to escape the guillotine. The main objection to retrospective legislation was based on its affront to human rights, and that the rights of corporate avoiders were respected more than those of individual avoiders said much about the times.

The Treasury had also lost its nerve on a general anti-avoidance rule even though there was still plenty to play for and the schemes continued to pour in. By 2008, 1,053 schemes had been reported (around a third flogged by the Big 4 accountancy firms) and used 13,797 times – around 14 users per scheme.[21] In 2007/08, 207 separate schemes were sold, and latest figures show this has fallen to around 120 being marketed each year.[22] This is still a substantial volume of artificial tax avoidance, and makes the 2005 statement from Dave Hartnett that within three years 'we will have made tax avoidance not worthwhile' look hyperbolic.[23] But he was right to foresee some improvement; one Big 4 partner explained that the regime 'definitely put off some of the big companies from going for the more contrived schemes' in order to avoid being branded as tax avoiders.[24] That at least was the mood in boardrooms that gave a toss what the taxman thought about them. One most definitely did not.

Banking on tax breaks

From their new headquarters in the Treasury's smartly refurbished Whitehall building, on a clear day tax officials could look up from the latest wheeze to hit their desks and marvel at the biggest single source of tax loss in Britain. Five miles to the east, behind the shimmering glass of the Canary Wharf tower, sat the precision fiscal engineers of Barclays Bank's 'structured capital markets' operation, performing activities that the bank's seventeenth-century Quaker founders certainly wouldn't have recognized.

The clandestine operation, then barely known outside Barclays and the Revenue, had its origins in the bank's investment banking arm, Barclays de Zoete Wedd. Although ditched in the late 1990s as an unloved underperformer, BZW did bequeath the bank a nice line in tax avoidance. It had been honed in the 1980s onslaught on tax reliefs for industry-boosting investment in plant and machinery which, post-Rossminster, had become the main field of play for big-time tax avoidance.

Only rarely and well after the event was the action glimpsed. Two schemes from the early 1990s eventually appeared in the courts a decade later to illustrate what was going on at BZW. In one, its subsidiary Barclays Mercantile Business Finance Ltd (BMBF) bought from Bord Gáis (the Irish gas board) an 'interconnector' gas pipeline spanning the Irish Sea to Scotland (originally built,

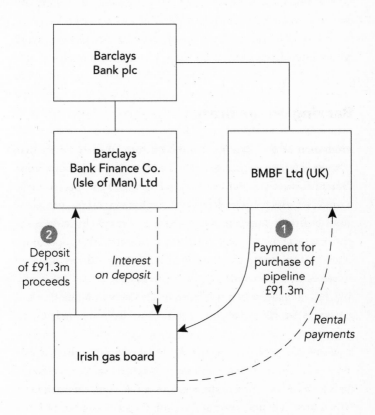

Fig. 5 Barclays buys a gas pipeline (or does it?)

incidentally, with a taxpayer-funded EU grant). But of course the bank had no use for a pipeline; this was just the first step in a ruse through which BMBF would lease the pipeline *back* to Bord Gáis. Meanwhile the £91m Barclays paid to buy the pipeline, and on which it claimed the tax allowances, was deposited by the gas board with a Barclays company on the Isle of Man, as collateral for its future lease payments.

In reality the gas board kept every bit of its pipeline, and the bank retained its money, albeit in a different pocket. But up popped around £30m worth of tax allowances for Barclays, the benefit of which would be shared with the Irish gas board. The Revenue, rehearsing all the arguments that held sway in the Ramsay case, contended that once again money had just gone round in a circle. But in the early 2000s the higher courts, led by the mercurial Lord Hoffmann – more famous for approving a series of executions in Britain's overseas territories while serving as an Amnesty International fundraising director – were swinging back towards a more literal interpretation of tax laws with a focus on 'statutory construction'. They hadn't entirely rejected the 'Ramsay principle' but still concluded that the Barclays company had incurred real costs – as the law stipulated – on the pipeline and could have its allowances.[25]

Such were the fine distinctions of tax avoidance. If a scheme went all the way through the courts, much would depend on the judges' preference for competing doctrines of legal interpretation. A literal, reductionist view would probably see a scheme work as it had in the first BMBF case; a more rounded view of the economic reality would strike it out as it had in Ramsay. It was a debate that felled a forest or two in learned papers, but for a major-league tax avoider like Barclays, the lesson was simple: boost your chances with quantity as well as quality.

The scores of schemes emerging from Barclays were a serious headache for an under-resourced Inland Revenue that could be tied up for years on any given scheme. The bank, meanwhile, wanted to bank its tax breaks as soon as it could. So an unholy truce was reached: every year Barclays would divulge the rudiments of its many schemes, against a few of which the taxman would take up the cudgels while nodding through the remainder.

This was expensive to say the least. When, in 2004, the Revenue took a closer look at the tax avoiders punching the biggest holes in Gordon Brown's finances, an internal report noted: 'Barclays produces structured capital markets products that are the subject of pre-return negotiations and enquiry. For example there were 20 products used/sold in the 2003 [accounting period], some more than once.' Under the reproachful heading 'Adjustments at company level that parliament did not intend', the Revenue noted that 'total tax lost in schemes for 2002/03 is estimated at £638m not including several schemes where tax saving is not in the UK (another £300m)'.[26]

As a one-stop shop creating, financing and selling tax avoidance schemes, Barclays 'structured capital markets' was a souped-up Rossminster mark II tax avoidance factory, with a crucial difference. In the age of open cross-border markets it was doing more than exploiting loopholes in domestic tax rules; it was gaming different countries' tax systems too, multiplying the tax avoidance possibilities. 'Tax arbitrage', as it became known, meant playing one set of tax laws off against another. It might involve engineering payments between countries, usually the UK and US, that would be tax-deductible in the country from which they were paid but not effectively taxed where they were received. No economic profit or loss, just a tax break. A US company, for example, could make a payment that the American taxman considered to be interest on a debt and for which it would give a tax break. But the same financial instrument could be designed so that under UK tax law it looked like a shareholding and the receipt from it would be a dividend. Many 'preference shares' for example, carrying a right to fixed annual dividend, might be viewed in the US as debts but under the UK's more legalistic tests would be shares. When the Revenue taxed a dividend on them it would also give a 'credit' for US tax paid on what it considered a distribution of the US company's profits, effectively *not* taxing it. This produced a tax break in one country, with no corresponding tax bill in the other. And the clever thing was that both countries' tax authorities would think their rules were just fine and it was the other that was being shafted.

Even smarter, a bank in the UK could lend, say, $1bn to a US bank in this way – generating tax-free income in the UK but a tax deduction in the US – and then simply borrow it back. For the second leg a different instrument could be used that generated tax-free income in the US and a tax deduction in the UK. The banks had simply swapped $1bn, to no economic effect beyond two tax breaks, while quite possibly keeping any mention of the debts off either's balance sheet. Such tricks – the creation of debt more for tax advantages than real business need – undoubtedly contributed to huge levels of inter-bank indebtedness that triggered the financial crisis. By 2008 Barclays, for example, had 'leverage' (the ratio of its debts to its shareholder funds) of around 37, while across British banking the ratio had risen from around 25 in 2003 to over 35 before the autumn 2008 crisis.[27]

The great disappearing tax trick could also be played with 'hybrid entities' that looked like different legal vehicles from opposite sides of the Atlantic. What might in the States be seen as a distinct US company, for example, could be viewed under UK tax law as a US branch of a British company. The trick had been simple to engineer ever since, in 1997, the deregulatory Clinton administration cut through complex 'entity classification' rules with a 'check the box' system allowing tax planners to classify legal entities however they wanted. A simple recipe then was to add some debt to one of these hybrid entities, leave to simmer for a few months to produce interest costs, then claim these against corporate profits both in the

UK – since the vehicle was merely considered a branch and thus a part of a UK company – *and* in the US where it was classified as a separate American company. The costs of corporate borrowing could thus be subsidized by two tax breaks adding up to over 60%.

When one arbitrage scheme – operated by Barclays in a 2003 partnership with US bank Wachovia – was exposed, the founder of the bank's 'structured capital markets' operation, Roger Jenkins, became known as 'King of the Double Dip'.[28] It was an unwelcome appearance in the spotlight for Jenkins, but with personal income reported at up to £75m a year, a glamorous Bosnian wife who mingled with the international jet set and an Olympic 400m medalist-turned-jailbird brother, the shaven-headed Jenkins at last gave reporters struggling with tax avoidance something to colour their reports.[29]

He was, though, merely one of a triumvirate who had joined Barclays de Zoete Wedd in the mid-1990s before taking their 'structured finance' tax business to the bank's investment banking reincarnation, Barclays Capital. Fuelling the effort with huge bonuses for its elite tax schemers was the boss of Barclays Capital, Bob Diamond, the American banker who had joined BZW after reportedly falling out with his old employer CS First Boston over a derisory £8m bonus. He would soon make BarCap the bank's most profitable arm on the back of its structured capital markets team before, in 2011, taking the chief executive position from which he would have to resign over the LIBOR-rigging scandal the following year. Tax avoidance was critical to the meteoric rise of one of the world financial crisis's most controversial characters.

No less important than these alpha males at the time was a bright Scottish lawyer and chartered accountant called Iain Abrahams, who arrived with a CV that for a tax avoider was like the Royal Shakespeare Company via RADA for an actor: Ernst & Young in London and New York, then the 'magic circle' law firm Slaughter & May. It was an education in the key tax disciplines of accountancy, law and banking that, allied with a certain kind of imagination that finds its natural home in tax avoidance, became the real motor in the Barclays tax avoidance engine.

Risky business

When the economy-threatening reality of big-time corporate tax avoidance dawned on the Revenue and, in 2005, it launched its 'serial avoiders' project to nail the main culprits, Barclays was inevitably the first name on the list. An exhaustive review of the company's tax affairs, codenamed Project Thames, was instigated to get to the bottom of some of the big schemes and, more importantly, make the company mend its ways. It was a model that, once politically correctly relabelled as the 'high risk corporates' project, would be repeated for thirty-eight companies over the following six years.[30]

Whether it worked with Barclays is far from certain. Around £300m in tax was extracted from the company on profits from controversial payment protection insurance. This was sold through a couple of Dublin subsidiary companies that wrote the policies but fell foul of 'transfer pricing' rules requiring them to pay for services provided from Britain. The tax would almost certainly have been recovered without Project Thames; indeed eyebrows were raised when – following the personal intervention of Dave Hartnett – Barclays was not charged a penalty for getting its tax return so wildly wrong in relation to the PPI business, when the Revenue's own rules suggested it should have been.[31] As for changing behaviour, it would take more than a few words from the authorities to wean a hardcore addict off the drug it had been hooked on for decades.

More emerged about Barclays' tax avoidance habit in the space of a few days in February 2009 – four months after the worldwide banking bailout – than had done in the previous twenty years. When a team I was working with from the *Guardian* newspaper reported the bank's by then somewhat dated tax avoidance history, a well-connected source decided now was the time, in the wake of the financial crisis, to get some things off his or her chest. In came a batch of internal memos documenting seven separate tax structures set up in 2006 and 2007, proving that neither the disclosure rules nor the 'high risk corporates' approach had dampened Barclays' ardour for tax avoidance. Among the new schemes were Project Knight, said to be 'not disclosable in the UK', under which $16bn was channelled through an array of partnerships and offshore companies, to 'double dip' tax relief on interest paid by US banks. Then there was Project Berry, involving the sale and repurchase of UK government securities between Barclays and a subsidiary company, generating an extra tax deduction for payments of 'manufactured interest' by Barclays. Another, authored by Iain Abrahams himself and called Project Valiha, enabled the bank to cash in profitable swaps with Credit Suisse tax free using a web of Cayman and Luxembourg companies and partnerships. All reached impenetrable levels of complexity, well above what a US senator bamboozled by tax avoidance once termed the 'MEGO' – 'my eyes glaze over' – threshold.

The schemes went a long way to explaining why Barclays had over 300 tax haven subsidiary companies, 181 of them in the Cayman Islands.[32] Most existed to exploit the havens' relaxed regulations and corporate laws (written at the behest of the finance industry) that enabled the wackier corporate manoeuvrings required for a tax avoidance scheme to take place very quickly, no questions asked. Reflecting the value of Barclays' work and its financial clout, the tax breaks on the schemes were split with the client either 70/30 or 80/20 in Barclays' favour (rates that would have turned Tucker and Plummer green with envy). And they were all signed off with legal advice from Abrahams' old firm Slaughter & May – which boasts thirteen 'tax-efficient financing' partners – plus accountancy advice from PwC.[33]

These stark revelations did not elicit the contrition expected of bankers in the months following their rescue by the taxpayer. Instead, in came a High Court injunction demanding removal of the documents from the *Guardian*'s website, though this was soon neutered when Lib Dem peer Matthew Oakeshott brought them up in parliament. His colleague Vince Cable fumed: 'It is incongruous and offensive that banks which are either directly or indirectly dependent on the government should be systematically finding ways to avoid tax ... Reputable banks don't turn tax avoidance into a profit machine.' Within weeks, two of Barclays' Project Knight clients had pulled out under political pressure, but it was clear that serial avoidance was alive and kicking in Canary Wharf. 'Every single thing SCM [structured capital markets] does is a tax trade,' said another source. 'The deals start with tax and then commercial purpose is added to them. We were told that in one year SCM made between £900m and £1bn profit [for the bank] from tax avoidance.'[34]

Barclays was not the only bank running elaborate tax rings round the government. Whistle-blowers exposed Lloyds TSB as being up to similar tricks, if not on quite the same scale. The bank – a recent recipient of £17bn of public money and by then 43% owned by the taxpayer – was even fighting to salvage a tax avoidance scheme through the courts. Before long bankers suffering crises of conscience had dumped details of now publicly owned Royal Bank of Scotland's 'arbitrage' schemes (said to be worth £500m) in the *Guardian*'s inbox, prompting the bank's new management to shut its 'structured finance' business down. 'The idea that we could take support from the Treasury with one hand and somehow pick their pocket with the other would be wrong on every level,' one banker said.[35]

Parliament's inevitable post-crisis questions met with thinly veiled contempt. John Varley, Barclays chief executive at the time, told MPs in the wilfully blind manner of a Murdoch executive

denying knowledge of phone hacking, 'I don't recognize this statement that we have undertaken tax avoidance schemes.'[36] A year later
his successor, Diamond, who couldn't credibly play the wise monkey,
budged a bit further. 'It is our obligation, when we do financing
for clients, to do it in the most tax-efficient way,' he claimed.[37] Tax
avoidance was not an optional sideline, but at the very heart of
banking the Barclays way, and it would not be until the humiliation
of other scandals, notably LIBOR-rigging, that the practice was
questioned under a wider reappraisal of the bank's culture.

Court short

Perhaps the most remarkable feature of the Barclays tax avoidance story was what it did *not* contain: any legal action against the
bank since its gas pipeline and other leasing schemes of fifteen
years earlier. In the intervening period it had almost certainly run
hundreds of separate tax avoidance schemes (one of the *Guardian*'s
sources put the figure at up to seventy 'tax trades' on the go in any
year). Each, by definition, exploited uncertainties in tax law that
the bank would prefer to see one way and the Revenue another. In
2002/03, the taxman had put the annual loss at over £600m, equal
to the running costs of over a hundred secondary schools. Yet not
once did a dispute have to be resolved in court. The bank might
have backed down from some schemes before litigation, although
Jenkins and his team were known more for macho bonding ritu-
als than climbdowns in the face of timid taxmen. Several insiders
vouch that the bank won far more of what battles it did have with
the taxman than it lost. As one of the *Guardian*'s whistle-blowers
put it: 'It is a commonly held view that no agency in the US or the
UK has the resources or the commitment to challenge [Barclays].'[38]

Not many corporate tax avoiders, for that matter, were being
seen in court. In five years from April 2006 the Revenue put just

eight corporation tax avoidance schemes – all of which took place before the end of 2003 – before the tax tribunal that is the first step in the legal process.[39] Although each case would determine the outcome for several other users of the scheme involved, this was still a derisory effort. The fact that, from 2007, HMRC's own rules stipulated that when it came to tax avoidance disputes the authorities would take an 'all or nothing' approach made the picture even more astonishing.

This small sample of cases seeing the light of day did at least indicate where the most contrived tax avoidance schemes were taking place. All but two were executed by banks and an insurance company: Hill Samuel (part of the Lloyds TSB group), Bank of Ireland, HBOS, Nationwide, a Morgan Stanley subsidiary and Prudential. What this showed was that tax avoidance had become one more financial trading activity for Britain's bankers, deftly marrying the markets and multibillion-pound transactions with the endless 'opportunities' lurking within the labyrinthine tax code. Every year, the latest 'asymmetries', 'arbitrages' and other tricks would reduce their tax bills. Such schemes were in fact essential for a bank looking to avoid serious amounts of tax because the financial regulations under which they operate close off the blunter tax avoidance instrument of shifting capital and profits wholesale into related companies in lower-taxed territories to secure permanently lower tax bills. For conglomerates outside the City, unencumbered by such restrictions, the international tax game offered even richer alternatives.

4
Foreign Adventures

Tax havens at the heart of Europe enable Britain's corporate elite to slash billions off their tax bills

---

Nestled awkwardly where France, Belgium and Germany's western border meet, the Grand Duchy of Luxembourg has been a continental battleground for hundreds of years; the scene of the last major German offensive of the Second World War. So in 1957 it was unsurprisingly an enthusiastic founder member of the European Economic Community. But while it signed up for the economic privileges that come with membership of what is now the European Union, Luxembourg also turned to lax regulation (eventually throwing up the infamous BCCI banking scandal) and secretive, predatory financial services to carve out a distinctive role for itself among its more industrialized neighbours, especially after its once successful steel industry collapsed in the wake of the 1970s oil crisis. By the 1990s an open world economy was presenting opportunities for what was now a financial centre that went far beyond the stereotypical 'Belgian dentist' suitcasing undeclared earnings across the border for deposit in anonymous accounts. The Grand Duchy was now the bolt-hole of choice for a far richer cross-border tax-dodger: the acquisitive multinational company.

Employing the standard tax haven ploy of adapting its law to suit companies looking to avoid another country's tax, Luxembourg boasts special rules for intermediate 'holding companies' through which a multinational business from one country owns companies in another. Among their advantages, Luxembourg holding companies are not taxed on dividends they receive from their subsidiary companies, nor on the gains they make when they sell these companies. Better still, the profits of these companies' foreign branches are also exempted from tax. Ordinarily, however, the countries hosting such branches *do* tax them, so this should not be a great tax avoidance opportunity. But if a company can find one that does not, the tax avoidance possibilities open up. Which is where Luxembourg's comrade in tax-avoiding arms, Switzerland, comes in.

The twenty-six regional cantons of Switzerland, local states-within-a-state enjoying a large degree of fiscal autonomy, are every bit as expert in designing tax incentives as they are expensive watches. Capitalizing on branch exemptions offered by the likes of Luxembourg, many offer special 'finance branch' tax rules that inhabit a fiscal make-believe world. These cantons ostensibly tax the profits of such local branches at normal rates, usually somewhere around 25%, but levy the tax on an entirely fictional profit. If the branch receives income of, say, €100m and has no expenses to speak of, because it is funded entirely by interest-free capital, its profit will also be €100m. But if a Swiss tax official is doing the calculations the branch will be *deemed* to be funded by interest-bearing loans and the profit for tax purposes will typically fall to well below €10m. Only on this smaller figure will Swiss tax be levied. The result is explained by leading tax avoidance adviser Ernst & Young in its brochure on the joy of Swiss tax: 'In several Cantons a finance branch may be taxed at an effective rate of less than 2% of its accounting income due to the notional interest deduction.'[1]

Swiss branches of Luxembourg companies are thus tax avoidance gold for a multinational group of companies. They can lend money to other companies in the group, which pay interest that reduces profits being taxed at perhaps 30%. If the corresponding income earned by the Swiss branch is taxed at less than 2%, that's a big overall saving without the group overall incurring any cost at all. This was the perfect tax break for a company in one country looking to invest billions in another.

Mobile capital

It wasn't hard to spot the British captain of industry in Room 111 of Dusseldorf's regional criminal court on the morning of 25 March 2004. He was the upright 55-year-old with neatly side-parted silver hair, sporting a dark pinstriped suit, crisp white shirt, sombre tie and cufflinks.

Sir Christopher Gent, recently retired chief executive of Vodafone, was about to take the stand in defence of half a dozen directors of German engineering and telecoms giant Mannesmann who were facing fraud charges dating back to the British mobile phone company's acquisition of their firm four years before. The €180bn deal had been the largest takeover in European corporate history, originating in a corporate strategy that Gent called 'hunt or be hunted'. Facilitated by bonus payments to Mannesmann's directors running to €57m, it pitted his aggressive brand of Anglo-Saxon capitalism against the more consensual Rhineland variety. But huge windfalls for the bosses weren't the only excess that freewheeling capital markets brought with them.

A cross-border takeover is to Britain's tax lawyers and accountants what a well-fed wildebeest with a limp is to a pride of hungry lions. And this one, the meatiest one ever to have lumbered across the savannah, would be devoured more greedily than any before or since. From the moment the takeover was conceived, 'tax planners' from City law firm Linklaters and accountants PwC were set to work. After a couple of decades of economic liberalization at home and abroad they had plenty of tools at their disposal: two different tax regimes in the UK and Germany to play off against each other, an international financial system allowing them to shift limitless amounts of capital across borders and a pick of tax havens, one of them helpfully within the European Union itself.

On the face of it, the Luxembourg company with a Swiss branch was the ideal conduit for Vodafone's German acquisition. By pouring funds into the German company as loans from this company, rather than directly from the UK, it could recoup some of its massive outlay in tax relief for no real economic cost. But was it open to British multinationals when their government had spent fifteen years shutting down a host of ruses to channel profits into the world's tax havens, and was considered to be among the best in the world at blocking the abuse?

Shut out

The 'controlled foreign companies' (CFC) laws, under which British multinationals' tax haven subsidiaries could generally be taxed in the UK even though they were not resident in the country nor performing any business here, served a crucial purpose in shoring up Britain's vulnerable tax base. But they contained a series of exemptions including one for holding companies that own legitimate foreign trading companies. If such a holding company's income was almost entirely from such companies, it wouldn't be taxed under the CFC laws because the trading companies would already have paid the appropriate amount of tax wherever they operated. Which would normally be fair enough, but by the late 1990s tax advisers had found a loophole in this reasonable exemption and were busily enabling their clients to avoid billions of pounds through it.

Here was the routine. First, set up a Luxembourg holding company and transfer to it the ownership of overseas subsidiary companies. Second, establish a Swiss branch of the holding company. Third, stuff the branch with free money in the form of share capital from the UK. Fourth, get it to lend this money to the subsidiary companies. They will receive tax deductions for the interest payments while, in the hands of the holding company with the Swiss branch that receives them, they are taxed at 2% or less. And crucially, since the income comes from its legitimate trading subsidiaries, the profits of the Luxembourg holding company (including its Swiss branch) still qualify for exemption from the CFC laws. In this way any British multinational buying an offshore business or funding existing overseas operations could dramatically reduce its total tax bill. As tax avoidance goes, it was fairly straightforward, and by the turn of the century scores of companies had been ushered towards the scheme by the big accountancy firms.

Limbering up for its Mannesmann takeover, this was exactly what Vodafone planned, but on a scale far grander than anything seen before. Once it had expensively persuaded the Mannesmann directors to accept its bid and had taken control of the German company, it set about the corporate restructuring needed to insert a Luxembourg company and win the big tax avoidance prize. The transactions themselves would be meat and drink to a corporate lawyer: Vodafone would swap its new shareholding in Mannesmann for shares in a new Luxembourg company, which would subsequently load the German company up with the debt that would work the tax magic.

Unfortunately for the tax planners, the Revenue's patience with what was the latest in a long line of schemes to undermine perhaps its most important anti-tax avoidance laws was already wearing thin. Officials had little difficulty persuading Chancellor Gordon Brown to shut the loophole in his March 2000 'Prudent for a Purpose' budget, which might have been expected to thwart

Vodafone's scheme there and then. But even after the failure of some heavy lobbying of HMRC and Treasury officials, as well as Gordon Brown himself, Vodafone decided to pursue its scheme anyway. It would seek to wriggle out of the CFC tax net by applying for a last-gasp let-out contained in the laws for schemes with no 'motive' to avoid UK tax. This was an optimistic call to say the least since, having just shut the Swiss branch loophole as a tax ruse, the Revenue was unlikely to accept that a company setting up just such a structure did not have a tax avoidance motive. Other companies, less brazen than Vodafone, had ripped up similar plans in light of the new legislation. So when the gory details of the biggest tax avoidance scheme in British history hit a seasoned tax inspector's desk one spring morning in 2000, with a request for a 'clearance' that there was no tax avoidance motive and the restructuring could go through, he wasted little time reaching for the 'reject' stamp.

But why let official disapproval spoil a good wheeze? Vodafone had nothing to lose by going ahead anyway, even with the taxman glowering from the sidelines. The tax break had always been a central element in the acquisition of Mannesmann, lined up before Gordon Brown's inconsiderate budget clampdown. And it still remained a one-way bet. If Vodafone could find a way of defending its tax arrangement it would make billions; if it failed, it would simply pay the standard amount of tax on its profits. And the odds, while slim, did not look impossible. For one thing, the 'motive test' let-out had never been tested in the British courts. For another, Europe's tax lawyers were becoming increasingly excited about overturning national laws against cross-border tax avoidance, such as the 'controlled foreign companies' legislation, on the grounds that they offended 'fundamental freedoms' enshrined in the Treaty of Rome that Luxembourg and its EEC co-founders had signed back in 1957.[2]

Caution: tax avoiders at work

Nothing ventured, nothing gained, Vodafone and its advisers set about erecting their cross-border edifice. Just like charity, however, tax avoidance begins at home. First up, in October 2000, they created a British company called Rapidwave which would own the Luxembourg holding company. So far, so simple. But, while it is easy enough to incorporate a company in the Grand Duchy, if the company is run from the UK, it will remain a UK tax resident. This much had been established ninety-four years before Vodafone's trip to Luxembourg when the British courts decided that one of De Beers' mining companies, although incorporated in South Africa, was in fact a UK tax resident because it was 'centrally managed and controlled' from the company's London office.[3]

To escape British tax residence, overseas companies within a British multinational group therefore must make their big decisions locally, not back home. Thankfully for the world's corporate tax-dodgers, advisers such as PwC are well versed in the rigmarole required to demonstrate this to the taxman. First, the company needs some local stooges – preferably with something meaningful on their CVs – to act as directors. So, to man the board of Vodafone's Luxembourg company, in came Guy Harles, a big cheese in the Luxembourg legal establishment, plus his assistant and a couple of Vodafone's Dutch directors. But the scheme was very much a British initiative and it was Vodafone's Newbury-based financial controller Robbie Barr – number two to group finance director Ken Hydon – who would be calling the shots, though he was careful to do so only when safely out of British airspace.

With the suits in place, by December 2000 Vodafone Investments Luxembourg sarl was born and the tax plan could be executed. Not that anybody strolling past the company's home at 398 route d'Esch (PwC's local offices) – nor past its Swiss branch at 37 Bottigenstrasse, Bern (a local accountant's office), would have guessed at the breathtaking scale of the financial scheming within. In no time VIL, as it would became known by the British tax authorities and courts, was the nondescript receptacle for €118bn (approximately £75bn) of Vodafone's wealth – equal to five times the gross domestic product of Luxembourg itself and over half of Vodafone's entire worth.

Of this money, provided from the UK via Rapidwave as interest-free share capital, €74bn was invested in shares in Vodafone's European subsidiary companies, mainly Mannesmann, while €44bn was lent to them through the Swiss branch, €42.5bn of it to Mannesmann (see figure 6).[4] This latter debt was the key to the tax avoidance trick, and its artificiality was betrayed by the fact that the whole of the Vodafone group, worldwide, was borrowing only *half* this amount.[5] The Mannesmann debt was a tax planner's creation rather than a commercial reality, though nobody need know. While Mannesmann and its acquisition merited 84 mentions in Vodafone's 64-page annual report for the period, there was not a word on the Luxembourg arrangement. The patriotic image of the company whose name was at the time emblazoned across the shirts of the England cricket team need not be tarnished by tax avoidance.

By 31 March 2001, just three and half months after opening up for business, VIL had earned €897m from its loans, with the payers of this interest picking up tax breaks on the costs. Its expenses, such as they were, came to €62,553 while the Swiss tax bill on the net profit was €7.3m, or 0.8%. By the same date the following year VIL's Swiss coffers were swelled by a further €2.9bn interest income, again earned at no meaningful expense, and its tax rate remained at 0.8%.[6] This was serious 'tax efficiency', wiping hundreds of millions of pounds every year off the company's tax bill.

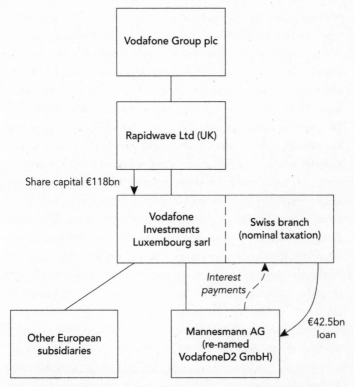

Fig. 6 Vodafone Group plc uses Luxembourg and Switzerland
to indirectly loan Mannesmann AG €42.5bn and avoid billions in UK tax

An inspector calls

Having told the mischievous child he wasn't allowed these sweets, the Revenue's tax inspectors were never going to appreciate seeing him reappear with mouth and pockets bulging with them. So when, in 2002, Rapidwave submitted its first tax return showing that Vodafone had done precisely what the Revenue had told it not to, the inquisition began. Out went a stiff missive from one of the Revenue's principal inspectors in the Glasgow outpost of its Large Business Office. Demanding details of the Luxembourg company's management, legal arrangements and board meetings, he intended to delve deep into VIL's business, probing whether it had in fact achieved non-resident tax status in the first place and, if so, whether it existed to avoid tax so that its profits should still be taxed as those of a 'controlled foreign company'.

This, however, was as far as the investigation would go. The Revenue, Vodafone's lawyers complained to a tax tribunal, could not even ask about the tax return of Rapidwave, by now renamed 'Vodafone 2', and its Luxembourg subsidiary or its Swiss branch. The laws that would defeat its scheme, they said, contravened the founding European Treaty and the taxman's enquiry should be strangled at birth. An epic, Jarndyce v. Jarndyce level legal battle ensued, as the tribunal referred the knotty European law questions governing the matter to the European Court of Justice in Luxembourg. But this referral was itself appealed by the Revenue, which thought that even if the law was uncertain it still had cause enough to ask Vodafone to turn out its filing cabinets. Eventually the procedural wrangle ended up in the Court of Appeal where in July 2006, more than six years after Vodafone first snaffled Mannesmann, it was decided that, yes, the European Court *should* look at the question.

As it happened, the Luxembourg judges were already mulling Britain's anti-tax avoidance laws in connection with Cadbury Schweppes' exploitation of 1990s' tax incentives in Dublin, where the company had located its money management arm and was sheltering interest received from the US following its acquisition of fizzy drink company Dr Pepper. And no sooner had the Vodafone file landed on their desks than the European Court judges concluded that Britain's controlled foreign companies laws could apply only to 'wholly artificial arrangements', not where the tax haven company 'carries on genuine economic activities', even if it was based in one of Europe's new tax havens purely for the tax breaks.[7]

On which note the European Court thought it had said quite enough on the subject already and declined to look at Vodafone specifically. It was left to the British courts to decide whether the UK's laws were compliant with EU law as clarified in the European Court's Cadbury judgment. Domestic legal battle was joined once more; Vodafone arguing that the CFC laws simply could not be interpreted in line with Europe's liberal economic strictures and so – as it had said from the start – the Revenue had no grounds to question its Luxembourg–Switzerland arrangement. Three more English court hearings later, on 22 May 2009 the Revenue's legal team, led by its mainstay David Ewart QC and leading European law silk David Anderson QC, sat in the Court of Appeal to hear Chancellor Sir Andrew Morritt deliver a comprehensive judgment in their favour. The Revenue's 'controlled foreign companies' laws *were* capable of being interpreted in line with European law.

Without question, this was a big victory for the taxman, confirmed when the Supreme Court finally slammed the door in Vodafone's face in December 2009. The taxman could now challenge the tax avoidance scheme. And since Vodafone had routed €42.5bn of debt through a Swiss branch of a Luxembourg company that employed one official on a junior accountant's salary, when the whole Vodafone empire combined had just €22bn, it looked well within even the European Court's narrow sights. So would the Revenue dust off the Glasgow tax inspector's seven-year-old letter and get stuck in?

Fig. 7 Behind closed doors: the locked office that is home to Vodafone's
Luxembourg companies' multibillion pound Swiss finance branches

Sale of the century

Things had moved on in the years since Vodafone's plans were first
given short shrift by tax inspectors and government alike. For one
thing, the Mannesmann investment, like many an overpriced, tax-
geared acquisition of the early noughties, had gone sour, prompting
a €50bn write-down of its investment value. This appeared to have
enabled VIL to cease using its Swiss branch as the Luxembourg
authorities generously agreed the paper losses could be set against
the company's interest income and wipe out any tax bill without

the Swiss detour. Comically, however, the branch in Bern would be maintained as an unoccupied locked room in an accountant's office so that loans could be 'parked' there for a few days over the company's accounting date and escape even the relatively minor Luxembourg wealth tax that was levied on assets held in the Grand Duchy at these times.

As Mannesmann and other companies continued to pay money into VIL, the tax avoidance provided some ongoing compensation for the flawed acquisition. Up to 31 March 2010, the Luxembourg company earned interest on its loans to fellow Vodafone companies of €16.8bn. In the same period, despite minimal expenses to set against these, VIL had paid €89m in tax, an overall rate of less than 1%.[8] If a renewed investigation could catch the profits of the Luxembourg company under the anti-tax avoidance laws, the taxman stood to gain the difference between this tax bill and UK corporation tax at up to 30%, plus interest. The stakes were now appreciably higher, but whereas a thorough investigation had been the order of the day eight years earlier, by 2010 less confrontational channels had opened up between large companies and HM Revenue and Customs.

Years of navel-gazing on the subject of large corporate tax administration had created an extremely business-friendly tax authority. At its apex sat HM Revenue and Customs' ambitious but impressionable 'permanent secretary for tax' Dave Hartnett, valuing his department's 'relationship' with big business above all else. Further down the HMRC chain the mood music had softened, too. The Glasgow official who in his searching 2002 letter had signed himself 'Principal Inspector' was by now a 'Customer Relationship Manager' in Reading. Where once the company had Taggart on its case, now it had David Brent.

HMRC's 'relationship' with Vodafone was closer than most. The company's deputy tax director John Connors had until 2007 been an HMRC director. Connors had some handy experience on his CV as right-hand man to Hartnett on a 2006 review of the department's relationship with business (conclusion: ease off). Another relationship was even more important. While the legal dispute had been rumbling on, Vodafone's finance director since 2006, Andy Halford, had regularly met Dave Hartnett under HMRC's 'board-to-board' agenda, purportedly aimed at instilling responsible attitudes to tax in Britain's boardrooms. Now it was time for some serious face-to-face.

And when it came to talking turkey, another familiar face in the world of tax turned up in the urbane person of Deloitte's senior British partner David Cruickshank. Over several years he and Hartnett had sat across the table negotiating settlements on some of the biggest disputes, the closeness of their relationship apparent from the later disclosure that in five years the pair had met forty-eight separate times.[9] Now he appeared as Vodafone's adviser and, although Hartnett would insist that Vodafone, not he, brought Cruickshank into the discussions, one Vodafone insider at least disagreed. '[Cruickshank] even held the first meeting in the Treasury building – we didn't know he was even invited!' wrote an informant to *Private Eye*. 'It was supposed to be an informal exchange of views with Dave Hartnett before everything kicked off. Instead we find the meter [ie Deloitte's billing] is already running.' Whatever the truth in this allegation, the Deloitte man's involvement betrayed the importance of personal relationships in determining what should have been cold questions of law. Cruickshank had no special expertise in the matter at hand; indeed there were scores of better qualified advisers on the subject. And, since his firm Deloitte was Vodafone's auditor, his appointment to advise on a multibillion-pound bone of contention posed a normally prohibitive conflict of interest that had to be cleared by the Vodafone board and specially noted in its annual report. But as Cruickshank was known for getting deals with Hartnett, he was worth it.

This particular deal was sealed at the Revenue's 100 Parliament Street headquarters on 22 July 2010 after the case had been, in

Hartnett's word, 'escalated' away from senior tax officials to his direct control. The influential Halford (who the week before had been appointed by Treasury minister David Gauke to his 'Business Forum on Tax and Competitiveness') and Cruickshank sat opposite Hartnett and HMRC's director general for business tax, Melanie Dawes. Dawes was a former Treasury economist with no background in tax law or investigations who would soon depart for the Cabinet Office. The businessmen had little trouble persuading the pair to take £1.25bn as a settlement covering the whole ten years of the scheme. But, since Halford didn't want to cough up more than £800m straightaway, the company would be given five years to pay £450m of the bill (with no interest). The settlement would also allow the company to report in its results announcement the very next day that no tax bill would arise on the offshore arrangement in future.[10] Since HMRC at the time was pursuing a policy of not applying its offshore laws to tax haven subsidiaries only if they sent a large proportion of their profits – upwards of 70% – back to the UK as taxable dividends, and later accounts would show that Vodafone was not doing this, the clearance was especially generous. As was the time-to-pay agreement. There was no statutory basis for extending a large company so much interest-free credit, and this was about as least deserving a cause for special treatment as could be imagined anyway. Not only did the bill arise from a tax avoidance scheme, but Vodafone was sitting on a £9bn cash pile,[11] one of the biggest in the corporate world, and paying over £5bn a year in dividends to shareholders. If ever a taxpayer might have been told to empty its pockets, it was this one.

Halford was as pleased as Punch. 'I think the CFC [settlement], although it is a reasonable sized cash outflow here, is actually very good,' he enthused to stock market analysts. 'We have got a lot of benefit from this over the last nine years, and it now secures the position going forwards, and a reasonable proportion of the group's free cash flow obviously does come from the tax efficient structuring we have got, and we have now got that certainty going forwards.'[12] In other words, a fair chunk of Vodafone's stock market-delighting cash flow, which grew from around £2.5bn to £7bn a year over the period, had been – and will continue to be – the fruits of tax avoidance.

It had not been hard to get the better of the Revenue. Hartnett and Dawes might have been the Revenue's top two business tax officials, but neither understood either the details of the Vodafone case or the legislation that governed it. What's more, they conspicuously failed to consult either their own experts in the area, including half a dozen tax inspectors manning a specialist CFC team whose working lives were dedicated to the matters in dispute. Nor did they consult any lawyers to assess the strength of their case, whether the Revenue's own or the external counsel who had taken the case through to the earlier Court of Appeal win. This was perhaps the most staggering feature of the case; what other organization would enter a multibillion-pound negotiation on a legal dispute without taking specialist and legal advice?

Had the Revenue's negotiators investigated and weighed up the case properly, they would have been far more bullish. While handling over €100bn of investments, the Luxembourg company was paying around €50,000 in staff costs, enough for no more than a junior accountant in Luxembourg or Switzerland, wherever he or she was. The company was lending out twice as much money as Vodafone had borrowed worldwide. If this was not 'wholly artificial', what was? As one well-informed tax blogger wrote in 2011, 'Would any court accept that employees being paid €50,000 are consistent with responsibility for managing a loan portfolio of €35bn?'[13] VIL was a far cry from the active cash management operation of Cadbury's Dublin subsidiary, which did meet the European Court's threshold of 'genuine economic activity'. Vodafone itself appreciated this. Soon after the Cadbury decision, in November 2006 Halford had told analysts: 'The Cadbury case, we think overall is slightly positive for us, there are still uncertainties – the Cadbury case does not apply directly to us therefore our situation will have to be looked at separately.'[14] Recognizing its vulnerability, some time in 2008 VIL had begun to employ a few more staff in Luxembourg, although these people appeared to be working on the finances, accounts and taxes of other Vodafone companies that were also exploiting Luxembourg's tax advantages. One boasted on CV website LinkedIn: 'I am currently working with Vodafone Investments Luxembourg, in charge of finance operations for Vodafone Roaming Services' (a separate Luxembourg company – itself highly profitable, incidentally, but paying no tax, thanks to Vodafone's paper losses). Another loyal VIL staffer described his task as 'to support the group's Luxembourg based businesses', adding that he was 'passionate about tax strategy'.[15] But putting a few staff on the books and charging them out to the companies they really worked for was hardly likely to convince a court that VIL's business was 'genuine activity'.

So the Revenue's 2009 Court of Appeal victory should have heralded a decisive offensive, not the hoisting of a white flag. The precise value of Vodafone's tax saving from the settlement is hard to quantify, but it was certainly several billions of pounds. As early as 31 March 2006 the company had set aside £2.2bn for the tax bill. There were over four more years in which VIL would earn more than €6.5bn on its loans, plus more in dividends from subsidiary companies that, if not taxed fully when earned, also would have come within the taxman's net. Meanwhile, interest would continue to run up on bills going back to the start of the scheme almost a decade earlier. Vodafone itself had set aside £900m for its interest bill but it was let off the whole amount. Since interest on late paid tax was first introduced in Hugh Dalton's 1947 budget as one response to a post-war slump, there was a deep irony in the 2010 authorities forgoing the charge in the teeth of the latest crisis. With a 'tax free' clearance given for at least a couple of future years and taking into account the opinions of senior officials, in September

2010 I reported in *Private Eye* that the deal could have cost the taxpayer around £6bn.[16] More remarkably still, I later discovered another similar scheme through yet another Luxembourg company with its own Swiss branch, Vodafone Luxembourg 5 sarl, that had been funding Vodafone's American investments (mainly its 45% stake in Verizon) since 2006 and itself had racked up over $10bn profit on loans by the time of the settlement. By 2011 it was earning $2.5bn a year (taxed at 0.03%), on a $27bn loan paying interest at a thumping 9%, which was not bad for a company with wage costs of less than $10,000. Since it too was cleared as part of the deal, the £6bn estimate now looked very conservative.[17]

When the report sparked the first 'UK Uncut' protest at Vodafone's Oxford Street store a few weeks later, HMRC dismissed the figure as an 'urban myth', but pointedly refused to explain why, citing its commitments to 'taxpayer confidentiality'. Some months later the *Daily Mail*'s Alex Brummer reported that 'Vodafone executives privately have acknowledged to me there may be documents in which a figure close to £6 billion crops up',[18] while an MP on the Public Accounts Committee came up with his own back-of-an-envelope £8bn figure.[19]

Cave-in men

Whatever the precise figure, why would the Revenue so readily concede what was certainly several billions of pounds? In truth, it did not *want* to collect all it could. Dave Hartnett shared the view of the captains of industry and bean counters he consorted with, that the 'controlled foreign companies' laws operated unfairly in these kinds of cases as it was other countries' tax that was being avoided. This much became clear when he later answered questions on the subject before the Treasury Select Committee. 'The profits to which the £6 billion allegedly relates arose in

Luxembourg from activities in Germany and Greece,' claimed Hartnett. In fact, the interest was a legitimate *cost* in these countries, as their tax authorities recognized by giving tax breaks for it. This was quite reasonable; funding businesses with a certain level of debt is commercially standard and revenue authorities around the world, not least Britain's, respect this. Strip away the tax avoidance structure and the economic reality – as the controlled foreign companies laws recognized – was that Vodafone in the UK lent billions to Mannesmann. Vodafone in the UK would have received taxable interest if it had not dog-legged the money through a Luxembourg company purely for a tax break. British tax was avoided; which is exactly how UK tax law had interpreted the arrangement for over twenty-five years, and that should have been the end of the matter for a taxman charged with applying the law on the statute book. But Hartnett was gulled into the view preferred by Vodafone and its advisers, that it was Johnny Foreigner's tax that was being avoided so the Revenue should apply its laws as generously as possible. A month after the Vodafone settlement he would tell the *Financial Times*: 'HMRC is packed full of very intelligent people but we are sometimes too black-and-white about the law.' Which might explain why he decided not to consult those intelligent people.

Among the few repeatable comments I heard from tax inspectors familiar with the case was that the deal was an 'unbelievable cave-in'. It was one that would have serious ramifications for other companies queuing up for their own deals on similar arrangements. At 31 March 2011 the Revenue had 134 of them under enquiry, with £3.74bn tax officially hanging on these, plus perhaps the same amount again in interest on the older bills. (In total, a fair estimate would be that at least something equivalent to the UK's annual £7bn overseas aid budget was hanging on them.) The Revenue's relaxed view of Vodafone's Luxembourg set-up would make a big difference to these companies, some of which found out what they could about Vodafone's deal, plonked the details in front of the taxman and demanded something just as good.[20]

Corporate Britain was certainly receiving far more sympathetic treatment than HMRC's own staff as an enquiry was launched into what was considered its most serious leak for years. All five expert tax inspectors with special responsibility for the controlled foreign companies' legislation were unceremoniously assigned to other duties, even though there was no evidence they had leaked anything, and the loss of expertise would be very damaging. But the purge was necessary 'in order to provide assurance to the markets and companies that work was being kept confidential'.[21] Not for the only time, the 'markets' took priority over the tax system.

At least the minister responsible for the Revenue, David Gauke, approved. 'I was pleased to see HMRC recently achieve the largest cash settlement in the department's history,' he explained in response to the UK Uncut protests against the deal. 'This has brought in extra revenue that has sat in financial purgatory for numerous years, and shows the department and business working to resolve long-outstanding issues.'[22] He was making his speech, appropriately enough, in the offices of Vodafone's adviser on the deal, Deloitte.

And he was wrong. The Vodafone settlement did not bring in 'extra revenue'; it threw billions away. It effectively pre-empted relaxations in the CFC laws that were being considered by the Treasury following heavy business lobbying, enabling the company to tell investors that 'longer term no CFC liabilities are expected to arise as a consequence of the likely reforms of the UK CFC regime due to the facts established in this agreement'.[23] Four months after that comment, Vodafone's deputy tax director John Connors appeared on the Treasury's 'monetary assets working group' looking at precisely how to change the laws determining the treatment of his firm's Luxembourg schemes.[24] So Britain's second biggest company appeared to be privy to legislative changes that had as yet gone nowhere near parliament, and it had a clairvoyant agreement somehow establishing future 'facts' in a way that meant the new laws would not touch its schemes. New laws that would, happily, be shaped with the help of its own tax director.

By 2010 a multinational company that was avoiding tax on a breathtaking scale could sidestep the law, write its own tax bill and simultaneously shape the rules that will govern its tax avoidance in future. Ten years after Anglo-Saxon capitalism defeated the German social model in Dusseldorf, it had conquered the British tax system too.

At home with the tax-dodgers

Luxembourg does not reserve its deluxe tax avoidance services for Britain's largest mobile phone company, as was to become strikingly apparent in 2011 when French TV journalist Edouard Perrin obtained a leaked cache of correspondence between the Duchy's tax authorities and PricewaterhouseCoopers.[25] It documented industrial levels of tax avoidance by hundreds of British companies using schemes put together by PwC and rubber-stamped with repetitive strain injury-inducing regularity by the director of the Administration des Contributions Directes, Bureau d'Imposition Sociétés (company tax division), Mr Marius Kohl.

Most of the schemes involved complex transactions but operated on a simple principle. They allowed multinationals to make payments into Luxembourg corporate structures that, just as with Vodafone's financing arrangements, would reduce their taxable profits in countries with 'normal' tax rates, such as the UK or US. But when the same payments were received in Luxembourg they would effectively not be taxed. This was the familiar tax avoidance trick, in other words, of moving money within the same corporate group in a way that generates a tax break in one country but no corresponding taxation in another. Not that Luxembourg explicitly exempts any income from tax; as a member of all the major economic clubs – most importantly the EU – it can't do anything so obvious. In theory at least, it does tax corporate profits at 29%. But it applies this standard tax rate to a *far lower* measure of profit than the companies created within its borders for tax avoidance actually make.

Engineering lower profit figures requires some artful scheming from the likes of PwC, along with the Luxembourg taxman's complicity. The routine was neatly illustrated by what Perrin's files showed the accountants had created for its client Pearson plc, publisher of Britain's financial newspaper of record, the *Financial Times*, as well as *The Economist*, Penguin Books and educational products around the world. A November 2009 letter from PwC to the Luxembourg taxman revealed a plan for the group to invest $587m in its US educational books business through a scheme in which, first, a British company called Embankment Finance Ltd (EFL) set up a branch in Luxembourg. EFL in London would pass the money to its Luxembourg branch, which would then invest it in another Luxembourg company, Pearson Luxembourg No 2 sarl, in return for shares in that company. It then lent the money to yet another Luxembourg company, FBH, for onlending to the American business.

The idea was that Pearson's US empire got its tax break on the ensuing interest payments while no British company, or any company anywhere for that matter, was taxed on the income. And that's what was achieved when the Luxembourg taxman Mr Kohl agreed with PwC that he should look at all the companies on his patch – including the branch of the British one – as a 'fiscal unity'. And crucially, the money passed from EFL's London base to its Luxembourg branch would be treated as a loan, even though legally – and for any accountancy purpose – it was nothing of the sort. All of which meant that, factoring in this fictitious borrowing, the various entities on Mr Kohl's patch had simply borrowed and lent equal amounts of money. And no taxman would expect to see much taxable profit on that. In reality, of course, the Luxembourg

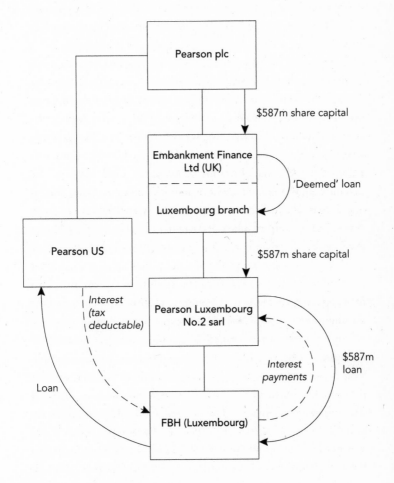

Fig. 8 Pearson US earns a tax break

entities had received money for free and lent it on at interest, making a decent profit in the process.

In return for hosting these fun and games, the Luxembourg authorities tax a fictitious level of profit on the principle that what they view as a 'loan in, loan out' arrangement would not generate much profit commercially. The amount depends on how much is involved, and in Pearson's case the Luxembourg taxman would be satisfied with taxing 1/16% (0.06%) of the $587m passing through his borders, equal to around £240,000 and giving an annual Luxembourg tax bill, calculated at 29%, of about £70,000. But if interest on the debt were estimated at 5%, tax relief would be given on interest of around £20m a year in the US. And critically, the company would claim nothing would be picked up by the British anti-tax avoidance laws aimed at profits diverted into tax havens by multinationals like Pearson.

Yet the artificiality of the arrangement became apparent when Perrin and I visited Pearson's Luxembourg companies at their 17 rue Glesener office, which turned out to be a room above a sports shop near Luxembourg's central station. It could be accessed only with a spot of public-interest trespassing through a private main door, then up a dimly lit stairwell, where the international financing activities of one of the world's leading financial publishers was announced by a piece of A3 paper listing eighteen companies (including the branch of the English one), pinned to a tatty hardboard door of the sort that normally marks the entrance to a student bedsit. It was not, of course, supposed to be seen by outsiders and when we knocked on the door we were not exactly welcomed. 'How did you get in? Who opened the door?' barked an expatriate Scot running CPC Business Services sarl, one of the hundreds of company administration services businesses doing silently lucrative work behind Luxembourg's closed doors and evidently responsible for Pearson's paperwork. A few unanswered questions and one threat to call the police later, we were back on the street, reflecting on the shabby day-to-day reality of international corporate tax avoidance.

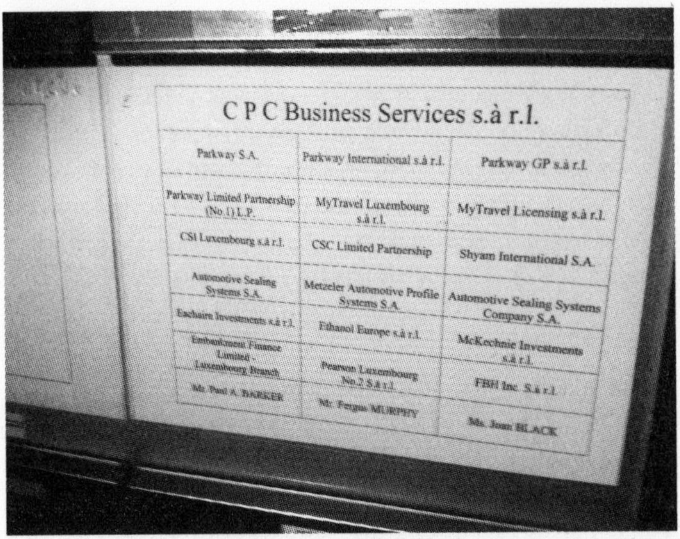

Fig. 9 The business service centre hosting
Pearson's Luxembourg companies and branches

Even Pearson's nugatory Luxembourg taxable margin looked expensive next to the 1/64% (0.016%) proposed for a scheme set up by Britain's biggest drugs company GlaxoSmithKline. The more a company funnels through the Luxembourg tax avoidance machine, the better its deal from the taxman, and GSK was among the Grand Duchy's highest-rolling customers. Its latest Luxembourg scheme, the documents showed, involved lending £6bn of profits that had racked up offshore back to the UK. Again, the UK company paying interest on this would get a tax break, but there would be no meaningful taxation in Luxembourg. The familiar result was achieved this time with a clever trick involving two Luxembourg companies, GlaxoSmithKline International Luxembourg sarl (GSKIL) and GlaxoSmithKline Holding (Luxembourg) sarl (GSKH). The latter earned the interest from lending the money back to the UK but could, PwC advised Mr Kohl, be judged to make no profit because it had obligations to the former under a 'zero coupon convertible bond'.

The overall result would be that while GSK in the UK received tax relief for hundreds of millions of pounds in interest at the 28% UK corporate tax rate then prevailing, there would be no profits to tax in Luxembourg beyond the 0.016% margin. And just like the other thousands of plans, the scheme was promptly returned 'approved' by the Luxembourg taxman.

Euro slash

Luxembourg has become a tax haven of its own government's and the tax avoidance industry's creation, and a pretty underhand one at that. It proclaims a standard corporate tax rate of 29% but allows multinational companies to turn this into something below 1% by using an array of abstractions: special companies and partnerships with tax-free foreign branches that hold debts, shares and abstruse financial instruments that can be either shares or debts depending on who's asking. The tax authority, through its biddable Bureau d'Imposition Sociétés, nods through schemes without delay, allowing billions of pounds, dollars and euros to wash through its territory for no purpose other than reducing tax bills. Vodafone sends billions from the UK to Germany and elsewhere via a Luxembourg company for no reason other than picking up a tax break. Pearson dispatches money from the UK to the States via the Grand Duchy for exactly the same reason. And these are just a few of the many hundreds doing so. As if to demonstrate how mainstream the practice is, even the publishing group half-owned by the Guardian Media Group, EMAP, has a tax-efficient Luxembourg financing scheme using hybrid financial instruments similar to those employed by Glaxo. It came as no surprise when a 2011 survey by ActionAid found that 55 of the

FTSE100 companies had subsidiary operations in Luxembourg, running to 336 separate companies.[26] So how does the Duchy get away with it?

An outwardly respectable member of the world economy, Luxembourg boasts a network of taxation treaties with all the countries it fleeces. These agreements ease international cash flows by stipulating, in most cases, that tax cannot be charged on payments such as interest by the country in which the payment is made, only by the country where it is received. The laudable intention is to avert 'double taxation' (where the same income is taxed in both countries), and in doing so make life simpler for trade and investment. But these agreements are predicated on income being taxed when it arrives in one of the countries and becomes profits of a taxpayer there. For this reason such agreements are never signed with territories that are recognized as tax havens. When a country such as Luxembourg sets out to become a haven that will effectively not tax certain cross-border income, it cynically subverts this system and turns its international tax treaties, signed by its partners in good faith, into instruments of tax abuse.

If a country such as Britain then seeks to recover the profits its companies have diverted into this tax haven, the companies can use Luxembourg's European Union membership to claim that such action breaches 'fundamental freedoms' under European law. It's a formula for big-time tax avoidance, allowing Luxembourg all the privileges of being in the club while pilfering from the kitty. In 1998 the EU did set up a committee called the Code of Conduct (Business Taxation) Group, at the behest of the British government, to police 'harmful tax competition' among its members. But this ponderous body has done no more than nibble at the edges of Luxembourg's parasitic tax code. Nor do the EU or its member governments show any appetite for amending the European law that, as European Court of Justice judgments such as the Cadbury case confirm, to some degree demands that tax avoidance arrangements are respected. To round matters off in favour of the avoiders, the world's tax officials certainly aren't going to turn up in the Grand Duchy to test whether thousands of Luxembourg tax set-ups meet the 'genuine economic activity' threshold required under European law to defeat national anti-tax avoidance laws. And all the while a cloak of euphemism shrouds the industry from public understanding, never mind scrutiny. PricewaterhouseCoopers Luxembourg invites companies to use its 'flexible and competitive tax structuring models'[27], not its tax avoidance schemes.

While British and other taxpayers get fleeced, the Grand Duchy and its elite prosper; replacing lost industry with tax avoidance has afforded Luxembourg the highest GDP per capita in Europe (double its nearest rival, the Netherlands, and more than double the UK or Germany) and the second lowest post-crisis budget deficit.[28] The future for its tax services looks equally bright, not least as the UK government gives the Luxembourg tax avoidance factory a major boost by relaxing its controlled foreign companies laws to the point of all but giving up on offshore schemes. Vodafone made this all too clear when it announced that its untaxed Luxembourg billions would be in the clear under the new rules.[29] The thud of rubber hitting paper will be resounding from Mr Kohl's office for some time yet.

Grocer profits

The scale of Luxembourg's tax avoidance industry became public only because of a major leak of confidential documents setting out hundreds of schemes in explicit detail. Without such whistle-blowing, tax avoidance is notoriously difficult to expose. First you have to find the pieces of the jigsaw, then piece them together without the box that has the picture on. Which explains why it has thrived in a state of pernicious secrecy for so long.

The *Guardian* newspaper discovered the difficulty to its cost in 2008, when it reported what it described as a £1bn corporation tax avoidance scheme run by Tesco through a series of offshore companies. In fact, while these companies were *registered* offshore, they were *tax resident* in the UK and not responsible for tax dodging on anything like the scale the *Guardian* had alleged. They were in fact set up to avoid much smaller amounts of stamp duty on property deals, not corporation tax on profits.

While the *Guardian* scrambled to limit the libel damage, I had a suspicion that Britain's favourite supermarket was doing more to 'manage' its evidently low corporation tax bills than it was letting on.[30] The obvious thing to look for was one of those Swiss branches which, with some help from a local journalist, I eventually found in the shape of the Zug outpost of something called Cheshunt Overseas LLP.

A corporation tax avoidance scheme loomed into view. Cheshunt Overseas LLP, named after Tesco's Hertfordshire base, was an English 'limited liability partnership' in which the partners were two Hungarian companies and an Irish one, the latter entitled to 99.8% of the profits. The genius of this foreign-owned English partnership with a Swiss branch (and, it was a claimed, a Hungarian management branch – neither with any staff) was that it made all these countries' tax authorities look the wrong way. British taxmen look right through partnerships and consider their profits to be those of the partners, in this case effectively just the Irish company, which as a non-resident earning its money abroad was beyond their reach. Irish taxmen are interested only in their companies' domestic returns and, since the profits were made in a Swiss branch, would leave them well alone. As for the Swiss, they live in a make-believe world in which branch profits are measured at a fraction of their true level. So money could be poured in from Tesco's growing overseas empire and incur minimal tax. The grocer, it seemed, had indeed found yet another loophole in the 'controlled foreign companies' laws. (Tesco's scheme rumbles on; up to February 2011 what would have been taxable profits of over £300m wound up in Zug and incurred a total tax bill of £13m, less than 5%.)[31]

Within a couple of weeks of reporting this wheeze in *Private Eye*, I had found more Tesco schemes, this time English partnerships whose partners were Luxembourg companies effecting a similar dodge but without the need for a Swiss detour. It worked because Luxembourg companies do not account for the profits of any partnerships they might be involved in, while HMRC does not tax partnerships, even English ones. As luck would have it, the 2008 Finance Bill wending its way through parliament outlawed these arrangements, one Treasury minister calling them 'highly artificial tax avoidance schemes'.[32] Whatever Tesco's protestations, there could be little doubt that – as the *Guardian* had alleged, albeit for the wrong reasons and not on the scale claimed – it was a corporate tax avoider.[33]

High farce ensued, as Tesco sought to exclude *Private Eye*'s revelations from the simmering libel action. In the High Court that summer the company's expensive silk Adrienne Page QC pleaded to a bemused libel judge that 'planning or efficiency that results in tax being avoided' doesn't make a company a 'tax avoider as a slur'. Adopting the tax industry's trademark obscurantism, she insisted: 'It is now more usual to divide "tax avoidance" into aggressive and non-aggressive tax planning behaviour. The claimant [Tesco] would readily put itself into the second category, but not the first.' Mr Justice Eady, who had spent the previous week getting to grips with more fathomable questions posed by Max Mosley's sadomasochism parties, looked puzzled. 'I'm grappling with the notion of passive tax avoidance,' he sighed, before admitting the *Eye*'s stories as evidence.[34]

Which was all very entertaining from the public gallery, but not such fun for the *Guardian* and its editor Alan Rusbridger. Although the paper eventually escaped with a limited apology, a small damages bill and a large legal one, it had been a bruising affair. Tesco's charming lawyers, Carter-Ruck, had thrown everything they could at the case. Not only had the paper libelled the grocer, they claimed, but Rusbridger had personally committed more serious 'malicious falsehood'. 'You have been caught out publishing lies . . . and you don't like it,' they sneered.[35]

The legal action plunged Rusbridger, a bookish Cambridge English graduate, into an unfamiliar world of 'baroque' tax avoidance. He was horrified by the obstacles to reporting a subject – wealthy companies dodging their dues to society – that should have been squarely within a liberal broadsheet's sights. The paper trail behind the erroneous story told of the herculean task facing non-specialist reporters trying to get to the bottom of tax avoidance by companies not inclined to be too helpful. A study from Oxford University, he noticed, described how most companies 'believed that corporation tax issues seem to be too complex or obscure for the media and the public to understand. Accordingly, the issues are not covered in the media or they go unnoticed by the public.'[36]

It was time, thought the *Guardian*'s editor, to lift this particular stone and show readers the nasties lurking beneath. What a team of reporters eventually found was a corporate Britain that was doing more than just diverting its financing offshore for the tax breaks. It was tearing itself apart in pursuit of tax avoidance.

5
Breaking Up Isn't Hard to Do

The companies that carve themselves up and send the pieces round the world for tax avoidance

Multinational enterprises have long understood that the most valuable things they possess are often not the bricks, mortar and machinery of their physical operations but their *intangible* assets: their know-how, patents, trademarks and brands. The profits to be made from a drug, for example, drop like a stone when a patent expires and ownership of the formula behind it lapses. Well-known breakfast cereals sell for a great deal more than 'brand X' not just because of the crappy toys inside the box.

With the growth of international trade in the twentieth century, such intangible assets could be increasingly turned to profit not just in their country of development but across in the world. In 1900 Coca-Cola sold its first bottle in Britain. By 1920 it had 1000 bottlers in countries all over the world. All were selling a product whose immediate value lay less in their physical operations but in a secret recipe and a brand name.

In the aftermath of the First World War it was also becoming clear that international businesses needed to be taxed on some basis agreed among all the countries involved. If, for example, Britain's Inland Revenue wanted to tax all the profits Coca-Cola made from selling the fizzy stuff here, because it was where the customers were, while the American taxman decided that he too would tax it because it was a US product, the same commercial profits would be taxed more than once. This could hamper the economic co-operation and development that the world hoped would accompany and cement peace. So a year after its formation through the 1919 Treaty of Versailles, the League of Nations convened an 'international finance conference' in Brussels, at which it identified the prospect of 'double taxation' as a 'serious impediment to international relations and world production, and therefore a threat to global peace'.[1] It began setting the ground rules for international taxation, stipulating that a tax authority could tax all the profits of enterprises resident in its territory but, when it came to 'non-residents', just those profits made by branches of the enterprise within its borders. So the US, for example, would not tax the foreign Coca-Cola bottling companies. The UK taxman would take a share of any US company's profits to the extent that they were made through UK branches (and then these companies' US tax bills would be reduced accordingly). That seemed to be the core 'double taxation' problem sorted, but within a few years it was obvious that this wasn't the only threat to the international economy. Many companies were already exploiting their growing international trade to *avoid* tax.

A multinational enterprise making a product in one country for sale in another generally transfers it first to an affiliate in that second country, which then sells it to the customer. The price at which the transfer occurs effectively divides the profits, and multinationals had already begun to manipulate these prices to ensure that greater profits arose in the country with the lower tax rate. If, for example a company made a batch of ball bearings in country A at a cost of $5 and sold it through an affiliated company in country B for $10, the transfer price between the companies might be $8, in which case the profit would be $3 in country A, $2 in country

B. But if country A had a much higher tax rate, the multinational could adjust the price to $6, diverting an extra $1 of profit out of country A into country B and thus pocketing a significant tax saving.

So how should the 'transfer price' be fixed? The League's answer, in 1935, was the 'arm's length principle', which following the Second World War, would be enshrined in an expanding network of bilateral taxation treaties agreed between the major trading nations. The UK's first such agreement, with the United States, was signed in 1945.[2] In fixing transfer prices, the world's taxmen were to imagine that the affiliated companies were independent from each other, dealing on 'arm's length' terms. Every physical good and service provided by one to the other should be priced accordingly.

The concept was refined when the body set up to administer the United States' Marshall Plan for the post-war reconstruction of Europe – what is now the Organization for Economic Cooperation and Development (OECD) – effectively became the custodian of the rules of international taxation (as before, smoothing out the wrinkles in international taxation was recognized as an important pillar of a stable world economic order).[3] Crucially, in its 1963 'model' taxation treaty, on which countries would base their bilateral agreements, the OECD made a point of ensuring that transfer prices must reflect the value of intangible assets such as patents and trademarks. This was logical: independent parties did indeed pay royalties for using such assets, the legal protections for which were also being strengthened across the world (making them still more valuable). Or the prices paid commercially for goods reflected the technology, know-how and brands that had gone into making and marketing them. As countries signed up to thousands of taxation treaties incorporating this OECD principle in the 1970s and 80s, the world's tax system became bound to it.

In the latter part of the twentieth century, however, the tax industry became expert at taking such principles and forging them into the tools of tax avoidance. Intellectual property was not only valuable, it was mobile. Rights, patents, trademarks, licences, sub-licences and much else could be transplanted at the stroke of a lawyer's pen to companies in low-tax areas that would receive payments for allowing related companies in 'normal' tax rate countries to use their new 'intangible' assets. And the international rules of the game – drawn up without foreseeing a time when multinationals would break themselves up for tax avoidance – dictated that the tax results of these arrangements must be respected.

For British multinationals there remained a major hurdle to overcome. The same 1984 'controlled foreign companies' laws that tackled British multinationals diverting financing income into tax haven subsidiaries applied equally to the parking of intangible assets in such offshore companies. In the same way that they couldn't stuff these companies with interest payments reducing taxable profits in countries with normal tax rates, neither could they use them as receptacles for royalties or other fees. But just as companies like Tesco found loopholes in these rules to shift financial property, i.e. money, into tax havens to great effect, so others with some smart advice could exploit the rules to get their precious intellectual property out of the country.

Spirited away

Johnnie Walker is about as British a brand as there is. Indeed the Scottishness of what began as Walker's Kilmarnock Whisky nearly 200 years ago is what sells it to the world's scotch lovers. It's still blended in Scotland by Scots. But when this became one of the first companies considered by the *Guardian*'s 2009 investigation, it became clear that, fiscally, it's not Scotch. It's Dutch.

The Johnnie Walker business had already been through a few hands in the century and a half before the merger of its owner Grand Met with Guinness to become Diageo in 1997. The new conglomerate swiftly moved its Johnnie Walker business to the Netherlands where it would pay far lower taxes. Or at least it moved the ownership and finances of the business there. Its Kilmarnock plant carried on blending the scotch, but now as a poorly rewarded – and consequently low-taxpaying – servant of a modern Dutch master.

Pulling off this switch required a bit more than just plonking a few filing cabinets on the Harwich–Hook of Holland ferry. First, the ownership of the business was transferred within the UK to a special company, UDV (SJ) Ltd, that immediately established a branch in Amsterdam, from which the Johnnie Walker business would be controlled. The Dutch branch then incorporated, becoming a new, legally distinct Dutch company, UDV (SJ) BV. It now owned the Johnnie Walker business for a short time before selling it to yet another Dutch company, known as Diageo Brands BV. All was aimed at securing a special Dutch tax break for 'intellectual property' like trademarks that would allow Diageo Brands BV to set what it had paid for the Johnnie Walker brand (to the first Dutch company) against its profits over a number of years. As the value of the trademark of the world's best-selling whisky was almost £6bn, it meant an immense tax break for one of the most profitable parts of the Diageo business and a correspondingly puny Dutch tax bill. Back in Scotland, meanwhile, the blending company – stripped of the brand and know-how – would be paid a small taxable margin as a contractor of Diageo Brands BV. The reorganization would all be free of UK capital gains taxes, too, in line with EU rules facilitating business reorganizations within the single market. (This is the same EU, incidentally, that boosts Diageo's profits by reserving the description 'scotch' for whisky produced in Scotland and banning it for foreign imitations. The wee irony is that it's largely the Dutch, not Scottish, profits that benefit.)

The technique was known by another great tax avoidance euphemism, 'outward domestication', and it was repeated over a

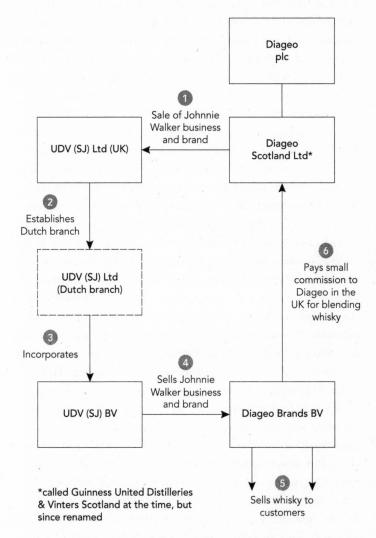

Fig. 10 Johnnie Walker goes Dutch

Diageo
plc

1 Sale of Johnnie Walker business and brand

UDV (SJ) Ltd (UK)

Diageo
Scotland Ltd*

2 Establishes Dutch branch

UDV (SJ) Ltd
(Dutch branch)

3 Incorporates

6 Pays small commission to Diageo in the UK for blending whisky

UDV (SJ) BV

4 Sells Johnnie Walker business and brand

Diageo Brands BV

5 Sells whisky to customers

*called Guinness United Distilleries & Vinters Scotland at the time, but since renamed

number of years for other major Diageo brands, including J&B, to remarkable effect. In both 2009 and 2010 Diageo's accounts showed no UK tax charge. Worldwide, the group paid 18% tax on its profits, well below the typical tax rates of the countries it operates in.[4] If even this small amount had been shared on the basis of physical rather than financial presence, its annual tax UK bill would have been in the hundreds of millions of pounds. Unsurprisingly the Revenue probed the arrangements to see if what was left of Diageo in Britain was being adequately rewarded, and therefore taxed, and whether Diageo Brands BV really was a Dutch tax resident doing enough to justify its profits. In 2008 a delegation of the tax authority's less demanding officials returned from Amsterdam to declare it as Dutch as Edam and agree a settlement with the company's advisers, Deloitte (led again by the partner who would soon help settle Vodafone's tax dispute, David Cruickshank). Diageo duly reported a 'tax credit' of £155m 'in respect of settlements with tax authorities'.[5] In other words, settling tax disputes, of which this was the company's major one, had cost Diageo £155m less than it had set aside. More importantly, the deal embedded the tax structure for good and Diageo's UK tax payments continue to flatline.

What worked for Johnnie Walker also did the trick for Walkers Crisps Ltd, founded in 1948 by Leicester butcher Henry Walker to occupy his staff while meat was scarce. Forty years later when the company was bought by PepsiCo it still clung onto its 'heritage', choosing local-boy-made-good Gary Lineker to front its advertising. But when it came to tax the approach was less homespun. One of Pepsi's first priorities for its acquisition was to slash its tax bill, so in 1999 the entire Walkers business – raw materials, finished product and of course trademarks – was transferred to Frito-Lay GmbH of Bern, Switzerland. Since then the Leicester plant, owned by a separate UK company, has fried the potatoes on behalf of this Swiss company in return for a limited fee. Walkers might to this day boast that 'we're proud our crisps are made from 100% British potatoes, and we love our home', but as soon as Walkers, or rather Frito-Lay, buys the spuds from the farmer they become as Swiss as the rösti for which Bern is better known. Again it works for tax, though; Walkers' UK company saw its profits and thus its tax bill quickly halve, and although the company had to pay £40m to settle a Revenue enquiry, the structure remains in place for the long term.[6]

The restructuring of these two British companies typified tax planning among multinationals with big names and big wholesale turnovers. They could get round the 'controlled foreign companies' laws that stopped cruder techniques such as simply parking valuable assets in tax haven subsidiaries. Instead, they moved entire businesses into them, minus the industrial bit, but still with enough of the economic substance required to escape the anti-tax avoidance laws. And the tax havens didn't need to be distant offshore islands; continental neighbours such as the Netherlands and Switzerland were tailoring their laws to become the very havens they needed. At the end of the twentieth century multinationals with big international consumer brands were the natural customers for these services. But in profiting from them they owed a debt to an industry built on more serious 'intellectual property' that had blazed the trail in the art of 'tax fragmentation'.

The drugs do work . . . for tax avoidance

Few companies have thicker files on the shelves of the world's tax offices than Britain's dominant drugs companies, GlaxoSmithKline and AstraZeneca. For decades tax inspectors have struggled to work out where the companies really make their profits on blockbusters that might be developed, manufactured and sold in separate countries, and for which the all-important patents might be owned somewhere else still. There's serious money involved. In 2006 Glaxo paid $3.1bn to settle investigations by the US's IRS, who considered the companies on their patch to have been under-rewarded. Five years later AstraZeneca – born of the 1999 merger of ICI's pharmaceuticals division with Sweden's Astra – paid $1.1bn to conclude its 'transfer pricing' enquiry, a year after it had handed £500m to our own HMRC to bring a fifteen-year investigation to a close.[7] There's an inevitability to these disputes given the dispersion of the businesses involved, but the structures used also build in some smart tax avoidance.

Since the early 1980s, the rich world's dyspeptic millions have slept more easily thanks to a wonder drug brought to the market by Glaxo. By the early 1990s stomach ulcer and indigestion treatment Zantac was bringing in over $3bn annually for the company. Most came from the land of the Big Mac and super-size fries, but this was really a British success story. The active ingredient, Ranitidine, which prevents excessive stomach acid production rather than just neutralizing it with chalk, was generated in British labs by the renowned Glaxo pharmacologist Sir David Jack and his team of largely British scientists. The patent and the trademark that allowed Glaxo exclusively to sell Zantac for sixteen years was also owned by a British company in Middlesex. Which might be expected to mean that, beyond some reward for American salesmen with one of the easiest pitches in the business, Zantac's towering profits would be taxed in the UK. Not if the tax planners could do anything about it.

While the men and women in white coats developed the winning drug formula, their colleagues in the tax department were devising a special supply chain to direct as much of its profit as possible into low-tax areas. In the same way that a freehold property can be leased and sub-leased, the use of a patent can be carved up, and the tax planners' first move was to sub-license the Zantac patent to a company in Singapore. It would manufacture the drug before selling it on at a hefty but lightly taxed profit to a Swiss 'sales hub'. This company then co-ordinated sales to Glaxo's operations in the major markets of the US and elsewhere (including back to the UK), taking its own low-taxed commission in the process. To round matters off, the Swiss and Singaporean companies' profits were then lent back to Glaxo in the UK (a so-called 'upstream loan') to generate further tax breaks on interest paid out to the tax havens, a set-up that remained in place until very recently. By the late 1990s much of the lending back to the UK would be routed through Luxembourg, latterly via the scheme exposed in Edouard Perrin's leaked documents (see last chapter).

Watching the fruits of British scientific genius wash from its shores, in the early 1990s the Inland Revenue's inspectors set about what probably remains their longest-running investigation. They finally extracted a few hundred million pounds from it a decade later by establishing that, through incorrect 'transfer pricing', insufficient profits had been allocated to Britain and excessive ones to companies outside the UK.[8] The snag was that the US authorities had much the same concerns about their own haul from Zantac and other drugs including asthma treatment Ventolin, believing that they were as much marketing successes as scientific ones. Which says plenty about the modern drugs industry, but also explains why international taxation disputes often resemble a tag wrestling contest in which rival authorities grapple first with a company and then with each other over taxing the same profits. In this bout, no sooner had the British taxman cashed his cheque than he became Glaxo's partner fighting claims from the American authorities on the Zantac profits. The $3.4bn cheque written by the company to Uncle Sam in 2006, a chunk of which had to be refunded by the British taxpayer, hints at who got the better of it.

At least Zantac/Ranitidine remained a British drug throughout the life of its patent, even if subject to the Singapore sub-licence. In the face of losses to European and Asian tax havens and the demands of the IRS, the British taxpayer could be grateful for that small mercy and took some share of the, albeit diminished, worldwide tax bill. But by the time the tax on Zantac's profits had been carved up by the world's taxmen, the supply chain that had been built around it twenty-five years before was about as cutting edge as the Sinclair ZX81 computer developed at the same time. Drugs and technology had moved on in twenty years, and so had international tax avoidance.

By the late 1990s the authorities' challenge to transfer pricing schemes in which key elements of businesses were farmed out around the world prompted a rethink by the world's tax advisers. If the taxman was going to quibble over the prices paid to offshore outposts providing services like packaging, sales co-ordination and sub-licensing, the answer might be to invert the whole process. Why not put the heart of the operation – the ownership of the drug itself – in the tax haven and pay just limited fees to the relatively high-tax countries where the companies themselves were headquartered and had their major markets?

So just as Walkers and Diageo transplanted their businesses to Switzerland and the Netherlands, so the big drugs companies found ways of ensuring that the next blockbuster, even if developed in Britain, would not be owned here. Early-stage patents and the trademarks associated with them were registered in offshore companies *before* they became valuable through the research that gets them to market. The white coats in Glaxo's Middlesex labs developing diabetes treatment Avandia and breast cancer drug Tykerb, for example, would work for Puerto Rican and Irish group companies enjoying special tax status. They would also, from 2002, simultaneously benefit from generous 'research and development' tax credits in Britain, currently running at 130% of costs.

The result is that, while few industries are more pampered by policy makers wondering where economic growth is going to come from, big drugs companies make little direct contribution to the Exchequer. In 2010 Glaxo reported worldwide pre-tax profits of £4.5bn but appeared to pay little if any

UK corporation tax, showing benefits from the tax credits and from using Singapore's special tax status of around £115m and £80m respectively.[9] AstraZeneca, a similarly enthusiastic tax haven user, in 1999 ensured that what would turn out to be its blockbuster anti-cholesterol drug Crestor (with sales over $5bn by 2010), was licensed around the world from the Caribbean tax haven of Puerto Rico.[10] The company now shaves several hundreds of millions of dollars off its annual tax bill by using such territories.[11]

'Tax-efficient supply chain management' – as it has become known in one of those obfuscatory tax euphemisms – offers huge scope for tax dodging as established and newer tax havens bend over backwards to host the management, intellectual property, financing and other facets of a business that can be commoditized, moved and priced. It has spawned an industry in what one of its leading exponents, KPMG, defines as 'incorporating tax arbitrage into supply chain structures (typically by optimizing the location of the key supply chain functions, assets and risks)'.[12] Strip away the jargon and this is corporate tax dodging on a global scale, increasingly sanctioned by the world's tax authorities. And it's not just Britain's own multinationals with their snouts in the tax efficient supply chain trough. Our biggest corporate visitors feed from it every bit as greedily.

Over here and under-taxed

The same post-war growth in international markets that allowed British multinationals to strike out abroad also opened up the domestic market's sixty million consumers to their foreign counterparts. And by the late 1990s 'tax efficient supply chain management' was enabling them to access this source of profit while making precious little tax contribution to Britain's public coffers.

135

The trick again is to own anything of any value somewhere convenient. So Nike's British stocks are owned by a Dutch company called Nike European Operations Netherlands BV while the business of selling them on its behalf is performed by British company Nike (UK) Ltd. The £70m a year it earns in fees, significantly less than it would from buying and selling the gear in its own right, translates after its costs into a profit of just over £10m.[13] Even this limited operating margin produces less than £1m in tax as the company also cuts its tax bill through the financial dealings of its UK parent company, Nike Vapor Ltd. It borrowed around £225m from its Dutch parent company, Nike UK Holdings BV (itself owned by a Bermudan company called Nike Cortez). The tax-deductible interest expenses on this debt all but wipes out the taxable profits of the official kit supplier to the England rugby team and – through its ownership of Umbro in the UK – the football team too.

Much the same goes for American clothes retailer Gap, which set up a similar system in the mid-1990s. Just like Nike's trainers, the jeans and T-shirts tumbling onto shop floors across the UK don't feature on any British company's balance sheet. The idea was that Gap's British commission agent, GPS (Great Britain) Ltd, would make a small profit and pay a correspondingly limited tax bill while the big European profits would be earned by a company owning the stock in Amsterdam, Gap Netherlands BV. It didn't quite go to plan, though, as a move upmarket into more expensive clothing flopped and the whole operation began to haemorrhage money. The tax strategy had backfired: losing money overall in Europe, the company had contrived to ring-fence some taxable profits in the UK while the losses that the company was making were racking up uselessly in Amsterdam. But just as there are routes out of the British tax system, so there are ways in. Like an escaped prisoner who realizes he'd be better off back inside, in 2002 Gap ghosted its Dutch company *into* Britain – by the established method of having its board meetings in the right place – so that its annual losses could be set against and eliminate its UK company's tax bill. Fast forward to 2009 and 2010, and the move provided some comfort for the struggling retailer. The £25m losses of Dutch-incorporated but UK tax resident Gap Netherlands BV swamped the profits of the UK commission company GPS (Great Britain) Ltd and the tax bill vanished.[14]

The effect of tax-efficient supply chain management on UK tax payments hit the headlines in 2012 when Reuters analysed a series of US companies' contributions and found that Starbucks had paid just £8.3m tax on several billions of pounds' worth of sales since 1998 and nothing for several years. At the same time it had been telling investors – as anybody strolling along a high street would agree – that its British operations were prospering. Again, the tax result could be put down to standard techniques including buying beans from a Starbucks company in Switzerland and paying royalties to use the global brand through a related Dutch company.[15]

American companies operating in the UK have long found tax relief not just across the North Sea, but the Irish one too. Tax poaching was always one of the Celtic Tiger's main stripes. It started in the 1990s with a 10% tax rate in a special financial services incentive zone in Dublin's regenerated docks area, combined with other breaks for high-tech companies and then, from 2003, an across-the-board 12.5% tax rate. Ostensibly aimed at luring companies to employ people in the country, the tax breaks have proved too good to resist for many companies seeking simply to divert profits as much as establish any real business. And they are greatly assisted in this by Ireland's network of tax with governments around the world that, just like those enjoyed by Luxembourg, allow companies to get money in and out tax free.

Among Ireland's tax-efficient visitors is the Microsoft empire, notoriously streetwise on tax matters. Rights to its technology in Europe are held by an Irish company, while its UK operation, Microsoft Ltd, is once again merely a commission agent paying very little tax. Employing 2800 British staff and serving millions of British customers, plus huge swathes of government, this UK company reported profits of £76m in Britain and a tax charge of £20m in 2010.[16] Its Irish company employing 700 staff, on the other hand, made €1.4bn (£1.2bn) profits, on which it paid €150m (£130m) tax.[17] So its Irish operation is seventy-five times more productive per employee than its British counterpart. Or not. Worldwide, Microsoft's local tax policies add up to big savings. For 2010 the group reported annual revenues of $60bn, profits of around $25bn and a worldwide tax bill of $6.2bn which, at 25%, was dramatically lower than the headline US federal rate of 35% and represented a good couple of billion pounds a year in tax saved.[18]

There are plenty of other huge American corporations minimizing contributions to national governments at the time of their greatest need. Not only do British advertisers pay a low-taxed Dublin company for getting their name up first on Google searches but this company itself pays royalties for using the Google name to an Irish-registered but Bermuda-tax resident company.[19] The payments go via a Dutch company interposed between these two companies in a 'Dutch sandwich' arrangement so that the money can leave Ireland tax free under the country's tax treaty with the Netherlands, which then allows its onward tax-free transmission to the Atlantic tax haven. The effect is that, courtesy of none-too-demanding Irish corporate tax laws and generous international agreements, companies can dodge even Ireland's low tax rate if they're greedy enough. Other users of the technique, including Facebook, Apple, Oracle and Pfizer, certainly are. Even firms earning large amounts of their income from the taxpayer are in on the act. In 2009 one of the UK government's favoured IT consultants, Accenture, moved its corporate headquarters to Ireland and at the same time transferred $7bn worth of 'intellectual property' to the country from Switzerland (dog-legging the transaction through Luxembourg, so that with the help of the Grand Duchy's rubber stamp, the increase in value would not be taxed). After paying to use the know-how, Accenture UK's £2bn turn-over – including the hundreds of millions derived from the British taxpayer – translated into a corporation tax bill of under £3m.[20]

Fill yer boots

Overseas ownership opens up a world of tax avoidance opportunity. And when it takes the form of ownership not by a single overseas corporation but by a group of investors through the private equity funds that since the turn of the century have accounted for increasing volumes of acquisitions, the effect can be the near elimination of corporate tax bills. The recent experience of one of Britain's best-loved high street names illustrates the point only too well.

The 2006 merger of Boots plc with Alliance Unichem of Zurich marked a major transformation for the company that began in the mid-nineteenth century as a herbal medicine store in Goose Gate, Nottingham, and which Jesse Boot pioneered across Britain with simple soaps, cosmetics and remedies. But this boom era corporate deal was a mere taste of what was to come the following year when the Swiss company's proprietor Stefano Pessina and US private equity manager Kohlberg Kravis Read teamed up for an £11bn takeover of the new Alliance Boots. The new owners quickly capitalized on the ample tax possibilities open to a Swiss-headquartered group that was ultimately owned by a Gibraltar holding company and a series of offshore funds but with around three-quarters of its business in Britain. Boots' tax bill before the merger with Alliance had been £131m in the UK alone in a single year, and as far back as 2000 it had handed over £154m to the Exchequer.[21] From 2010 to 2012 the new Alliance Boots managed to pay tax to all the countries in which it operates of just £156m (most of it likely to have been to the UK), while making pre-tax profits of £1.8bn, an effective tax rate of under 9%.[22]

The precipitate drop in tax payments was accounted for not just by the huge interest costs incurred on the external debt that characterizes private equity buy-outs but also tax-deductible interest paid by UK companies to associated overseas companies *within* the now Swiss-controlled group itself. The accounts of Boots' new UK holding company, AB Acquisitions Ltd, showed that in 2009 and 2010 the company paid £658m interest to its bankers and £479m to offshore related companies, the latter costs alone shaving over £100m off the tax bill. The offshore structure allowed for another move, too, as Alliance Boots set up a series of 'limited liability partnerships' to hold much of its property. British Boots companies pay tax-deductible rent to these partnerships, the profits of which belong to a Cayman Islands company that can escape the UK anti-tax avoidance 'controlled foreign companies' laws, given the new Swiss control of the group.[23] And such control is easily established. When in 2012 I called on the Swiss company, Alliance Boots GmbH, at its 94 Baarerstrasse, Zug address, it turned out to be one of around fifty unrelated companies dealt with by a local business service company, the proprietors of which were none too pleased with the visit, and had no Boots personnel present. It was a far cry from the 'common hopes, common sympathies and common humanity' that enlightened businessman Jesse espoused a century before.

Similar destruction of tax bills was reported in just about all the big private equity takeovers of the 2000s, including those at Debenhams, motor insurance company AA and oldies' service company Saga (outlined by Robert Peston in his 2008 book *Who Runs Britain?* under the unambiguous subheading 'We are all subsidizing private equity').[24] Others would chronicle the effects even on companies profiting from providing increasing amounts of publicly funded healthcare. Spire, for example, the owner of what were BUPA hospitals and now a significant NHS service provider is just one, wiping out its taxable profits by paying interest offshore at 10%.[25]

The technique of using large levels of debt to strip out a company's profits through tax-deductible interest payments, which often end up in some low-tax territory, is known as 'thin capitalization'. It is open to the vast stock of foreign-owned business in the UK – currently running at around $1 trillion's worth – and has, unsurprisingly, never been popular with the taxman.[26] The recent takeover of another British company with honourable origins, Quaker-founded Cadbury, by US food company Kraft, had devastating consequences for the company's UK tax payments, not to mention the jobs of some its British employees. What's more, the process demonstrated how the UK's generous tax breaks for interest payments act as a public subsidy to foreign takeovers that can distort Britain's industrial base.[27]

For thirty years, in fact, the Revenue has been combating the practice of thin capitalization using laws that limit tax relief to what would be available if a foreign-owned British company's debt were at genuinely commercial levels, i.e. what it could borrow in its own right if it weren't supported by its usually far larger overseas parent company. The rules prompted a group of companies operating in the UK to launch a decade-long battle in the European courts, arguing that effectively restricting debt between companies within the EU was unlawful under the European Treaty. They ultimately failed, with the European courts approving the Revenue's laws restricting tax relief for interest to that on no more than commercial levels of debt. But the private equity funds owning companies like Boots were still able to claim that in their brave new, financially liberated world, rampant debt levels *are* commercial. That's the point. You gear up, strip out costs from a business and multiply the value of your investment within a few years – all aided by tax relief for the debt financing the process.

All too often the taxpayer-subsidized result was the decimation of jobs, while the funds' managers extracted eye-watering returns for themselves. So when parliament's Treasury Select Committee of MPs turned its attention to private equity in 2007 it recommended that 'the Treasury and HM Revenue and Customs examine whether the tax system unduly favours debt as opposed to equity [i.e. share ownership], thereby creating economic distortions'.[28] The answer might have been obvious; even a right-of-centre review of taxation policy four years later would conclude that this was one distortion that should go.[29] But the Labour government had become intimate with the industry through contacts such as Gordon Brown's close adviser and Apax private equity group founder Sir Ronald Cohen, while the same new friends were filling party coffers. New Labour was never going to pull the MPs' recommendation out of the 'pending' tray.

The problem was certainly appreciated early in 2010 by the then Conservative opposition. When one national champion fell into highly geared foreign hands, the party's tax spokesman David Gauke protested that 'the current structure of our tax system appears to encourage the situation whereby a successful and profitable business like Manchester United becomes loaded down with debt as a consequence of a leveraged buy-out . . . This may be a tax efficient structure but it is difficult to see how this is good for the long term interests of the club, good for football or good for the country.'[30] Once in government Gauke would, however, quickly U-turn on this one.

Hedge of darkness

If private equity grew up under the indulgent parenting of successive deregulating, tax-cutting governments, so did its equally spoilt cousin: the hedge fund industry that took full advantage of the 1990s explosion in new financial instruments including arbitrage, short-selling and any number of products 'derivative' of regular financial transactions, such as swaps and options. All could be executed at a pace that made the banks look leaden-footed, while late twentieth-century 'light touch' financial regulators gazed on approvingly. Offering returns even in falling markets – if far from consistently delivering them – this was a game that appealed even to once conservative investors like pension funds. So alluring was it that an in-demand hedge fund manager could squeeze investors in its funds for a 2% annual management fee plus a further 20% of the profits made by the fund. By 2010, the worldwide hedge fund market was put at $2 trillion of investments, around $420bn of which was based in London.[31] Apply the 'two and twenty' standard for management fees and profits shares to that and there's a lot of profit, and tax, at stake.

Large dollops of money and a sprinkling of financial brain-power are just the ingredients for a tax avoidance recipe. Both are eminently mobile and can be placed almost anywhere in the world the tax planners choose. So over $400bn of 'London' investments are to be found in funds registered in the Cayman Islands or one of the many Swiss cantons that offer favourable tax deals to those bearing ambitious business plans. But stroll around Mayfair, pausing to gawp at the Aston Martins and outrageously priced restaurant menus, and it's clear that many of the funds' managers are actually nowhere near the Alps or a small coral island in the Caribbean.

The 'hedgies' revel in the London life without the fruits of their toil facing any meaningful taxation here. This is largely thanks to a generous tax exemption introduced in 1970 to give the expanding City of London an edge in the market for managing what were then more sedate 'offshore funds'. Without this concession the profits of such funds were likely to have faced UK taxation because their management in London would, in effect, have made the profits those of a UK branch. The 'investment management exemption', expanded to cover greater levels of management by Tory chancellor Ken Clarke in 1995, keeps the funds' profits out of the taxman's grasp. But it applies only if the managers are paid for (and thus taxed on) what they do in the UK at what the law calls the 'customary' rate, which is one of those words that makes pound signs spring up in a tax adviser's eyes.

The funds' advisers in the big accountancy firms ensure that what is done in the UK is something for which a very low return is indeed 'customary'. The typical outcome was neatly summarized in a 2003 paper by the industry's most public tax adviser, Chris Sanger, a Deloitte partner who from 1997 had spent four years on secondment as a special adviser on tax to Gordon Brown. 'Overall,' explained the Oxford engineering graduate who like many of his generation now found high finance a more rewarding use of his talents than making things, 'the aim is to ensure: no taxation of the fund . . . minimisation of the taxation worldwide of the fund management company (or companies); and maximisation of the allowances/reliefs from capital gains for the founders.'[32] The method he outlined is now standard: an offshore fund manager in the tax haven where the fund is based and a 'sub-manager' in London. While the Mayfair hedgies work for this latter company – often under employment contracts with another offshore company for further tax advantages – it receives and is taxed on just a small proportion of the fees.

Evidence of UK tax payments by hedge funds is mixed at best, even if you know where to look among the publicity-shy firms. One place to start is with the hedge funds whose founders feature six times in the top ten recent donors to the Conservative Party.[33] The most successful of them is the Australian-born, British-based 'arbitrage' specialist behind Caymans-based hedge fund CQS, Michael Hintze, who has given £1.25m to the Tories. His fund is managed in London by a limited liability partnership called CQS

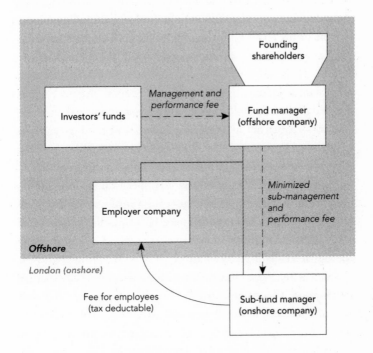

Fig. 11 A sample structure that a London-based hedge fund might use to minimize corporation tax

(UK) LLP, which in 2010 received a healthy $175m in fees but, as a partnership, is not itself taxed. Its partners are, but the one entitled to the income is a British company called CQS Management Ltd, which paid just £51,000 tax for the year. This limited bill came about because it paid out its hundreds of millions of pounds in income to the Jersey company that employs all CQS's staff, CQS (Global Services) Ltd. At which tax-efficient point the trail runs cold.[34]

A similar set-up is found at the hedge fund chaired by current Tory treasurer and multimillion-pound donor Stanley Fink, International Standard Asset Management, which boasts 'offices in London and New York'. In fact the company earning the real money from managing funds worth around $700m is again based in the Cayman Islands. It reimburses the UK operation for its £1.5m a year costs (including the £160,000 paid annually to Fink personally for renting its Queen Anne Street, Fitzrovia, office) plus a small mark-up of less than 5% which leaves the ISAM companies' UK tax bills at less than £20,000 a year.[35]

Next to the hedge fund managers' total returns these amounts are infinitesimal. The man in charge of Deloitte's lucrative hedge fund advisory practice put the tax at stake into some kind of perspective. If a fund has $1bn in assets sitting offshore and earns 20 percent in a year (the kind of returns many funds look for), he commented, 'that's $200 million of gain potentially not being taxed in the UK at rates of 30 percent to 40 percent,' adding somewhat unnecessarily: 'We are talking big numbers here.'[36]

Little is known about the Revenue's reaction to these arrangements; my enquiries revealed only that the authorities didn't even know how many cases they had looked at. Rumour circulated in 2006 that the taxman was finally applying some pressure, but he could do no more than enforce rules that, as Deloitte's Sanger's 2003 exposition made clear, allowed for serious tax 'minimization'. The only known outcome of this was that the largest publicly listed hedge fund manager, Man Capital, had had a run-in with the inspectors. But even after this, the firm that Stanley Fink turned into the biggest hedge fund manager in the world, and split between Geneva and London, reported an effective tax rate of around 15% and disclosed a tax saving of £574m over four years through the 'effect of overseas rates compared to [the] UK'.[37] That's about a major new hospital every year, just on the tax saved by a single hedge fund company listed in London but carving itself up between the UK and Switzerland.

Just like the big-name multinational corporations with long histories selling food, drink, drugs and much else, the hedge funds and private equity industry at the cutting edge of twenty-first century capitalism discovered the joys of fragmenting their businesses and parking the profitable parts in the world's tax havens. And an indulgent government was not going to make any of them pay tax at reasonable levels. Rules governing multinationals' offshore subsidiaries would be relaxed. Private equity's almost unlimited tax breaks for interest payments, understood on all sides to be a harmful distortion, would continue. A 2006 HMRC review of hedge funds' central tax concession, the 'investment management exemption', set off with the aim, duly achieved, of 'continuing UK attraction'.[38] These footloose outriders of British capitalism, flattering and funding the governing classes one minute, quietly pointing out their own international mobility the next, were to be appeased at all costs. Besides, the millionaires running the private equity and hedge funds, like the rest of Britain's high earners, at least paid a fair slug of personal tax. Didn't they?

6
A Rich Man's Kingdom

The special tax breaks that make Britain a playground for the international jet set, while the rest of us pay the price

Lehman, Clichy, Cygan, Lauren, Toure, Eduardo, Pires, Vieira, Bergkamp, Henry, Almunia, Senderos, Fabregas, Flamini, Van Persie. When these Arsenal players ran out at Highbury on 14 February 2005 to give Crystal Palace a 5–1 thrashing, the six Frenchmen, three Spaniards, two Dutchmen, Brazilian, Ivorian, Cameroonian, Swiss and German became the first professional English football team without a single English player among them. These were some of the most gifted players of their generation but their dominance of the Premier League champion's starting line-up was as much a product of smart fiscal formations as their talent for the beautiful game. This was arguably the most tax-efficient sporting outfit in history.

Thirteen years after its creation, the Premier League was awash with the billions of pounds poured into elite English football by its sponsors, new broadcaster Sky and overseas club owners bearing fortunes of questionable provenance. Restrictions on moving footballers around the world and on the numbers of foreign players within teams had been swept aside by the European courts.[1] What remained was a free-for-all over the services of the world's best players, in which those unencumbered by a British birthplace came at drastically reduced cost.

To go with more assured ball control nurtured on warmer or more enlightened training grounds, overseas players also had a serious edge under Britain's tax code. Foreign players coming to Britain would immediately become UK tax residents but, since they would not be expecting to remain permanent residents, would sit in a kind of anteroom to full tax status as 'not ordinarily resident'. The status was brought in by the chancellor, David Lloyd George, in 1914 to exempt 'the official carrying on the Empire abroad, who pays an occasional visit to this country' from his new law taxing UK residents on all their worldwide income, whether or not they brought it into the UK.[2] Now it allowed foreign footballers to escape any tax charge on what they earned from playing abroad, for example in lucrative European matches, as long as the income remained offshore. But even better than this tax perk, these players would be permanently 'non-domiciled'.

'Domicile' is a nebulous concept in English law based on a person's background and lifelong affiliations. It has its origins in the rules of Empire and the idea that in whichever far-flung corner of the globe an Englishman found himself he remained attached to the mother country through his English 'domicile'. The 'non-dom' notion entered the tax code in 1914 when Lloyd George excluded those who were not domiciled in the United Kingdom from the new tax charge, because they had little long-term connection to the country even if they might be resident here at the time. 'The citizen of the Empire who lives in one of our Colonies, and is not domiciled in this country, is exempt from this taxation,' explained Financial Secretary Edwin Montagu.[3]

Instead the 'non-doms' would be taxed on foreign income only if they 'remitted' it to these shores. There was nothing in this for the English football league champions of the time, Blackburn Rovers, and its home-grown team, but for their more exotic successors 90 years later, and all the other 300 non-domiciled players and managers by 2005, Lloyd George's concession – clearly never intended for ultra wealthy immigrants – was to prove a goldmine.[4]

Ten years before he appeared in the all-foreign Arsenal team, Dutchman Dennis Bergkamp blazed the trail for tax-efficient enrichment. Arriving in north London from Inter Milan as an established international, he was in a prime position to ensure his multimillion-pound income didn't bear the full brunt of income tax and national insurance. The Premier League player as celebrity could profit not just from what he did with his boots on but from his image, an intangible commodity as pregnant with income tax possibilities as a drugs company's patents were for its corporation tax bill, especially for a privileged 'non-dom'.

Bergkamp already had a company set up in Curacoa, one of the Dutch Antilles, to receive income from promoting coffee, chocolates and footwear when he was in Italy. So when Arsenal agreed to pay separately on top of the star's salary for the use of his image which, ran the theory, would enhance the club's commercial success, the Caribbean company proved an ideal receptacle. Arsenal would get tax relief for the payments as if they were wages but Bergkamp would not be taxed on them as long as the money stayed offshore. It was a departure from the days when players simply received wages and win-bonuses, their images available for the clubs to use as they wished, and unsurprisingly it didn't impress the taxman, to whom it looked like no more than 'a smokescreen for additional remuneration'.[5]

When a tax tribunal came to consider the set-up five years later, unsuccessfully using aliases to protect Arsenal's and the Dutchman's identities, it noted Bergkamp's appeal among the Highbury faithful: 'Sports [Arsenal] has sold more replica shirts bearing the name Evelyn [Bergkamp] than any other name.' This was a bona fide arrangement and, although the Gunners had not made as much out of Bergkamp's image as they might have done, the scheme worked.[6]

As it did for 'Jocelyn', aka ex-England international David Platt, who had come a long way from his early days at Crewe Alexandra. A year after hitting footballing stardom by hooking in a Gazza free kick at Italia 90, Platt had moved to Italy to further his career at Bari,

Juventus and Sampdoria. When he signed for Arsenal at the same time as Bergkamp, he, too, would be paid a salary while his company received fees from the club for allowing it to exploit his image. Although the Lancastrian Platt was no non-dom, an image rights company (based in the UK) still brought with it significant benefits in the form of a lower corporate tax rate, as opposed to PAYE tax on income, and the avoidance of national insurance contributions. In the event, the England man's image proved of limited value as injury and a receding hairline consigned him to the fringes of both the Arsenal first team and the world of product endorsement. But at least, agreed the tax tribunal, the tax trick worked.

Back of the netto

Evelyn and Jocelyn[7] opened the floodgates for England's elite players. Their agents could now demand spiralling 'wages' *and* insist that chunks of them were paid to companies for the use of their man's image, the value of which they were not prone to underestimating. The tax benefits were many and varied, especially if the money was not extracted until some point far into the future, possibly when the player had moved to the next international port of call out of the British taxman's reach. In the meantime, the basic salary in the UK was usually sufficient to keep even the flashiest player happy while he was here.

By the late 1990s, an image rights company was as routine for a leading player as the sports car and mock Tudor mansion. It provided a staple story for the Sunday newspapers, the *Observer* reporting the day before England left for the Euro 2004 championship that just about every senior member of the squad, including David Beckham, Michael Owen and publicity-shy Paul Scholes, had an (onshore) image rights company.[8] The list was updated six years later by the *Sunday Times*, which found the same set-up operated by current stars Wayne

Rooney, Gareth Barry and Jack Wilshere. For many of their clubs, looking to slash the pay-as-you-earn tax cost of wage bills that in football's Alice-in-Wonderland financial world approached or even exceeded total revenues, the temptation to pay as much as possible into a player's image rights company rather than through the payroll proved irresistible. When Portsmouth player Sol Campbell sued his club in 2010, he revealed that on top of his £30,000-a-week wages, his 2006 contract included £20,000 a week for his image, to be paid into a Geneva-based trust fund.[9] The set-up was legal, but there was evidence that the clubs were routinely over-allocating players' fees to image rights, and under-allocating them to conventional wages. By 2011 English clubs were being pursued for £100m in tax, Manchester United declaring its own £5.3m dispute on the issue.[10]

In a liberal transfer market, increasingly powerful top players could insist that their clubs bore the risk of the taxman's wrath. They were interested in net wage and image rights fees and demanded that if the Revenue were to challenge the contracts, it would be the club, not the player, that picked up any tax bill. In footballing parlance, these were the 'netto' deals negotiated by any agent worth his salt, and by the late 1990s they were pushing clubs to find ever more tax-efficient ways to pay. And once again the Gunners were at the cutting edge of football finance.

Parlour games

One of the players who made way for the influx of foreign stars into the Arsenal dressing room was Ray Parlour, a midfielder good enough to win ten caps for England but with his share of personal troubles. As his 2001 divorce was played out in the courts over the following years, more was revealed about football's tax affairs than many in the game wished. The man who opened the scoring in his team's 2002 FA Cup Final win was, it emerged, taking home around £1.2m a year from gross earnings of £1.55m. At 20%, this was around half the standard 40% for high earners and was explained by 'the fact that such bonuses as he receives in addition to his salary are made available to him through sophisticated and tax-efficient channels'.[11] These channels included what in the late 1990s became the tax tools of choice for big earners: the offshore employee benefit trust (EBT) and the offshore share scheme, deployed for the Gunners by tax advisers Deloitte in much the same way they were using them for bankers' bonuses (see chapter 3).

In Arsenal's case a company called Sevco, in which the players were shareholders, made payments to a Jersey trust called Fidus, from which the players received dividends taxed at 25% rather than their usual 40%, or not at all if they were non-domiciled and kept their dividends offshore.[12] An even more effective mechanism for bonuses, it was hoped, was the EBT which would *lend* the players money representing their bonuses. The player would be taxed merely on the benefit of not paying interest on the loan, worth perhaps 5% of what he was receiving and producing an effective tax rate of around 2%. Of course the loan would never be repaid, but that unmentioned fact was incapable of generating a tax bill. These schemes naturally provoked the Revenue, and Arsenal was presented with a £11m bill when the courts found that companies' payments into EBTs generally weren't tax-deductible for companies.[13] But such arrangements remained attractive for many other football clubs that have no use of tax deductions against corporate profits since, living beyond their means, they have no taxable profits anyway.

Most of the beautiful game's tax schemes work far better for foreign players. The Arsenal team trotting out that February 2005 evening would not have surprised a tax adviser. As 'non-doms', they can keep their image rights income offshore in a tax haven company entirely untaxed, while their British colleagues are forced to use UK companies (which would at least pay some tax) in order not to fall foul of laws written in the 1930s to stop some of the Vesteys' tax avoidance. Share schemes for bonuses are more valuable to non-dom players who can leave them offshore and not suffer even the 25% tax the Brits were forced to pay. The same 'netto' wage for a foreign player thus costs a club far less than it does for a native one. So for the same total cost the club can get a better overseas player. It's a competitive advantage that goes some way to explaining why the Premier League, which had just 11 non-British or Irish players in 1992, boasted 250 of them by 2007.[14] As a result, talented British youngsters struggle to find places at the top level and the national team plumbs new depths of under-achievement: failure to qualify for Euro 2008, a dismal showing at the 2010 World Cup and a further also-ran finish at Euro 2012. Football is one more business that has been distorted by tax avoidance. But at least the Premier League now has a fitting sponsor: Barclays.

There was a telling postscript to the exposure of Premier League tax avoidance in the divorce courts. The Parlours were put in an awkward foursome with another couple whose case raised similar issues. The other husband, Kenneth McFarlane, was a 'corporate tax planning' partner at Deloitte, the very firm that had advised Arsenal on their 'sophisticated and tax-efficient channels'. The bean counter was earning similar amounts – £1.3m in 2002/03 – to the England footballer. He was also using some tax-efficient channels of his own, having bought a £3m property in one of London's swankier suburbs, Barnes, through the Big 4 accountancy partnership in order to obtain higher rate tax relief on the mortgage interest under rules intended to encourage investment in business. The arrangement, more valuable than the basic rate tax relief for mortgage interest that itself had been scrapped by Gordon Brown in 1997, was described by a judge as 'very generous' and was subsequently outlawed. More revealingly still, a later round in McFarlane v. McFarlane showed how much more rewarding a career in premier league tax avoidance is than even life at football's higher reaches. By 2008 Kenneth's net pay hit £1.1m, suggesting around £1.8m gross, and he was contemplating a few more years on a seven-figure income before retiring at 55.[15]

Ray Parlour had just seen out his playing days at Hull City and was scratching around for media work.

Hello! to tax avoidance

Star-struck onlookers gasped as she emerged from a chauffeur-driven midnight blue Jaguar, her floor-length rose pink and organza-sequinned Jenny Packham evening gown glittering in the paparazzi's flashlights. He stylishly complemented his stunning new wife in a classic black dinner jacket. The date was 9 June 2011, the occasion the annual ARK gala dinner at Kensington Palace, the guests of honour Prince William, Duke of Cambridge, and his Duchess, Kate. (I include the haute couture detail, courtesy of the ever-reliable *Daily Telegraph*, not just as a desperate corrective to the previous blokeish passage, but to show where real glamour is to be found in twenty-first-century London.)[16]

ARK stands for Absolute Returns for Kids, a charity established by Swiss/French hedge fund manager Arpad 'Arki' Busson, whose leonine looks and list of exes (Farah Fawcett, Elle Macpherson, Uma Thurman), make him no Compo in the glamour stakes. More annoyingly still, Arki, whose personal wealth is routinely put in the nine-figure bracket, is universally rated an all-round good guy. In ten years his charity has raised over £150m for disadvantaged children at home and abroad. It sponsors seven publicly funded academy schools in England and donates to life-saving immunization programmes in Africa. Here was someone with whom our future king could do philanthropic business.

So once the yellow-fin tuna carpaccio, roast Kobe beef fillet and trio of desserts including blackcurrant soufflé and apple and sorrel sorbet had settled, William was able to announce a tie-up between his own foundation and ARK. Together, he informed guests including Elisabeth Murdoch, Mariella Frostrup, Matthew Freud, Liz Hurley,

Jemima Khan and Colin Firth, their joint venture would 'generate opportunities in education for young people in the United Kingdom and then later expand beyond our shores'.[17]

As well as hopes for the future, the gala dinner raised £18m for charity immediately. But amid the self-congratulation nobody stopped to ask whether the shindig really was such a great occasion for the world's disadvantaged children. Didn't such small, if star-studded, charitable fund-raising pale next to what could be achieved if the world's richer countries met their commitments to the United Nations Millennium Development Goals and spent 0.7% of their gross national incomes on development? Wouldn't children at home fare better if sounder government finances didn't necessitate the closure of Sure Start centres, for example? At the heart of which questions is of course the thoroughly unglamorous matter, not discussed at Kensington Palace on 9 June 2011, of tax.

The hedge funds themselves, as we've already seen, make precious little contribution to the nation's finances. Busson's British firm EIM (United Kingdom) Ltd, from whose Mayfair Place offices Arki operates, reports annual profits averaging less than £500,000 and tax bills below £200,000.[18] While he can assemble the cream of British socialites for a charity ball, his hedge fund deftly avoids performing in this country the work that makes the real money from managing an estimated £10bn of assets. London, according to EIM's website, performs 'client relations' and 'research' while the big money is earned on 'portfolio management' in the low-tax Swiss canton of Nyon, which of course does not require companies to publish any accounts.[19] It then pays some limited fees to the UK company for its research and client management. But what of the hedgies themselves, the (almost invariably) men signing the cheques to share an evening with the royal couple, whom successive governments have been so keen to entice to Britain?

Though apparently tax resident in Britain, Arki himself is eminently qualified to adopt 'non-domiciled' status. This would make it straightforward to avoid tax on what he earns from a business that he owns offshore through a series of Luxembourg and Swiss companies and a trust called, without apparent irony, Albion. Although it is all hidden from view, there is thus no reason for the profit shares that make up the bulk of a hedge fund manager's income to come anywhere near the UK and incur a tax bill for a non-dom. For some reason, my requests for clarification of Arki's tax status went unanswered.

As with football players, the competitive advantage for non-doms in the hedge fund business is overwhelming. By 2008 one senior hedge fund lawyer estimated that half of London's hedge funds were run by non-domiciled individuals, several hundred times the proportion of the UK population claiming non-domicile status.[20] Since around 700 hedge funds are thought to be based in London, that would put the number of non-dom hedge fund bosses in W1 at 350, without counting the lavishly rewarded managers beneath them.[21] And it means that a very large proportion of those fawning over the heir to the British throne at Kensington Palace were avoiding tax by virtue of a greater allegiance to some other country. Earning several millions of pounds a year – one commentator estimated in 2008 that 200 London hedgies were earning over £20m[22] – their tax concessions cost far more than anything charities such as ARK put back in.

Non-domicile tax status works so well for the international jet set by turning UK tax residence, which might be thought a fiscal handicap, into a major asset. Under the UK's network of international tax agreements, residence here automatically converts an individual into a non-resident back home and thus no longer taxable there. The UK then privileges its new resident with non-dom status and thus tax exemption for income that he manages to keep offshore (but with plenty of wrinkles to allow it back in if, for example, he wants to snaffle up some prime UK property). The non-domicile tax break thus becomes not just a UK tax avoidance tool but a global one.

It also represents a major subsidy from taxpayers to the businesses whose owners benefit most from it, such as the hedge fund industry. This is a business that has played a major part in inflating international finance to a level that dwarfs productive industry, creating the conditions for the 2008 financial crisis.[23] It provided much of the market for the exotic financial products that triggered disaster – in which the 2007 collapse of a series of (non-British) hedge funds played a central role – and has been repeatedly implicated as a source of destabilizing volatility in any number of markets including oil, food, foreign exchange and commodities. Whatever the benefits its proponents would still claim for it, a subsidy from Britain's and the rest of the world's taxpayers is the last thing it needs.

Privates on parade

There were to be special tax privileges for others inside the financial bubble, too. In his 1998 budget Chancellor Gordon Brown announced that 'for those who build businesses or stake their own hard earned money in them, the long-term rate [of capital gains tax] will be reduced even more from 40p to 10p, the lowest rate ever achieved'. He was unveiling tax breaks for the army of entrepreneurs that New Labour was sure would galvanize industrial performance and reinforce its own unproven economic credentials. As with most benign tax intentions, however, it was soon re-engineered for tax avoidance, and turned into a major public subsidy for yet another business model of questionable value to the British economy.

The new tax break went way beyond the budding entrepreneur toiling to return Britain to fabled greatness. Available on 'business assets' generally, it could be exploited by remote investors in businesses, and not just new businesses. So it had great potential for those whose trade was the buying up and selling on of businesses using largely borrowed money. This was the British private equity industry, investment in which had already trebled in five years up to 1999.[24]

The fund managers that would go on to snaffle up major British companies like the AA, Debenhams and Boots were soon exploiting their new tax break even if its full tax benefit, the 10% tax rate on profits from selling businesses, could be enjoyed only if those businesses were held for ten years, which was beyond private equity's usual horizons. More importantly they were also lobbying heavily, and effectively, for its improvement. Private equity astutely associated itself with the pioneering end of investment under the umbrella of the British Venture Capital Association, even though less than 5% of its investment was in 'early stage' businesses. Buying and selling long-established companies was not exactly boldly going into the commercial unknown but the corporate financiers were determined to piggy-back Britain's more genuine entrepreneurs to get at their tax breaks.[25]

By the end of Labour's first term, with private equity's lethal effects on jobs and corporation tax receipts yet to be laid bare, Gordon Brown's Treasury had been converted to the private equity cause. Two powerful businessmen were swaying opinion in Whitehall. Fund manager Paul (later, as a minister, Lord) Myners was officially recommending greater investment by Britain's pension and insurance funds in private equity, lauding its 'crucial combination of capital, business mentoring and financial discipline to help and encourage enterprises to realise their growth potential'.[26] At the same time, Brown had grown particularly close to the Egyptian-born founder of Britain's leading private equity manager Apax and chair of the BVCA. Ronald Cohen, who would become Sir Ronald in the 2001 New Year honours and later that year a six-figure party donor, impressed Brown with more than just the size of his cheques marked 'Pay Labour Party'. He convinced the chancellor that private equity was the golden industrial future and that its subsidies should be enlarged. In 2002 Brown dutifully extended the 10% tax rate to gains made after just two years rather than ten. 'Cohen was over the moon,' recalled BBC business editor Robert Peston (who had had several discussions with him). 'His lobbying had been extremely effective.'[27]

This was the kind of time frame the private equity industry, which typically hangs around three to six years before cashing in, could deal with. Its leading lights made their serious income by putting in a small amount of their own money, typically between 1 and 3% of the investment in a fund, in return for perhaps 20% of the fund's profit. Treated as a capital gain on an investment, this so-called 'carried interest' would be taxed at a quarter of the top income tax rate, or even less after other allowances. As the industry took off over the following years, expanding six-fold to attract £34bn worth of investments in 2006, the private equity fund managers scooped the jackpot.[28] One of their number, alas, forgot to put his cross in the 'no publicity' box.

Cleaning up

'Any commonsense person would say that a highly paid private equity executive paying less tax than a cleaning lady or other low-paid workers can't be right,' admitted chairman of the SVG private equity group, Nicholas Ferguson, in June 2007.[29] By the time parliament's Treasury Select Committee took its withering look at the inequities of private equity that year, Gordon Brown – now prime minister – was already promising to rein in the tax concessions he had introduced a few years earlier with eyes wide open but now, in the face of public outcry, disingenuously referred to as an unintended 'loophole'.

The Treasury nevertheless remained in thrall to private equity and when Brown's chancellor Alistair Darling acted he did so at minimum cost to the industry's luminaries. His officials still trembled at their threats to leave the country, citing the cost to the untouchable City – £3.3bn a year in fees – should they disappear. But even the private equity bosses could see the writing on the wall in a country growing disillusioned at widening inequalities. Duke Street Capital boss Peter Taylor magnanimously informed MPs, 'I do not think a rate of 15 or 20% [instead of 10%] would be a material disincentive to entrepreneurs like ourselves.'[30] Darling duly agreed a blanket 18% capital gains tax rate, less than half the top income tax rate. The plugged-in Peston later observed that, having named their own tax rate, 'partners of big private equity firms could not believe their luck'.[31] Although the coalition government has since lifted the rate to 28%, supposedly in line with Lib Dem tax policies that included taxing capital gains 'at rates similar or close to those applied to income', the rate remains little more than half the top income tax rate of 50% that they would otherwise incur.

For many private equity fund managers, the non-dom tax break, coupled with some rudimentary tax planning involving an offshore trust to keep their gains out of the UK, enables even the 28% tax to be avoided. Some estimates put the proportion of London's private equity partners who are non-domiciled at 80%.[32] Others dispute this figure but the proportion is certainly high. Very few come clean, although when the hostile Treasury Committee summoned a group of leading industry figures it was to the credit of one, Dominic Murphy of private equity manager KKR, that he came out as Irish domiciled for tax purposes. The self-assured 45-year-old Liverpool University graduate (pre-tuition fees), described by one interviewer as exuding "a quiet English charm",[33] had evidently prospered on Britain's education and healthcare systems. But since Murphy's parents were Irish he could exploit the 'non-domicile' legacy of Empire to create the opportunity to escape tax on potentially spectacular earnings.

Completing the private equity circle of tax avoidance, Murphy's most significant investment is almost certainly in Alliance Boots (on the board of which he sits), which we have already seen avoiding tax at both the corporate level by paying vast sums of interest offshore, and at the ownership level through Swiss and Gibraltar holding companies and trusts. Now its British, but non-domiciled, private equity manager sitting in London can escape tax when he cashes in his 'carried interest'. KKR's sale in 2012 of just half of its stake to an American chain for a £3bn gain suggests the non-dom tax break could prove highly valuable.

It was soon reported that Murphy was one of seven out of KKR's eight UK partners to claim the advantageous tax status, the others not British-born.[34] The non-dom tax break, it was clear, was handing a competitive advantage in the battle for control over expanding swathes of British business to those with little attachment to the country. When Cadbury was taken over by US food giant Kraft in 2010, shutting down a factory despite promises not to do so, business secretary Vince Cable promised to rein in overseas takeovers that erode the British industrial base (although nothing would come of that commitment). The non-dom tax break in the hands of private equity is in fact a far greater source of the influence he feared. It acts as a kind of reverse protectionism in which overseas control is favoured over home control and can only militate against a sustainable domestic economy.

Congratulations, you have a beautiful baby non-dom!

'What do you call 100,000 Frenchmen with their arms up? The army.' With this and twenty more 'jokes', the *Daily Mail* greeted the news in March 2009 that France was rejoining NATO after forty years' absence.[35] None of the gags was quite as amusing, though, as the revelation just the month before that the jingoistic newspaper's proprietor claimed to be domiciled across the Channel.[36]

The Honourable Jonathan Harmsworth was born on 3 December 1967 in Hammersmith Hospital, heir to the Rothermere media dynasty and its Associated Newspapers empire. His early life prepared him for his inheritance: private schooling at Prince Charles' bracing alma mater Gordonstoun, followed by business education in the States before a whistle-stop tour of senior positions in the family newspaper group. By the time his father Vere Harmsworth died in 1998 the cherubic Jonathan, now the 4th Lord Rothermere, was just about ready at the tender age of thirty to run the multinational corporation of which Associated was now part, Daily Mail and General Trust plc.

The 4th Viscount inherited more than his father's newspapers and his mother's curly hair. Through quirky laws not explained in *Burke's Peerage*, he was also bequeathed the French domicile of his tax exile father. Although Vere had revelled in his status as a peer of the British realm – taking his Lords seat at various times on the Conservative, Labour and cross benches – Rothermere *père* had since the fifties been a Parisian exile. And because he had intended to, and did, live out his tax-efficient days there, he acquired a tax 'domicile of choice' in France, which was passed on as an equally French 'domicile of origin' to his son Jonathan. It might be as bizarre as inheriting a straight nose from a naturally bent-beaked parent who'd had plastic surgery, but this Lamarckian tax genetics can be extremely valuable. Not only did the Rothermeres' non-dom status ease the offshore transfer of the DMGT empire to the 4th Viscount inheritance-tax free, it continues to enrich the family.

Jonathan's own family eventually outgrew the Rothermere home in London's *Upstairs Downstairs* heartland of Eaton Square, so in 2004 he commissioned from architect Quinlan Terry a neo-Palladian house deep in the Dorset countryside. By 2006 even this £40m pile, surrounded by 220 acres of grounds, wasn't enough and new east and west wings were needed at Ferne House. The money came in the form of bank loans for which Rothermere pledged eight million of his DMGT shares, worth around £50m. Except they weren't *legally* his shares. They belonged to the Bermudan company through which

Rothermere family trusts control the *Mail* empire, Rothermere Continuation Ltd. In this way Jonathan could fund his new house without bringing any of his own earnings into the UK and triggering the tax bill that, through the offshore company and trust structure, he had managed to avoid in the first place. By sending £10m a year of DMGT dividends through Rothermere Continuation Ltd and the trusts of which he and his family are beneficiaries, Jonathan had converted them into 'overseas' income that for a non-dom would not be taxed unless 'remitted' to the UK.[37]

Since Rothermere had little more interest in France than occasional holidays at the Dordogne chateau his father had bought shortly before his death, and had now acquired a sizeable chunk of Dorset for a permanent home, there was a chance that he had involuntarily relinquished his foreign domicile. Tax inspectors had worked up a case for investigating precisely this, and towards the end of 2008 had their plans approved by HMRC's strategy board, before they were mysteriously dropped following the intervention of HMRC boss Dave Hartnett.[38] The conspiracy theorist might have suspected that, already facing appalling publicity over lost discs and other fiascos, the last thing the tax authorities needed was to rile one of Britain's most powerful press barons. Others thought that pursuing Rothermere's domicile status – a difficult thing to change given its deeply personal nature – would be a wild-goose chase on which Hartnett was wise not to send his inspectors (though this ought to have been something for the more expert members of the strategy board). Whatever lay behind the decision, the result was that the English-born, British-educated proprietor of the guardian of middle England's prejudices could carry on avoiding tax on the strength of his father's tax exile a generation before.

Rothermere's status, like that of all non-doms, was a closely guarded secret until I was able to report it in *Private Eye* in 2009. The news sparked a pointed protest from activist-comedian Mark Thomas, who in full, frothing *faux* Richard Littlejohn mode fumed:

'It's political correctness gone mad that the French are now running the *Daily Mail*. They are tax-dodgers, they are spongers. He's almost an asylum seeker.' Beside him outside the *Mail*'s Kensington office supporters waved mocked-up *Mail* front pages: 'WHAT A BLOODY GAUL!', 'DODGY FRENCH TOFF IN NON-DOM TAX ROMP' and 'ROTHERMERDE!'[39] But still, beyond a line in the *Guardian*'s diary column, this fairly significant information went unreported.

The novel tax arrangements of other Fleet Street proprietors, such as the *Telegraph*-owning Barclay brothers – personally resident in Monaco and with an offshore-from-offshore redoubt on their own Channel Island, Breqhou – might have explained the silence.[40] Political indifference to such a wealthy Briton's tax privileges, meanwhile, hinted at the influence of this and many other wealthy non-doms. Reform had often been mooted, most seriously in 1988 when Tory Treasury minister Norman Lamont proposed bringing non-doms into the same tax net as everyone else. The plan was approved by his boss, Chancellor Nigel Lawson, but he was swiftly put back in his box by Margaret Thatcher after lobbying from Greek shipping owners living in London. This yielding to offshore wealth infuriated a young opposition firebrand called Gordon Brown who, as shadow chancellor a few years later would promise: 'A Labour Chancellor will not permit tax reliefs to millionaires in tax havens.'[41]

Filthy rich

Tax relief for millionaires using tax havens was, however, exactly what Gordon Brown permitted and extended over thirteen years at nos 10 and 11 Downing Street. His imperviousness to his own previous convictions was, for some reason, strongly correlated to the generosity of a group of non-dom Labour Party donors, including Ronald Cohen and industrialists Lakshmi Mittal and Lord Paul, who had rallied to the New Labour cause. Between 2001 – when party donations were first published – and 2010, the non-doms donated around £10m, more than the cost of a typical general election campaign.[42] After a promising 2001 contribution of £125,000, for example, Mittal weighed in with separate £2m donations in July 2005 and January 2007. These were the new friends whom New Labour architect Peter Mandelson delighted with his admission to being 'intensely relaxed about people getting filthy rich'. He would later be at pains to point out that he had added 'as long as they pay their taxes', though he preferred not to dwell on the fact that *their* taxes were substantially lower than everybody else's.

The non-dom question became what ought to have been an embarrassment for New Labour. It wasn't until 2002, with the innovation of published party donations revealing the extent of non-dom largesse and New Labour's obeisance to wealth disillusioning many voters, that Brown announced a review of the domicile rules. But with the shipping magnates' successors in the hedge fund and private equity worlds reminding Brown that they too could swan off if asked to pay their fair share, and big name non-doms posting fat cheques to party HQ, budget after budget passed with no action on the tax break. Only in 2008, when Brown's successor as chancellor Alistair Darling was upstaged by his Tory shadow George Osborne's idea of a £25,000 non-dom levy, was the domicile 'review' hauled from the long grass. Darling quickly produced his own entirely original proposal for a £30,000 charge on claiming the status, but only for those who had been in the UK seven years, which the Treasury put at 4000 of the estimated 112,000 non-doms.

For the Mittals and Cohens this was loose change, but the move was defended on the grounds that non-doms – most of them well-paid City bankers employed by generally foreign financial institutions – did at least pay £3bn tax on what they declared as earned in the UK.[43] [44] Later figures put the total at nearer £6bn.[45] As for how much the non-doms avoided, that was anybody's guess since there is no requirement to report 'unremitted' offshore income. Tax campaigner Richard Murphy made a valiant stab at a number, estimating £4.3bn annually based on the typical income that might be expected of a non-dom working in the businesses, such as banking, where most lurk.[46] But this seemed to overlook the stratospherically rich who might be escaping tax bills running into tens or even hundreds of millions thanks to Britain's positioning as their own tax haven.

In 2006 accountants Grant Thornton estimated that in the previous year Britain's fifty-four billionaires, mostly non-doms, paid tax of £15m on combined fortunes of £126bn. A quick look at the *Sunday Times* Rich List 2012 suggests that fifteen of the top twenty would almost certainly qualify for non-domiciled tax status given their origins.[47] Mittal's fortune alone is estimated at £12.7bn, largely through his Luxembourg-based ArclorMittal steel group, which would be expected to produce annual income for the boss in the high hundreds of millions. Similar guesswork right down the rich list – via Roman Abramovich's £9.5bn at no. 3, the Selfridges and Fortnum & Mason-owning Weston family with £5.9bn at no. 10 and even Lord Rothermere's estimated £760m fortune at a respectable no. 99 – indicates several billions of pounds avoiding the Exchequer's grasp even from this small group. In principle, of course, the non-dom elite should be taxed on their offshore income when they bring it back into the UK, which, to judge by their lavish spending, they were certainly doing. But the figures seemed to confirm that the techniques deployed by armies of tax advisers to circumvent this law remain pretty successful.

Perfect solution

The tax case for non-dom concessions is that if the footloose elite were fully taxed, they would either leave or not come here in the first place and Britain wouldn't pick up even their contributions on what they earn here. But since most of this tax comes from bankers' UK earnings that would remain unless the banks themselves left London, this argument is overstated. The economic case for running 'the tax economy of this country as a large-scale version of Chelsea football club' – as one former Labour MP put it[48] – is that doing so attracts talented foreigners to sprinkle their entrepreneurial genius over Britain. 'At a time of growing economic uncertainty it is vital we do all we can to keep wealth generators and their businesses in the country,' claimed CBI boss Richard Lambert when the non-dom levy was proposed, 'not make them feel unwelcome and drive them out.'[49] It seemed not to bother the representative of British industry that the non-dom tax break directly discriminates *against* British entrepreneurs, the majority of whom can't claim non-dom status. So it might not be the smartest way to grow a sustainable economy.

The reasoning can't of course apply to born-and-bred non-doms who are going nowhere, like Lord Rothermere, and must merit their special treatment in some other way. But while the Labour government accepted that advantageous tax status was fine for those controlling big chunks of the British media, it did eventually recognize that it was incompatible with public life. In 2010, following the revelations of the non-dom status of major Conservative Party donor Lord Ashcroft (despite prior promises to become a 'full UK taxpayer' when he donned the ermine years before) and Tory MP Zac Goldsmith, one of the Labour government's last acts was to disqualify parliamentarians from claiming non-dom status. It wasn't much to show for a thirteen-year opportunity to do something about 'tax reliefs for millionaires'.

When a new coalition government of Tories and Lib Dems with a strong anti-tax avoidance flavour to their election manifesto had another look at the tax break across the board it did no more than raise the levy to £50,000. Even this incremental rise was too much for some. One of KPMG's leading tax avoidance advisers, David Kilshaw, whined: 'You cannot overestimate the psychological damage if people think any time there is a change in government there is another attack on non-doms.'[50] This is typical of the argument. The 'attack' amounted to no more than asking certain members of the club, who were enjoying all the privileges of full membership, to pay marginally higher subs but still at far lower rates than everybody else. Yet to Britain's tax avoidance practitioners the idea of telling a rich man to pay even a slightly fairer share is on a par with extraordinary rendition and waterboarding.

As well as entrenching the non-dom tax break in return for a paltry rise in the levy, the Treasury was also making it easier for non-doms to get their offshore incomes into the UK without having them taxed. The proviso is that the funds are invested in business, but it's a condition that tax advisers are busily crawling over for loopholes that will enable them to get their spending money into the country. And their colleagues over at the Home Office were going one better. They were encouraging the world's tax tourists to use the UK by relaxing immigration rules for those with £5m to place in a UK bank account (and making them easier still for those with £10m). This money could even be borrowed as long as the rich immigrant, who will inevitably become a non-dom, has twice the value in assets somewhere. It is an open invitation to use Britain while protecting untaxed offshore fortunes, betrayed when the minister responsible, Damian Green, turned to a leading tax avoidance consultant for endorsement. 'International wealthy individuals and families need effective, interesting solutions that can be implemented swiftly,' drooled a Jersey-based tax planner from a firm called Henley Partners in Green's press release, 'and this new policy gives these people those possibilities.'[51] Britain was now a 'solution' for the global tax-dodger, which is not a bad definition of a tax haven. Another Henley Partners' executive was soon addressing a Zurich conference for advisers to wealthy Russians on the question of 'Foreign passport shopping – what are my options?', with the UK one enticing possibility.[52]

This is more than Britannia showing a bit of ankle; it is the tarting out of an economy, for which nobody can identify any real benefit. If non-domicile status were withdrawn from UK tax law, only those non-doms with sufficient offshore wealth and limited UK personal connections would even contemplate leaving for a tedious life in some other tax haven. Such people may spend some money here, but they are rarely big UK employers and certainly don't base any real business decisions on living here personally for the tax breaks. The ArcelorMittal steel empire belonging to Britain's richest non-dom, Lakshi Mittal, has no physical presence in the UK beyond the self-aggrandizing 'Orbit' in the Olympic Park.[53] Chelsea football club would employ no fewer players or staff if it weren't owned by a non-dom oligarch. The most economically active non-doms are in the hedge funds and private equity firms. If a non-dom hedgie trades the London life for Alpine ennui, who loses beyond a few Mayfair estate agents and restaurateurs? Would Britain be any poorer if the private equity manager pumping Boots full of debt did so from the Riviera rather than the City? Barely, if at all. Yet the UK persists with a tax bribe that, like other bribes, skews both its own and the world's economy.

Non-dom businessmen, footballers, bankers, hedge fund managers and entrepreneurs all have a competitive advantage over their home-grown rivals. Highly geared private equity-owned businesses generating high but risky returns for their owners and less security for their employees can exploit the non-dom advantage to gain an edge over more traditionally owned companies. Meanwhile, by poaching tax residents, the non-dom rules also rip off other nations, many of which won't have been well served in the creation of the non-doms' all too often dubious personal fortunes in the first place. Britain becomes a tax haven, pure and simple. As one tax commentator put it, 'We might as well go the whole hog and apply to become the 27th Canton of Switzerland.'[54]

7
Sell-Out

How Britain's tax system became the servant of big business

'Dear Saddam,' began the spoof letter doing the rounds of the Inland Revenue's Large Business Office some time in 2002, 'we are trialling a new weapons inspection regime modelled on the Inland Revenue's approach to large corporate taxation. All you have to do is tell us you don't have any and we'll go away. Yours, Hans Blix.'[1]

As the UN inspectors scoured the Iraqi deserts for non-existent weapons of mass destruction, back in Britain one of that era's lesser-known dodgy dossiers had driven a despairing tax inspector to satire. It was the Inland Revenue's own sexed-up 'Review of Links with Business' and it marked what many old-school tax officials saw as the abandonment of the hard-nosed analysis of big companies' tax affairs in favour of something fluffier. 'The Revenue's strategic direction is to be an enabler as well as a regulator' droned the paper in third-way Blair-speak, promising a 'customer-focused, supportive and enabling approach' to go with the obligation to collect tax. All was aimed at 'understanding companies' business drivers' and 'bringing business and the Revenue closer together'.[2]

A raging tax avoidance epidemic, against which a serious fight might have been in order before making nice with big business, was not going to stand in the way. 'There are a small number of corporates for whom aggressive tax planning is the norm and who do not want to enter into an open relationship with the Revenue,' declared the report, brushing aside evidence in the department's own records and private sector studies showing that most big businesses were under investigation for some sort of dodge. As with preparations for war in Iraq, the facts had to fit the policy, not the other way round.

The report, commissioned by Gordon Brown after regularly having his ear bent by captains of industry at 'business breakfasts', immediately became known as the 'Hartnett Review' after its lead author and new head of policy at the Revenue, Dave Hartnett. It firmly announced the arrival at the summit of British taxation of the career tax inspector who, as the Inland Revenue's lone 'commissioner' with any experience of tax enquiries, more or less seized control of everything to do with tax avoidance, from directing his department's policing of the activity to advising on the government's legislative response to it. The war on tax avoidance had already been slipping through the Inland Revenue's fingers since the early 1990s, as Conservative governments all but froze the recruitment of tax inspectors and left the department hopelessly outgunned. In its place was a growing emphasis on a co-operative rather than confrontational approach to taxing the largest companies. But Hartnett's review took things one stage further. First, it directed the most senior tax inspectors away from investigating companies towards co-ordinating more routine customer service work. It also designated the section of the Revenue responsible for advising government on business tax policy a 'champion for business'. It was heaping favouritism on top of already declining enforcement, reflected in damning reports in the *Guardian* a few months later under the headlines: 'Cosy relationship keeps corporates happy but could cost £20bn in taxes' and 'Poor leadership, missed chances and billions down the drain'.[3]

Although in keeping with the New Labour trend of taking Tory deregulatory policies and rapidly accelerating them, in fiscal terms the retreat from the fight with Britain's biggest tax-dodgers was

badly timed. Tax-avoiding multinationals were draining billions from
public finances just as they were entering their (ongoing) downturn.
Within a couple of years the mistake would be obvious, prompting
limited legislative action in 2004 and 2005. But although some of
these measures would prove long-term successes – notably the laws
requiring disclosure of tax avoidance schemes – the rot had set in
to tax administration. And any hope that the Revenue had got its
eye back on the tax avoidance ball was about to be swept away in a
calamitous reorganization and a tsunami of management initiatives.

Merger most foul

A dark cloud already hung over the Inland Revenue following
parliamentary condemnation and scathing press coverage of the
sale of the country's tax offices to a Bermudan company in 2001,
while a sequence of collapsed VAT fraud trials had exposed management failings at Customs and Excise. Cabinet Secretary Sir Gus
O'Donnell took a long look at the accident-prone authorities and
concluded – largely, it appeared, on the 'something must be done'
principle – that the Inland Revenue and Customs and Excise
should merge.

To perform this task O'Donnell turned, as was the fashion,
to a captain of industry, in the stout, grumpy shape of one David
Varney. Having recently de-merged mobile phone company O2
from BT, he was, O'Donnell judged, just the man to merge and
chair two bodies with little common heritage. But the acumen for
which Varney had been recruited translated into little more than
a contract for management consultants McKinsey (past successes:
Enron and Railtrack). Far from streamlining the two agencies, the
consultants lumped them together and fragmented the new HM
Revenue and Customs, from April 2005, into an incomprehen-
sible matrix of 'customer units', 'operations', 'products/processes'

and 'corporate functions'. The idea, straight out of the McKinsey playbook, was to make different parts of the organization transact rather than co-operate with each other. Nobody understood what this meant, still less how to do it. Morale plummeted as the new body was flooded with management consultancy-inspired initiative after initiative. By 2007 the malaise was painfully apparent in the minutes of a typical HMRC board meeting:

> Chris Hopson [marketing director] briefly outlined the purposes of the new Change and Capability function, distinguishing it from the Departmental Transformation Programme through its involvement in the Strategic Framework and broader changes across all parts of the Department. The strategic framework bridges the gap between the high level Departmental Ambition and directorate level planning . . . There is a need to have clear and consistent links between the DSOs, Internal Departmental Targets, and the Framework, and all of these need to be hardwired into business as usual and the transformation programme.[4]

Three months later two discs containing seven million families' child benefit details went missing. The man brought in to investigate the scandal noted drily that HMRC was 'not suited to the so-called "constructive friction" matrix type organisation in place at the time of the data loss'.[5] The situation wasn't helped by 25,000 job cuts under a 2004 'efficiency' programme that even the Treasury and HMRC managers knew would cost the Exchequer far more in lost tax than it saved in staff cuts.

Rave review

Meanwhile, the large companies caught by what were far from punitive legislative changes, such as the requirement to disclose their tax schemes, were not taking them well. 'These measures are effectively a covert means of extending the tax base to raise revenue,' bleated the CBI's chief economic adviser Ian McCafferty in November 2005, adopting what was to prove a winning tax whinge formulation, 'and have impacted on the UK's attractiveness as a place to do business.'[6] Later the same month Gordon Brown stood obligingly before the organization's annual conference and delivered what would become his infamous promise of 'not just a light touch, but a limited touch' to business regulation. This model, he continued, 'can be applied ... to the regulation of financial services and indeed to the administration of tax'.[7] Just as Northern Rock could gear up its perpetual mortgage machine undisturbed by irksome regulators, so multinational companies must be allowed to structure their tax affairs without too much hassle from prying tax inspectors.

Brown's fawning before the CBI precipitated yet another 'review', this time with Varney's name at the top but in reality an extension of the 2001 exercise run by Hartnett, who sat sagely alongside Varney on the latest effort's 'consultative committee'. They were joined by finance directors from some of the biggest multinational tax avoiders in Cable & Wireless, HSBC, Cadbury Schweppes and AstraZeneca, all of them in dispute with tax inspectors over offshore arrangements. Running the project day-to-day was director of the 'Large Business and Employers Customer Unit' created in the McKinsey mash-up, John Connors, who would soon move on to become tax director of one of the more vocal companies in the review, Vodafone. All were ably assisted by a secondee from tax avoidance adviser KPMG.[8] Their conclusions would not disappoint Mr McCafferty. For starters, there would be fewer, shorter tax investigations for big businesses. Each multinational would have its own 'customer relationship manager', mimicking the way a private bank serves its wealthy customers. HMRC's priority would be 'taking the business perspective into consideration in everything it does, from implementing policy decisions to designing systems and processes'. As one whistle-blower would eventually write, these managers, soon appointed for the wealthiest individuals too, 'often find themselves trying to mitigate the effects of any HMRC enquiries so as to maintain the absurd concept of a client relationship'.[9]

The 'Varney review' also provided the pretext Hartnett needed for his increasingly frequent personal involvement in the most contentious cases. It formally offered the biggest companies the opportunity to 'escalate' their disputes away from any tax inspector who might prove awkward, right up to the point of getting Hartnett to deal with it himself. And his decisions on the largest tax disputes would be effectively unchallengeable; he was the only HMRC board member with any tax experience and was surrounded by fashionable but functionally useless 'commercial' non-executives who had little interest in taking on tax avoidance. The department's 'ethics' committee, for example, was chaired by former HBOS banker Phil Hodkinson, who simultaneously earned six figures jetting off for board meetings of a Guernsey-resident insurance company called Resolution Ltd.

In the closed world of large corporate tax administration, none of Hartnett's ensuing interventions would appear on the record, but tax inspectors familiar with this period report his personal involvement in major disputes involving GlaxoSmithKline, Diageo, Lloyds TSB, Royal Bank of Scotland, General Electric, Shell, BP, HSBC, Daily Mail and General Trust, Reckitt Beckinser, Hanson, Cadbury, Prudential, RSA, WPP, National Grid and Tesco. The details of all these cases remained secret but the result of one could be teased out from certain companies' published accounts. Barclays' efforts to divert profits from payment protection insurance to a low-tax subsidiary in Dublin, it emerged, were contested by the Revenue and led to a £300m tax bill – indicating a £1bn misallocation of profit – but, following Hartnett's intervention, and remarkably given the margin of the mispricing, no penalty. In many more disputes, senior officials promoted by Hartnett enthusiastically stepped in to ensure the new business-friendly approach was reflected in investigation settlements. As one former tax inspector told me: 'HMRC began to change from impartial policeman of the tax regime enacted by parliament, smoothing its rough edges in exceptional cases through negotiation and compromise, into a self-appointed adjudicator, policing the law only to the extent that it did not interfere with the global ambitions of multinational enterprises.'[10]

A treasury of tax breaks

At the political level, Labour's third-term government was riding a doomed economic boom, spending far more than it was taxing and paying the price in stubbornly high budget deficits. A sensible response might have included extending the clampdown on tax avoidance of 2004/05, but a government abasing itself before big business was more susceptible than ever to its grossly overblown threat that only more tax breaks would keep it in Britain paying anything at all.

'Business leaders believe the UK's corporate tax regime is more burdensome than it was five years ago, and that this is making the UK less attractive as an international business location,' declared CBI Director General Richard Lambert in 2006.[11] The multinationals that had captured the CBI – which should have spoken for business big *and* small but on tax at least was the mouthpiece of its larger members – wanted more than just a friendly tax administration, welcome though that was. They demanded nothing less than a rewrite of corporate tax law governing multinational businesses. There were two big gripes. First, British multinationals bemoaned the unfairness of having to pay UK tax on profits made in lower-tax countries when they were brought back home as dividends, to bring the overall tax charge up to UK rates. Second, they didn't like the way the 'controlled foreign companies' laws brought in by

Nigel Lawson in 1984 taxed profits diverted by multinationals into tax haven companies even if, they complained, those profits were made outside Britain.

These were in fact far from draconian laws. They only ever required a multinational to pay tax on profits at what were by international standards relatively low corporate tax rates (reduced to 28% by 2008) and achieved the economically rational result that the fruits of offshore and onshore investment by British companies were taxed equally. The pitch against them, however, was simple and persuasive to politicians (not to mention a tame and incurious financial press) who didn't understand the limited reach of tax law: taxing British companies on foreign profits made Britain less competitive.

Big business was pushing, if not at an open door, then one with a very dodgy latch. Since 2005 the Treasury's business tax work had been led by a true-blue City lawyer recruited from Simmons & Simmons, Edward Troup, who had been the last Tory chancellor Ken Clarke's special adviser and whose approach was encapsulated in his 1999 statement that 'taxation is legalised extortion and is valid only to the extent of the law', while spending money on tax avoidance advice 'is not immoral'.[12] And before long the job of amending the offshore tax laws was placed under the purview of a new 'Business-Government Forum on Tax and Globalisation'. Finance directors from British multinationals with major overseas operations including BP, Rolls-Royce and GlaxoSmithKline, along with the indispensable Professor Devereux of the Oxford Centre for Business Taxation, sat down with senior government officials and Labour's well-meaning but credulous tax minister of the day, Stephen Timms, to create a new, less onerous world of business tax.

By the spring 2009 budget a crucial pillar of Britain's international tax rules had been knocked down. Profits repatriated from overseas operations as dividends were exempted from tax, creating an incentive to divert income into tax havens in the knowledge they could be brought back and returned to grateful shareholders without further tax charge. Meanwhile those 1984 laws designed to stop companies shifting profits into tax havens in the first place would, it was promised, be rewritten under a 'liaison committee' made up of the big beneficiaries of any relaxations including HSBC, AstraZeneca and Cadbury.

Trough at the top

You don't find many tax inspectors plying their trade in the chic Monte Carlo Bay Hotel & Resort. But this was to be home for Britain's most senior, if ever so slightly dishevelled, taxman for one balmy September night in the land of the Grimaldis, Grace Kelly and Tina Green. Dave Hartnett had come a long way from the grey West Midlands tax offices in which he had cut his teeth.

He was, nevertheless, in familiar company. The occasion was KPMG's 2009 partners' conference, where he was to give a broad-ranging interview on 'the future of tax' before the Big 4 firm's top brass. Back in Britain's tax offices, meanwhile, Hartnett's inspectors were poring over the tax avoidance schemes marketed by his Cote d'Azur hosts, and battling the firm in the courts over a raft of major personal tax avoidance schemes run through tax havens (see chapter 3).

After many years in charge of the official response to tax avoidance, Hartnett was spending a great deal of time in convivial surroundings behind what might have been thought enemy lines. Following a protracted freedom of information battle, I established that in twenty-one months up to December 2006 he had been entertained by the Big 4 accountancy firms on seventeen occasions. KPMG took him to dinner five times, including at up-market London restaurants Mirabelle, the Cinnamon Club and Simpsons, and had put him up in the Park Lane Hilton ahead of the firm's annual tax symposium.[13] When similar FoI requests forced all Whitehall departments to start releasing top mandarins' hospitality lists, Hartnett gained recognition as 'Whitehall's most wined and dined civil servant'.[14]

There is no suggestion that Hartnett accepted hospitality in return for illicit favours, and the meals and hotel rooms usually accompanied some form of legitimate speaking engagement. This was no great conspiracy; the frequency and nature of the hospitality simply brought such intimacy with a tax avoidance industry, which had once been kept at arm's length, that its views fatally infected the tax administration's approach to avoidance. Right at the top, the Revenue began to see taxation issues affecting large companies in the way that the tax avoidance industry did, not in the way that tax inspectors seeking to apply the law might be expected to. What started out a decade before as an attempt to tax big business through 'a relationship of mutual trust' became one that involved, in the words of the Varney review, 'taking the business perspective into consideration in . . . implementing policy decisions' and then strayed alarmingly into applying tax laws as companies wanted them applied, not as parliament had decided they should be.

Friendly takeover

It doesn't take a degree in constitutional theory to appreciate that parliament makes laws and the executive arms of government, such as HM Revenue and Customs, implement them. But this centuries-old principle came under severe strain towards the end of the twenty-first century's first decade through the corporate capture of the tax authorities.

When in 2009 insurance company RSA, formerly Royal Sun Alliance, threatened to move its head office out of the UK because the 1984 anti-tax avoidance laws would catch the overseas profits it shifted into tax havens, the Revenue responded by offering a deal under which the company could put its overseas reinsurance business in Dublin (to be taxed at 12.5%) without falling foul of the rules, giving RSA all the benefit of moving its head office offshore with none of the hassle. Or, as the company's spokesman told me: 'We have developed a structure which delivers significant shareholder value without the need to re-domesticate.'[15] It reflected, said the company's chief executive Andy Haste, 'a very good relationship with HMRC'.[16] Just as banks serve their big clients through 'relationship banking', the tax authorities were now practising 'relationship taxing', with tax bills tailored as much to corporate wishes as the law and the Revenue's published policies at the time, which still had it that such profits would be caught by the 1984 laws.

But these rules, it was obvious to those in the know, were soon to be drastically revised under the changes promised by the Treasury. RSA was in the loop, as its finance director sat on the 'liaison committee' rewriting the rules, and its deal effectively pre-empted the changes. HMRC's press office even told me: 'Understanding and managing companies' reactions to the application of legislation is an important element of HMRC's administration of the UK tax regime.'[17] If you don't like the law, in other words, we'll see what we can do.

Yet until Vodafone's similar, if much larger, deal sparked the UK Uncut protest movement, blowing some desperately needed fresh air into the fetid world of big business taxation, the received wisdom was that the Revenue was doggedly chasing down corporate tax dodging. By 2011, HMRC never tired of pointing out, the six-year-old 'high-risk corporates' programme had raised over £9bn from settling tax disputes.[18] It gave the impression of an aggressive tax authority bearing down on tax avoidance. But it was a charade.

Surrender!

The high-risk corporates programme in fact just accelerated the settlement of large disputes that could rumble on for several years and was as likely to cost the Exchequer in tax forgone as it was to bring in extra cash. BT was one of the first companies through the programme and actually got money *back*: 'We reached a settlement with Revenue and Customs which will result in a repayment to BT of just over £1bn' (about half the company's annual pre-tax profits), finance director Hanif Lalani explained to the markets in February 2007. 'This repayment relates to the settlement of substantially all outstanding items in respect of the 10 years through to March 2005.' His contented chief executive Ben Verwaayen put it in context: 'earnings per share up 14% and nice to know that we have a £1 billion credit from the taxman'.[19] The lesson of BT's deal was not lost on the rest of Britain's multinationals, which were soon queuing up to go on a programme that was supposed to be a clampdown. But since, under the Revenue's system for measuring the fruits of its investigations, any settlement shows up as a gain for the Exchequer, ignoring possibly greater amounts of tax conceded, the game suited both sides. Vodafone's deal, for example, would count as a £1.25bn success, the billions relinquished simply ignored.

At the core of the programme were meetings between Hartnett and the avoiders' senior directors 'to change behaviour from the top down' with the promise of a lower 'risk rating' in HMRC's books. Sceptics, including even the business-funded Oxford Centre for Business Taxation, thought this was wishful thinking (as it certainly was for Barclays).[20] But it was the carrot extended to 'serial avoiders' including Tesco, BT, National Grid, Citibank, Lloyds TSB, Swiss Re, Hanson, and Daily Mail and General Trust.[21] There was, however, no stick hovering over them, no risk of their tax avoidance activities becoming publicly known as their special treatment effectively precluded these 'serial avoiders' being challenged in the tax tribunals and courts over their schemes (none ever has been). Without impressive leaks, nobody would even have known that Barclays was avoiding tax on an economy-shifting scale. One senior Revenue source concluded of the programme: 'To concentrate scarce resources on high-risk cases was very sensible. But what's happening is that litigation is seen as a failure of "engagement" and there's a danger that high risk corporates end up with better deals than other companies.'[22] The broom that should have been cleaning up large-scale corporate tax avoidance was sweeping it under the carpet instead.

As the Revenue cashed in early at major discounts, the more important tasks in policing big business's tax contributions were, it appeared, simply being abandoned and the value of tax issues under investigation was dropping like a stone (from £35.1bn in 2007 to £25.5bn in 2011, which was, perversely, presented as a success).[23] Fundamental to protecting the UK tax base is ensuring that the trillions of pounds' worth of transactions in and out of the country but within the same multinational enterprise are priced appropriately. As Barclays proved with its Dublin arrangement, mispricing these leads to substantial profits being diverted from the taxman's clutches. But by 2011, just £680m worth of tax covering several years' business was at stake on this 'transfer pricing' question and the related issue of multinationals stripping out profits from British operations in financing costs (see chapter 5).[24] Since £680m tax equates to less than £3bn worth of cross-border payments – roughly the level of business that one big multinational might have with overseas affiliates in a single year – the evidence that the British tax authorities had surrendered the tax border was clear. The amount of tax recovered from these enquiries from the 770 companies dealt with by HMRC's Large Business Service dropped to £273m by 2010/11 from a high of £1.6bn two years before.[25] At the same time, designing financing schemes to funnel interest into tax havens and 'tax-efficient supply chain management' – i.e. transfer pricing schemes – for the biggest companies to siphon profits out of the UK into lower tax areas remain among the major accountancy firms most profitable lines of tax work. Without serious resistance from the tax authorities, which is essential to recover lost tax and to deter companies from pricing their transactions too unfavourably to the UK, the practice costs the Exchequer billions. Yet, as one tax partner of a major accountancy firm told me, 'there is no meaningful activity from HMRC'.[26] Which, as much as the clever tax planning, is likely to explain why companies like Starbucks could operate successfully for so long in Britain while paying trivial amounts of tax.

Even when large businesses do face a tax inspector across a desk, they encounter nothing like the suspicion faced by smaller ones, their conduct considered all but beyond reproach. By 2010 penalties for fraudulent or negligent understatements of income charged on all 770 companies dealt with by the Revenue's Large Business Service had dropped to £0.4m, or around 0.01% of the tax they had under-declared on their tax returns.[27] This was around 200 times lower than the rate applying to other businesses. In part the discrepancy reflected the fact that outright tax fraud – concealing income or inflating expenses – is indeed rarer among larger companies, mainly because it would have to involve dishonesty by more people. But the threshold for penalizing a company is supposed to be 'negligence', of which large companies are routinely guilty, for example when they over- or understate the 'transfer prices' of cross-border transactions with other parts of their enterprise. So the stats did betray the feebleness of the Revenue's challenge to big business, something for which it had already been criticized by parliament's Public Accounts Committee in 2008 based on far *higher* penalties of £20m in the previous two years.[28] At the time the Revenue promised to do better. But lacking the stomach for a fight in the age of 'relationship taxing', it simply gave up instead.

Amateur dramatics

Abdicating core duties was a matter of capability as well as choice. Among senior staff, knowledge of matters such as taxation was deeply uncool, even career-threatening. Their suitability for promotion was measured on intangible 'competences' in 'delegating' and 'leading' under performance management systems imported across Whitehall from yet more management consultants. Meanwhile the cadre of expert tax inspectors schooled in the seventies and eighties push-back against the onset of endemic tax avoidance was slipping into retirement. More often than not they were doing so despairingly early, bitter valedictory speeches marking the regular leaving parties. One youthful retiree ruminated on the Revenue advertising campaign fronted by newsreader Moira Stewart: 'I thought "tax doesn't have to be taxing" was a mildly witty play on words to get people to fill in their tax returns. Now I realize that for big business it meant what it said on the tin.'

When HMRC's more dubious settlements came under the parliamentary spotlight in 2011, MPs were struck by the fact that of all the HMRC board members, only Hartnett had a background in tax and nobody at his level could question his decisions. This was indeed a corrosive decade-long concentration of power, but what was probably even more damaging was that at the director and deputy director levels immediately below him – where the big cases should have been capably turned over – expertise was vanishingly hard to find. The shortage was also acute in the crucial legal arm of HMRC. Since 2008 it had been run by a government lawyer, Anthony Inglese, who readily admitted to MPs: 'I am not what you call a tax lawyer.' Which might have been fine, but all three of his directors were also 'not what you would call tax lawyers'.[29] For tax inspectors, promotion to the higher levels was awarded for loyalty to senior management, not ability. Expertise was atrophying as senior jobs invariably went to what one uncharitable former inspector called 'airheads' with no track record in taking on avoidance or its perpetrators. It was as if Ministry of Defence pen-pushers who had never picked up a weapon were appointed generals, air marshals and admirals. The companies, accountants and lawyers they were up against were, of course, expert from top to bottom and by now ran rings round an embarrassingly amateurish Revenue.

This was more than just neglect of essential skills; the hollowing out of the effort against tax dodging was a fairly deliberate process starting from the top. In making himself a very public figurehead, combining bold pronouncements with personal deals on big cases, Dave Hartnett mimicked another fashion: that for high-profile 'leaders'. It was a phenomenon expertly skewered by economist and *Financial Times* columnist Professor John Kay who, reflecting on recent corporate failures, wrote that:

> The cult of the heroic chief executives has gained wide acceptance, especially among chief executives. But the abilities of such figures typically fall far short of those required to exercise all the functions relevant to good decisions. Worse, maintaining that self-confidence requires that you surround yourself, not by trusted advisers with a variety of technical skills, but by courtiers who will defer to your exceptional wisdom. You thus shut yourself off from the range of analysis and information which effective decision making requires.[30]

Where business's 'heroic chief executives' made ill-conceived mergers and acquisitions, the tax authority's heroic leader struck dubious deals with the likes of Vodafone and Goldman Sachs without consulting those who knew better.

There are long-term consequences, too. When, in 2012, Hartnett retired after heavy criticism of these deals, a decade or more of undervaluing expertise surfaced in the identity of his successor as head of HMRC's tax professionals. Edward Troup, the Treasury mandarin and former City lawyer, certainly had the technical ability for the job, but was no instinctive tax collector. There had been nobody in Britain's tax authority up to the job. And Troup was just one half of a double appointment marking the handover of HMRC to the tax industry; he would be overseen by a new lead non-executive director and chair of the HMRC board in Ian Barlow, the man who had run KPMG's tax practice during its late 1990s and early 2000s heyday of highly contrived avoidance (see chapter 3).

Among the senior tax inspectors and lawyers on whom success against big-time tax avoidance depends, the mood had already darkened. Their union, the Association of Revenue and Customs, had long been as conciliatory as its name suggests (partly because the Revenue's senior managers often shrewdly joined the union). But the worm eventually turned, and in 2011 it told parliament: 'Staff find that they are subject to minute and petty scrutiny and at times deals are done on cases over their heads.' It was a complaint backed up by a later National Audit Office report that noted 'the frequency of [large corporate] taxpayers requesting the involvement of Commissioners on specific issues as settlement discussions are continuing'.[31] Stripped of the spending watchdog's trademark *délicatesse*, this described the habit of big companies going straight to the top knowing that was where they would get the best deal. The HMRC officials' union complained that its members' 'professionalism in doing the job is increasingly undermined'. And with one final heartfelt twist of the knife, the Revenue officials said: 'Members feel that they work *with* people who genuinely care about what they do but they don't feel that they work *for* people who genuinely care.'[32] (The officials were also up in arms about yet more counterproductive job cuts, internal figures showing that between 2011 and 2015 the numbers of tax officials at the professional grades that pay for themselves tens or hundreds of times over were to be cut from 3550 to under 3000.)[33]

The war on even the more contrived corporate tax avoidance schemes had stalled, as one remarkable fact showed. By 2011 not a single corporation tax avoidance scheme unearthed by the 2004 disclosure rules – of which there were hundreds, at least – had been taken by the Revenue even to the first tax tribunal.[34] HMRC had shied away from serious confrontation with big business. Or as Hartnett put it to an audience of Indian businessmen and tax advisers at a Mumbai conference in 2010, a few months after backing out of the legal fight with Vodafone: 'In my opinion winning tax disputes at all costs is no way forward in the modern world.'[35]

The all-carrot-no-stick approach to corporate tax avoidance was a huge waste of what should have been the increasingly effective weapon of litigation. Corporation tax avoidance transactions dating from before 2004 but by now reaching the higher courts were regularly going the taxman's way as judges reasserted the 'Ramsay' principle of looking at schemes in the round. Of the last eight such cases, the Revenue had won five. Income tax avoidance schemes were almost without exception being decided in the Revenue's favour. But in the international taxation 'race to the bottom' that the government was keen to accelerate, an easy ride from the tax authorities was paraded as a competitive national advantage just like plummeting corporate tax rates and lax offshore avoidance laws. Treasury minister David Gauke spelt it out: 'How companies experience the UK tax system is as important to tax competitiveness as the headline rates that we set.'[36] Multinationals, he was pleased to report, were telling him that 'HMRC compares very favourably' with foreign tax authorities (small business would not have been so complimentary).[37] The government and the country's most senior tax inspector had become salesmen, and what they were selling was Britain's tax system.

Haven help us

From his New York apartment in the early hours of 24 March 2011 Sir Martin Sorrell, voluble chief executive of advertising and public relations multinational group WPP plc, was on a transatlantic phone line to BBC Radio 4's *Today* programme. 'We're delighted to say,' he told bleary-eyed breakfast time listeners, 'that, subject to the legislation being enacted, we'll look at coming back to the UK.'

The legislation in question would effect the comprehensive relaxation of the taxation of British multinationals' overseas profits under the 'controlled foreign companies' laws that George Osborne had announced in the previous day's budget. And what was really behind Sorrell's sleepless night was a chancellor desperate for cover for what was just the most significant of a raft of tax breaks for big business in a budget that was full of tax rises and spending cuts for everybody else. 'I want Britain to be the place international businesses go to, not the place they leave,' the chancellor had told parliament. And in came Sir Martin bang on the news agenda-setting *Today* programme the very next morning with a promise to return his company's HQ to the UK, three years after it had moved it to Dublin (following years of scheming to get round the controlled foreign companies laws).

In fact, contrary to Osborne's suggestion, there had been no corporate exodus in the first place. In four years up to 2010/11, twenty-two companies departed in response to the Revenue's laws against offshore avoidance.[38] Just four were from the FTSE350, including the patriotically named Brit Insurance (successor to Vodafone as England cricket team sponsor). And only WPP was from the FTSE100. Even these companies remained taxable in the UK on their real UK business and their establishment of offshore letter box HQs made little difference to their UK tax bills.

The PR stunt with WPP had taken shape in the Treasury's Whitehall HQ at a meeting between WPP and minister David

Gauke a few weeks before the budget and, at the other end of the building, the customary pow-wow with Revenue boss Dave Hartnett to line up a settlement of longstanding disputes over WPP's offshore schemes.[39] The whole episode betrayed the politicization of tax administration, prompting furious rows among Treasury and HMRC officials, the latter balking at reaching a tax settlement as part of a deal to provide a political fix for the government. But the Treasury was desperate for some kind of cover for its austerity-era generosity to the biggest corporations, one official warning internally: 'a big focus [in budget press coverage] will be why there is this big giveaway to business in a time of spending cuts'.[40] The return of WPP would show the unappreciative newspapers exactly why.

And what a giveaway it was. Not only did Osborne accelerate corporation tax cuts to the lowest rate of any major Western economy – 23% by 2014 (since cut to 21%) – he also took an axe to the offshore anti-tax avoidance 'controlled foreign companies' laws and announced a tax emption for companies' tax haven branches. The package would slash the largest companies' tax bills by around £7bn over four years, the Treasury estimated. It was paid for in part by a reduction in tax allowances for business investment in plant and machinery, cutting against the widely supported notion at the time of 'rebalancing' the economy away from finance towards industry.

The structural changes represented a profound rewrite of business taxation. The idea was to relinquish UK tax claims on profits diverted into tax havens by UK-headquartered multinationals' overseas operations as payments for, say, the right to use intellectual property such as trademarks or interest on loans from tax haven companies. Which meant that a company like WPP could move its head office's tax residence back to the UK and retain the benefit of its tax haven schemes. It also meant every other company could use the dodges, too. As one tax writer put it, 'in order to claim the PR for WPP's return, George Osborne has relaxed the rules . . .

meaning that every other UK multinational with no intention of leaving the UK is ecstatic'.[41]

It would now be straightforward for a company to fund its overseas operations by borrowing in the UK, generating tax-deductible interest expenses to reduce its taxable profits here, while ensuring that the profits from using this money aren't taxed here – or anywhere else for that matter. UK Co plc investing in, say, the US will now borrow not in the US but in the UK, place the money interest-free in the standard Luxembourg set-up, which will lend it on to the US operation.

The result is tax breaks in both the US and the UK for the same amount of borrowing, where previously there would have been just the one in the US. Or, as Deloitte's leading international tax partner Bill Dodwell put it: 'Since the UK is one of those territories where many international groups will already be earning some profits, it means there is a profit base that can absorb those [interest] deductions.'[42] Under the relaxed offshore tax rules, the tax haven finance company will be taxed at between 0% and 5.25%. The rates were fixed so low, Edward Troup cheerfully told a parliamentary committee, because 'the Dutch have a rate of 5%'.[43] Precisely, in other words, to compete with a tax haven.

One well-informed tax specialist blogged, under the heading 'Corporate tax reform and the death of UK corporation tax for large multinationals', that the changes 'will likely lead to most large multinationals paying significantly reduced or no UK corporate tax'.[44] It is a prophecy of doom – or joy for the tax-dodgers – that is shared by Britain's leading tax advisers. KPMG was quick to produce a pamphlet advertising that, with its services, the change 'gives UK-based multinationals an opportunity to significantly reduce their tax rate', estimating that 'for every £1m of finance income received in the UK, the finance company regime could save cash tax of £172,000'.[45] That's 'cash tax' straight out of public services into the biggest multinationals' coffers. Another Big 4 tax partner, admitting to me that clients were being advised to put as much debt in the UK as possible for the tax breaks, was even blunter: 'Nobody in the private sector could believe what they [the government] did,' he told me. 'It was just so stupid.'[46]

The sting

The trashing of the corporate tax system was a stunning and artfully executed victory for big business and its champions in the Treasury in the face of what, before the 2010 general election, was already growing public disquiet over tax avoidance. In the tortuous coalition negotiations of May 2010, the Tories had agreed that the Lib Dems' tax policies – largely set by leading tax avoidance critic Vince Cable – would enter the new government's programme. Which meant action against tax avoidance, and it wasn't long before one coalition agreement box could be ticked by dispatching leading tax silk Graham Aaronson – the Revenue's courtroom adversary on many a scheme over the years – to think about the long-mooted but never-delivered 'general anti-avoidance rule' (GAAR) favoured by Cable. He would be helped by a small group including retired law lord, Lord Hoffmann, whose judgments a decade or so before (such as in the Barclays leasing case described in chapter 3), had marked a more tolerant judicial approach to tax avoidance. Whatever Aaronson produced, however, it could only ever tackle schemes sufficiently artificial to meet the official definition of 'avoidance'. In the event, he narrowed his proposed GAAR yet further to what would have to be 'egregious, or very aggressive, tax avoidance schemes', which meant it would touch just a tiny proportion of real world tax avoidance that the courts generally overturned under existing law anyway. And by effectively endorsing anything that isn't 'egregious', claimed the senior tax inspectors' union, Aaronson was 'actually facilitating avoidance'.[47]

Changes to the offshore business tax rules governing far more important real world tax avoidance, on the other hand, had for some time already been matters of 'modernization' to accommodate 'current business practice'. They were the province of Treasury mandarins and the multinationals with whom they were already working closely through the previous government's various forums and liaison committees. So, while the Lib Dems were appeased with the sight of Aaronson and Hoffmann kicking a GAAR through the long grass before emerging with something not very useful, back on the main field of play Chancellor Osborne and his junior minister David Gauke could ease the offshore tax rules to the point that Britain would become a corporate tax haven where contrived avoidance schemes aren't needed anyway.

Six months after the election Gauke duly unveiled the next stage in the relaxation of the offshore tax laws: a 'corporate tax roadmap' to be navigated by a new business 'liaison committee' of finance directors from companies including Tesco, Reed Elsevier, BP and others with immediate, multimillion or even billion-pound interests in the results. The all-important details were left to a series of working groups comprising the tax directors of forty multinationals including Vodafone, Tesco, RSA, HSBC and Cadbury's new owner Kraft. All were owners of vast offshore empires. Most striking was the presence of ex-Revenue and by now Vodafone tax director John Connors on the 'monetary assets' working group, deciding how to tax offshore financing of exactly the sort his company was running through Luxembourg and Switzerland for hundreds of millions of pounds in tax savings every year.

And when it came to piloting their new rules through parliament in the 2011 and 2012 Finance Bills, there was never going to be any meaningful scrutiny as the Labour opposition team were briefed (free of charge) by PricewaterhouseCoopers – the accountancy firm probably standing to gain most from advising on the offshore opportunities opened up.

The intimacy between government and business and the extent of their tax-cutting ambition was never more obvious than when, in September 2012, tax minister David Gauke and his senior officials were corralled into a trip to Washington DC. They were to appear at a seminar hosted by notorious tax-dodger General Electric – represented by its UK tax director and chairman of the HMRC-Industry Business Tax Forum, Will Morris – at the right-wing American Enterprise Institute. The title was 'UK Tax Reform: a Roadmap for the US?' and it was part of a concerted campaign to get US tax rates and offshore tax rules reduced to something like the UK's in the global race to the bottom. The international tax-slashing circus would not, of course, have been complete without the Oxford Business Centre's Professor Devereux jetting in to provide his contribution. 'We [the UK] have been quite fortunate in our leaders over a few years,' he remarked by way of explanation for getting the offshore corporate tax breaks on the statute book.[48] Or as Morris had put it a few months before: 'We have business talking to government, we have government talking to advisers, we have everybody essentially trying to move in the same direction.'[49]

This was supposedly the modern way to make policy. In fact, a mere 235 years earlier, Adam Smith had seen the same kind of thing in action and observed:

> The proposal of any new law or regulation of commerce which comes from this order [businessmen], ought always to be listened to with great precaution, and ought never to be adopted till after having been long and carefully examined, not only with the most scrupulous, but with the most suspicious attention. It comes from an order of men, whose interest is never exactly the same with that of the public, who have generally an interest to deceive and even oppress the public, and who accordingly have, upon many occasions, both deceived and oppressed it.[50]

The offshore tax changes had been demanded by an 'order of men' from the multinationals standing to gain most from them, and certainly didn't receive any 'suspicious attention'. One internal Treasury briefing explained that since the current rules 'limit a group's ability to manage its overseas operations and the effective tax rate, [controlled foreign company law] reform is a **priority area for business**'.[51] (Emphasis *not* added.) And business gets what business wants.

The government's biddability has spawned some lucrative lobbying opportunities. Ernst & Young has a 'tax policy development team', run by former Treasury special adviser Chris Sanger that draws up tax-cutting legislative changes for its clients. 'Tax policy development offers the company a chance to create a new environment in which it can achieve its objective,' runs the pitch, 'and where there has been considerable media coverage on particular "tax avoiders", policy development offers a low risk alternative.'[52] If you don't fancy scheming round the tax law, we'll get it changed for you.

The implications go beyond immediate tax loss. Tax breaks available only to the largest multinationals hamper the competiveness of smaller ones that can't cut their tax bills with an offshore finance company or by shifting their brand names into a tax haven. What's more, tax concessions for diverting profits into tax havens will *take* jobs out of the country. In simple terms, if a company can easily send its foreign profits into a tax haven using the standard tax tools of interest, royalties and other payments, but has more trouble doing so with its UK ones, it has an incentive to locate real activity, such as a factory, *outside* the UK. The Tories, who nearly thirty years ago brought in the controlled foreign companies laws that their successors were now discarding, certainly understood that tolerating offshore tax dodging made no economic sense. Debating the laws' introduction in 1984, the then Treasury chief secretary Peter Rees (who, as a former Rossminster adviser, knew a thing or two about tax dodging) remarked that the rules 'on controlled foreign companies, will make it more attractive to take a profit here than overseas. These measures will be good for business, good for enterprise and good for jobs.'[53] Conversely, tearing them up will be bad for business, bad for enterprise and bad for jobs.

The companies that George Osborne now wants to call Britain home will come not to do real productive business employing real people, although they may create some work for the accountants and tax lawyers needed to exploit the new rules. This much was demonstrated in January 2012 when US insurance giant Aon became the first big firm to announce it was relocating its head office to London. It already has a substantial UK business or, as Deloitte's Dodwell would doubtless have it, 'a profit base' to absorb costs. The principal effects, it confirmed, will be just *twenty* staff coming to the UK (almost certainly 'non-doms') and 'a significant reduction in our global effective tax rate'.[54]

In 2013, working with BBC's *Panorama* I approached the big accountancy firms posing as an adviser to a number of multinational groups and was advised by KPMG that the new rules could 'wipe out' my clients' UK tax bills. The rules governing offshore financing produced a 'net sort of minus 15%' tax rate, said one.[55] By the following year, when US drugs giant Pfizer announced takeover plans for the UK's AstraZeneca using a UK holding company in order to reduce its worldwide tax rate from 27% to around 21%,[56] it was apparent that Britain as a corporate tax haven was perversely shaping global capitalism.

By 2012, the richest multinational corporations had put themselves beyond what was officially considered tax avoidance. Writing their own laws, they had created the offshore opportunities to reduce their tax bills way below headline rates, but now with a parliamentary seal of approval. And if parliament approves, on the official definition it can't be tax avoidance. This was a happy ending for some. 'We do have a good news story now,' beamed Dodwell: 'We can indeed compete with the Netherlands, Luxembourg and Switzerland.'[57] Big business, tax avoidance advisers, and the government they had captured had got what they wanted: Britain, the premier twenty-first-century tax haven for the world's multinationals.

8
Hear No Evil, See No Evil

The taxman turns a blind eye to offshore tax crime

It was at least in keeping with the deregulatory times that Britain's official response to legal tax avoidance so heavily favoured those indulging in it. What was more surprising was the tolerance shown by the tax authorities towards some thoroughly *illegal* tax evasion.

Undeclared offshore accounts have long been a familiar fact of life for tax investigators. Banks are required to notify the authorities of interest on – and thus the existence of – UK bank accounts, so the smarter tax evader keeps his secret stash in an account offshore. These boltholes often come to light when a tax-dodger is the subject of a more general investigation and either comes clean or has his documents seized by the authorities. But other than in these relatively few cases, offshore cash generally remains hidden from the tax authorities.

So when, in 2004, tax inspectors received a wealth of intelligence on UK credit and debit cards linked to offshore accounts provided by Britain's biggest high street banks, they were determined to make the most of it. The information contained details of about 9000 offshore Barclays accounts, most of them in the Channel Islands and the Isle of Man, held by people with UK addresses. But these accounts, based on limited if valuable intelligence, were clearly just the tip of the iceberg, and investigators wanted details of all of them. Barclays, stressing confidentiality obligations whatever its customers were up to, was not going to hand them over without a fight, and forced the investigators to make their case to a tax tribunal the following year. It turned out to be a pretty impressive case, the taxmen's calculations indicating disturbing levels of tax evasion. The 9289 offshore accounts already known to investigators had led to the declaration of offshore income on just 327 tax returns (a rate of 3.5%). Investigations into 206 offshore accounts (not all Barclays) suggested £2.1m tax had been evaded on 110 of the accounts (around £20,000 a go). Over half of the accounts, in other words, were hiding income that should have been declared, compared to the 3.5% that actually led to declarations. The inspectors projected that in total Barclays' offshore accounts would throw up £1.5bn in evaded tax and penalties. Though the number of their accounts estimated to be being used for tax evasion was not spelt out, some simple arithmetic suggests the Revenue reckoned it was around 75,000.[1] The bank argued that the exercise was a 'fishing expedition', but the inspectors were dangling their rods in rich waters and Barclays were forced to hand over the details the taxmen wanted. After similar battles over the following months so were HBOS, HSBC, Royal Bank of Scotland (owner of Coutts), and Lloyds.

This success stretched only to the offshore accounts of British banks' customers, however. Many hardcore evaders preferred the services of smaller overseas operations or the Swiss banks whose smug 'wealth management' arms could be found advertising in many a top-end British newspaper and magazine and were conveniently outside the limits of a British tax inspector's investigatory powers. And in any case there were simply too many undeclared offshore accounts – running into the hundreds of thousands – for a tax authority in the middle of a 25,000 job-cutting 'efficiency' programme to track down, compare to tax returns and then investigate. The Revenue's conservative Tax Gap estimates included £3.1bn – equal to half the overseas aid budget – in tax lost through offshore evasion every year, with just 7% of offshore income estimated to be declared.[2] Others put the cost at over twice as much.[3] If the government was serious about recovering the loot, it needed a rethink.

Amnesty irrational

As any police chief trying to get knives off the streets or teacher asking kids to spit out chewing gum would testify, amnesties offering exculpation for those who come clean must be used sparingly and be followed by tough sanctions for those who don't take up the offer. If they're ever to work again, the carrot has to be followed by the stick.

It's a principle that HM Revenue and Customs has grasped well in theory, but failed spectacularly to apply in practice. In 2007 the department offered offshore tax evaders a simple deal: own up and all you have to pay is your back tax bill, interest and a 10% penalty instead of the maximum 100%, and you won't be prosecuted. But heaven help you if you keep quiet and we still find out about you.

It *sort of* worked, raising £400m from 45,000 voluntary disclosures; still a fraction of total offshore leakage but valuable cash nonetheless for an economy about to career out of control. More promisingly, it foreshadowed a draconian legal clampdown, HMRC announcing as the amnesty deadline approached that 'within weeks' offshore tax evaders would be in court. 'Some will have to pay gargantuan sums of tax . . . We will get those in the magistrates court quite quickly.'[4] But the deadlines and the weeks passed with no wealthy offshore dodgers joining the grim line of tax credit and benefit fiddlers trooping before the nation's beaks. Then the months went by, and still none. Then the years.

Oh all right, one more chance. The cry of capitulating parents everywhere, this was also HMRC's next move, in the shape of the 2009 'New Disclosure Opportunity'. There would be another six-month period for evaders to come forward, from which the Revenue expected to pull in anything up to an oddly precise £792m.[5] It was accompanied by more than the usual bombast, plus blood-curdling threats. 'We've got more than smoking guns: smoking tanks, smoking howitzers,' Hartnett told the BBC's *Panorama* in February 2009 when asked if there was evidence of serious evasion.[6] And in an ominous YouTube message he insisted the second amnesty was 'one final chance to avoid penalties and avoid prosecution ... make your disclosure to HM Revenue and Customs by 30 November 2009 because there won't be another chance.'[7] By now this had all the authority of a supply teacher pleading for classroom order. £85m trickled in. Of all the offshore loot representing years or possibly decades of evasion, under £0.5bn – or less than one sixth of one year's conservatively estimated offshore dodging – had been handed in.

HMRC certainly did have some ammunition. Two years before it had bought a disc containing details of around 150 Brits with undeclared money stashed in Liechtenstein Global Trust, a bank already exposed in the US as home to rampant tax evasion. So would the prosecutions come now? No, there would be yet another 'disclosure facility' to spike those smoking howitzers. This time it was tailored for evaders using Liechtenstein accounts – not exactly at the forgivable end of the market – and again promised minor 10% penalties and no prosecution, with a generous five-year period to come clean even for dodgers who moved their swag from other havens just to get the special terms. It was all part of a deal Hartnett negotiated in April 2009 with the micro-state's ambassador Prince Nikolaus, whose brother Prince Philipp happened to chair the Liechtenstein Global Trust organization that was home to the suspect accounts divulged to HMRC. This was a family affair.

It was also cheerily, and without precedent, agreed between the two governments that it would be 'highly unlikely to be in the public interest of the United Kingdom to undertake a criminal investigation' into Liechtenstein's bankers for facilitating tax evasion.[8] The gnomes of Vaduz – one or two of whom might *just* be less than squeaky clean – were effectively being released from criminal liability. But at least the people actually evading tax using Liechtenstein remained in the frame if they didn't own up – in theory at least, although in practice none would be prosecuted. The tiny principality's neighbour, paymaster and home of banking secrecy, Switzerland, would negotiate an even cushier deal that let everybody off the hook.

In Swiss bankers we trust

In the same August 2011 week that Prime Minister David Cameron promised Britain's rioting feral underclass 'we will track you down, we will find you and we will punish you' and magistrates jailed a youth for stealing £3 worth of water, it was with a special kind of upper-class insensitivity that the Prime Minister's fellow Bullingdonian George Osborne granted immunity from prosecution to the feral financial classes who were looting the economy of billions.

This was more or less what was written on the piece of paper in Dave Hartnett's hand when he stepped off the last of several flights from Zurich after hammering out the latest tax deal. This one simply asked the Swiss banks to hand over a proportion of the money in accounts held by Brits, without naming them. The proportion, which Swiss bankers estimated was likely to average between 20 and 25% (the longer you'd held the account, the less you paid), would be far less than the tax and interest evaded. And that was only for accounts that the Swiss bankers could trace through the myriad trusts, foundations and shell companies favoured by most Swiss tax-dodgers. Even then, the accounts still had to be open in May 2013 for the levy to be applied, giving tax evaders over eighteen months to whisk their hidden fortunes off to another tax haven. Within weeks of its signature, the Tax Justice Network had identified ten separate escape routes in a comprehensive trashing of the deal, 'The UK–Swiss Tax Agreement: Doomed to Fail',[9] and it duly did: by the end of 2013 it had brought in £440m against a predicted £3.1bn for that period.[10] The deal also decriminalized a swathe of serious tax evasion and its facilitation by bankers, whose prosecution was 'highly unlikely to be in the public interest'. It was for these reasons that a similar deal signed between the Swiss and German governments was later overturned by the Berlin parliament. Here, the principle that all were equal before the law had been sold very cheaply indeed.[11]

A few weeks later the depths of credulity behind the deal became a bit clearer. When Conservative MP Jesse Norman asked how the Revenue would get behind the structures put up to hide assets, Hartnett told parliament: 'Swiss banks will require disclosure to them of beneficial ownership, and if that shows a connection to the United Kingdom, there will be withholding [tax] against those investments, and the Swiss tax authority will audit this in relation to the Swiss banks. It has a pretty fearsome reputation for the way in which it audits Swiss banks.' HM Revenue and Customs really had outsourced tax collection to a foreign government. Not just any foreign government, either, but one that for centuries has operated as little more than a servant of its banks and whose auditors were now supposedly to be set to work for another country's taxpayers. Asked why he had offered the banks immunity, Hartnett nudged the rose-tinted glasses back up his nose and claimed 'it was very unlikely indeed that we would get evidence against Swiss bankers during the course of this'.[12]

Fig. 12 Dodgers' charter:
Exchequer Secretary David Gauke (seated centre) and HMRC permanent
secretary Dave Hartnett (seated right) sign the agreement with Switzerland
that effectively decriminalizes tax evasion (Credit: HMRC)

This last observation flew in the face of very recent, never mind historical, evidence of what Swiss bankers were capable of. The firmer stance of the US's Internal Revenue Service on offshore evasion – a more productive process of high-profile prosecutions and only then amnesties – had brought convictions of Americans using Swiss accounts at UBS and of several of the bankers who assisted them. One was sent down for forty months for arranging for a property developer to hide $200m in Switzerland and Luxembourg using safety deposit boxes, artwork and other tricks, while UBS itself signed a 'deferred prosecution' agreement with the IRS in return for handing over details of all US residents' Swiss accounts.[13] Was it really so unlikely that Swiss bank employees in London should act in anything like the same way as they did across the Atlantic?

At this stage it might be asked whose interests the Swiss and Liechtenstein agreements really served. These states' banks, of course, approved because the deals showed to the new rich class in the Far East whose wealth they were targeting that they would always remain secret. But there were others for whom raising the carpet and applying a swift stroke of the brush was the ideal way to deal with tax evasion, too. While Hartnett was negotiating the deal in Zurich, back at the office his investigators were poring over the details of 6000 Swiss accounts held by British HSBC customers and passed to them in April 2010 by the French authorities, who themselves had received them on a disc from a former HSBC employee. The Swiss private banking arm of HSBC soon reported that it was expecting significant fines from the IRS for helping US customers evade tax. One was a surgeon who picked up $100,000 'bricks' from his HSBC banker in Zurich then posted the cash home in twenty-five separate envelopes. The banks were being forced to close down Americans' accounts and didn't want electronic transfers revealing their existence. Over in Spain, members of the Botín dynasty behind that country's biggest bank, Santander, had coughed up €200m for decades of hiding fortunes in HSBC's Geneva arm. It could not be clearer that this British bank for one was selling its customers Alpine secrecy.

As a result of the deals, how many highly influential British people would not now come under a tax inspector's gaze and avoid having some very dirty linen washed in public? The suspicious mind might also reflect that, with prosecutions for bankers ruled out, there could now be no investigations into the conduct of HSBC's private banking arm, which had been chaired until 2010 by the HSBC chairman who was now trade minister Lord (Stephen) Green.

What was indisputable was that, while the Revenue was taking tough and often effective enforcement action against other tax crimes, the one favoured by the wealthy and powerful – offshore tax evasion – had been almost decriminalized. In 2009/10 there were 263 prosecutions for excise fraud, 95 for VAT offences, 67 for tax credit frauds and 30 for all income tax offences.[14] For the tens of thousands of offshore accounts used to evade billions of pounds in tax? Zero. It was only in July 2012 that the first tax fraud conviction centred on an offshore account was recorded, when a property developer was fined over a Swiss HSBC account containing the proceeds of a legacy on which he evaded £430,000 inheritance tax.[15]

Another of the Revenue's tax 'amnesties' – offered to specific trades that HMRC didn't have the resources to police – was accompanied by far more rapid collar-feeling. Just three months after the expiry of a 2011 opportunity for tax-dodging plumbers to come forward, five who hadn't done so were picked up in dawn raids. 'These arrests send a clear message that HMRC will take action against those who choose not to come forward and pay the tax they owe,' said a criminal investigations chief.[16] The offshore dodgers against whom HMRC had a mountain of evidence and who had also ignored the taxman's peace offers, meanwhile, were sleeping far more easily.

TIEAs of a clown

Tax dodging is certainly not the limit of the economic delinquency facilitated by tax havens. 'Offshore financial centres', as they prefer to be known, also provide the regulatory conditions that enable financiers to do things that they would find either impossible or more difficult onshore. By tailoring their corporate laws to the bankers' demands and offering with trademark euphemism 'tax neutrality', offshore havens became, for example, perfect locations for the 'special purpose vehicles' that package up dodgy debt and dump it on the markets. The most notorious 'collateralized debt obligation' of the era, the Abacus 2007-AC1 sold by Goldman Sachs and profitably bet against by a related hedge fund – leading to a $500m regulatory settlement for the bank – was set up in the Cayman Islands. Serious reform of the malformed financial system therefore had to take in the tax havens that were pumping toxic financial products through its banking arteries. As British prime minister Gordon Brown rhetorically asked a special gathering of the US Congress on Capitol Hill in March 2009: 'How much safer would everybody's savings be if the whole world finally came together to outlaw shadow banking systems and offshore tax havens?'[17]

The following month in London, at what was billed as the most economically important gathering of governments since the post-war Bretton Woods conference sixty-five years before, the G20 came together to forge a way out of the crisis. This was where the world would answer Brown's Washington demand and unite to defeat tax havens. So went the hype, anyway. In the event, the best opportunity ever to assail the tax havens' post-war ascendency was comprehensively fluffed.

Heads of state and finance ministers struggling to comprehend the enormity of the economic chaos were grateful that for one of the many aspects they barely understood, namely tax havens, there was a ready-made initiative to latch onto. The OECD had been ruminating for over a decade on 'harmful tax competition', as it described the scourge of tax havenry. Invigorated by the post-9/11 impetus to frustrate terrorist financing, this work had focused on picking away at the secrecy of tax havens through a programme of 'tax information exchange agreements' (TIEAs) under which the havens would divulge details of money stashed in their terri-tories. But the initiative was always more symbolic than practically useful and certainly not up to transforming the offshore system, never mind ending it. TIEAs simply allow a country that suspects its tax is being dodged to request from the tax haven details on a named taxpayer's finances. The taxman thus has to know the evader has an undeclared account in the tax haven in the first place. If it sounds implausible to ask for secret information from secret jurisdictions, it's because it is. The whole point is that the tax authorities don't generally know who's dodging their tax or where they're doing it.

But this was the flawed initiative on which the G20 leaders in London would pin their hopes. Tax havens, they agreed, would be put on the international naughty step until they signed twelve TIEAs. It is hard to describe the inadequacy of this response. The hundreds of TIEAs signed so far have enabled all the world's havens with the exception of Nauru, Niue and Montserrat (which had signed eleven the last time I looked, just one to go!) to come off the step and carry on playing with their toys. [18] But they achieve next to nothing. That the Cook Islands, for example, has recently signed up to its twelfth exchange information agreement with Greenland (pop. 56,000) and is thus considered to meet internationally acceptable standards of tax transparency, when it has no arrangements with, say, the UK (pop. 63 million) or the US (pop. 311 million), illustrates the absurdity.

Even the TIEAs that have been signed don't work. The UK, for example, has had agreements with Bermuda and the British Virgin Islands in force since December 2008 and April 2010, yet the number of information exchanges under them is so small – fewer than five each – that the figures can't be disclosed as doing so would risk identifying somebody (supposedly). Similar provision in a pre-existing agreement with Switzerland, home to hundreds of thousands of undeclared accounts and other more sophisticated tax dodging, has yielded no more than three snippets for British tax investigators in any of the seven years on record. [19] Tax authorities aren't even that keen on using them. At one of the joint HMRC–Industry Business Tax Forum meetings in 2010, officials reassured the tax director of HSBC, purveyor of offshore services par excellence, that 'if the concern was that there would be a sudden flood of requests [from the UK to the Swiss authorities], this was very unlikely'. [20]

The best that can be said for the G20 deal was that it generated plenty of tub-thumping rhetoric from politicians around the world, and this might have scared some potential offshore dodgers for a short time. It is, of course, spun differently.'The era of bank secrecy is over' was the wildly misleading title of the OECD's October 2011 evaluation of the deal.[21] The truth is that the emptiness of the deal has already been rumbled by the world's secret bankers. A 2011 study by Christian Aid and the Tax Justice Network found that 'despite [the] G20 commitment two years ago to curtail the activities of tax havens ... the level of secrecy in international financial services is intensifying'.[22] Data from the Bank of International Settlements showed that two years after the financial crisis, deposits in tax haven accounts had remained stubbornly consistent at $2.7 trillion. The academics who crunched the numbers concluded categorically that 'the era of bank secrecy is not over'.[23]

Since 2011 the tax information exchange programme has gathered momentum through European Union directives and OECD agreements insisting on automatic exchange of information between member countries and their overseas territories, spurred on by action taken in the US to force offshore banks to hand over details of US citizens' income under its Foreign Account Tax Compliance Act. But none of this addresses the fundamental flaw in the process: that tax havens have neither the will or the laws or the capability to gather much of the information in the first place. And while the information exchange negotiations continue front stage, behind the scenes, the bankers, lawyers and accountants that serve tax havens regroup. They continue tax-evading, regulation-sidestepping businesses but now with international endorsement.

The tax information exchange pantomime has scuppered the best chance there was for meaningful change to the offshore world that subverts not just tax collection but all onshore financial regulation. The price of this failure will be far higher even than the lost tax billions.

9

On Her Majesty's Offshore Service

Selling Britain's public services for tax avoidance

Gordon Brown had a big circle to square when he became Chancellor of the Exchequer in May 1997. He, Tony Blair and Peter Mandelson had just engineered an election victory by persuading a sceptical electorate that, twenty-one years after the International Monetary Fund bailed out the last Labour government, their party could be trusted with the nation's finances. It was a promise that needed to be kept if Blair's 'new dawn' was not to prove a false one, and came first with a commitment to stick to the previous Conservative government's tax and spending plans, immediately bolstered in the new chancellor's first budget by two 'fiscal rules' that would govern his stewardship of the economy.

The more unforgiving, less easily fudged of these strictures was the so-called 'sustainable investment' rule limiting the government's indebtedness to a frugal – by international standards – 40% of gross domestic product, some 5% lower than the figure inherited from the Tories. This was quite a constraint for a new chancellor who, while preaching 'prudence', had also promised to reinvigorate Britain's creaking public services. Somehow he would have to find new investment without extra tax or borrowing.

Happily, a fix was at hand in the shape of the private finance initiative first thought up by the Conservatives five years before and already by this stage funding small amounts of new investment, mainly in roads and prisons. Under the scheme, private companies – rather than the government – borrow money to build and then own infrastructure that they provide to the taxpayer for a fee over thirty or more years. Economically the arrangement amounts to borrowing to fund the infrastructure, but unlike conventional borrowing, these thirty-year commitments usually don't appear on the government's books as debts.

Here was the answer to the conundrum of investing without taxing or borrowing up front, and within days of taking office Brown instructed his loyal paymaster general Geoffrey Robinson, complete with industry-led 'taskforce', to turbo-charge PFI. Before long the businessman-turned-minister had rewritten the PFI rule book. Private companies, bearing far less risk on the deals than their Tory predecessors had insisted they shouldered, could be sure of thirty-year income streams vastly exceeding their costs. The floodgates opened, and in Labour's first term, PFI contracts for £11bn worth of investment, including several major new hospitals, were signed. By the end of its second term in 2005, the figure had reached £50bn worth, for which the taxpayer would pay £7.5bn a year over the following three decades.[1]

From the outset PFI was saturated with ironies. In the same summer 1997 budget speech in which he boasted of having 'reinvigorated' PFI, Brown had promised he would 'not tolerate the avoidance of taxation'. Yet this was an initiative that would itself put public services themselves at the service of the tax avoidance industry. It was not entirely new in this respect; many of the Thatcher government's privatizations – also motivated by ridding the government's books of the debt required for investment as much as by political ideology – had already fallen under the tax avoidance spell. Twenty years after it became the first major business sold off in 1984, BT, for example, was among the companies placed in the Revenue's 'serial avoiders' programme. And a quick look at the fate of many utilities now in foreign hands shows that their vast quasi-monopoly profits rarely return much to the Exchequer in tax payments. The capital's water supplier, for example, although still known as Thames Water, is controlled by Australia's Macquarie group through a Guernsey holding company, and ultimately owned by a series of offshore funds managed by the group. Through this structure, operating profits of over half a billion pounds a year leach faster than water from the company's antiquated pipes in the form of tax-deductible interest costs, much of it on debt owed to the offshore investors. In the two years up to March 2011, from a £1.2bn operating profit the group that owns Thames Water paid UK corporation tax of £19m.[2] A similar outcome can be found at the company that since 1996 has owned Britain's dilapidated military housing, Annington Homes Ltd. Sold to funds now managed from Guernsey by the Terra Firma private equity group, the ample income that Annington receives for renting the houses back to the military produces almost nothing in the way of tax payments. Healthy operating profits of around £140m are entirely eliminated by interest payments to its offshore investors.[3]

A year before his party's 1997 election win, Peter Mandelson had written of the need to 'move forward from where Margaret Thatcher left off rather than dismantle everything she did'.[4] As the successor to her privatization programme, PFI certainly fitted this bill when it came to tax avoidance. The structure was an open invitation to extreme tax planning. To start with, the PFI companies that brought together builders, financiers and service providers could borrow up to the hilt since, earning government-backed income in the form of fees from public bodies that would not default, they were safe bets. This meant large tax-deductible interest expenses for the companies, especially in the early period of their contracts. And the tax planners could also ensure that the costs of constructing the school or hospital, which might otherwise be considered non-tax deductible capital spending on an asset to be used in the business, itself became tax-deductible. To achieve this result a PFI contract would be structured in such a way that the PFI company could be considered to be not just the provider of, say, a hospital, but to be in the business of building *and* providing the hospital for use by the health service. The company would be a 'composite trader' with building part of its trade. The hospital would not appear on its balance sheet and the construction costs would be deductible in working out its taxable corporate profits.

Of course, a chancellor adhering to strict fiscal rules and boasting 'prudence with a purpose' most certainly didn't want the infrastructure and the commitments to pay for them on his government's books either. So billions of pounds' worth of public service assets were consigned to an accountancy fourth dimension where they were nobody's assets, on nobody's books. The flexible PFI accountancy guidelines ushered in with Robinson's reforms allied with some smart lawyering and accountancy allowed both government and company to have it 'off the books' in order to harvest their own advantage. When I looked at a sample of ten major hospital PFI deals signed up to 2001, the nine that were off the government's books, such as the £160m Norfolk and Norwich, were also off the PFI companies' balance sheets.[5] The Iron Chancellor had, in the words of one Tory MP, become the Enron Chancellor.

Whitehall farce

This 'double-off' and other techniques meant that PFI companies would for many years incur no tax bills and even run up unused tax losses to wipe out future ones. By 2010, for example, the consortium running the Norfolk and Norwich hospital since 2001, Octagon Healthcare, had paid just a few hundred thousands of pounds tax on its £30m a year PFI fees, largely because of its helpful tax status – the hospital was off both public and private books – and interest payments at 12% on £30m worth of debt from its shareholders.[6]

It was a pattern repeated right at the heart of government. The company that owns the modernistic £200m Home Office building in Marsham Street, Annes Gate Property plc, which like the hospitals enjoys 'double-off' status, has not paid a bean in corporation tax since the PFI contract was signed in 2002 (the building opened in 2005) and by the end of 2010 had 'tax losses' of £57m to set against future profits.[7] This didn't mean the building's owners – investors brought together by HSBC – weren't getting their money, though. Through their Guernsey investment vehicle they were earning millions of pounds tax free in interest on the 'subordinated debt' that they owned in Annes Gate Property plc. This debt ranked below ordinary debt in security, so in the event of the PFI company going bust its holders would be towards the end of the queue for getting their money back. It thus commanded a generous 14.75% interest charge, but was still a pretty safe bet given the company's government-backed income. And just as importantly, it would drastically reduce the taxable profits of the PFI company.[8]

Much the same tax efficiency could be found at the companies owning the offices in which the rules they were exploiting were written. Since 2003 the Treasury and HM Revenue and Customs head office building at the bottom of Whitehall has been owned and operated under a PFI contract with the Exchequer Partnership plc group, which has also paid no tax in the eight years it has been up and running and has £6m tax losses for future use. The tax result is achieved by setting the refurbishment costs against its income and paying high rates of tax-deductible interest on bonds held by the company's investors – here 15% on around £6m worth of them.[9]

As the absence of tax payments was to a large extent explained by the fact that costs of building the infrastructure were set against income relatively early in the contract, these PFI deals were at least pregnant with the future profits that should be substantially taxed in the years to come. Unless, that is, the financial engineers could do something about it. And, funnily enough, they could.

Once a new PFI building has been built and the PFI company has sub-contracted the basic services for which it was responsible, it has to do little more than sit back and watch the money roll in. At which point, with the big risks out of the way and the income carrying a copper-bottomed government guarantee, its bankers relax. The PFI company can then repay its initially expensive bank loans and replace them with cheaper ones. Even better, with lower interest payments on the same level of debt, it can now afford to borrow some more and use this extra money not to invest in the business but simply to pay its investors for all their not-so-hard work. This 'refinancing', as it's known in the trade, thus allows PFI's private owners to extract their profits early in the life of the contract. Very lucrative it is, too. And, naturally, tax free.

'Refinancing' explained why, when the Queen cut the ribbon on the £230m Norfolk and Norwich hospital, she was unveiling what would be described in 2006 by the then chairman of the Public Accounts Committee, a Thatcherite called Edward Leigh, as 'the unacceptable face of capitalism'. His committee had just surveyed the PFI refinancing scene and found some eye-popping gains for its backers. The company behind the Norfolk and Norwich PFI contract had refinanced it just a couple of years after the hospital opened and immediately generated a £116m windfall for its investors. Under a code negotiated by an embarrassed Treasury, 29% of the gain was returned to the public sector, but this was simply a recognition that the contract, like most others written in the great PFI splurge, had been dramatically overpriced in the first place. The PFI company's owners – John Laing plc, Barclays, Serco and PFI investment fund Innisfree – still shared £82m tax free, representing their accelerated profit from the contract and increasing their return on the deal from a hardly unrewarding 16% to a 60% super return. Such ratcheting was repeated on contracts for buildings from hospitals in London to schools in Essex.[10] And it all stayed out of the taxman's hands. The Treasury eventually forced PFI companies to hand over a more realistic 50% of their gains on future refinancings, but the PFI industry was already another tax-efficient leap ahead. It had discovered how to extract its profits tax free by turning Britain's public services into tradeable commodities.

Off to market

It is unlikely that many officials sitting in HMRC's Whitehall head office in recent years would have appreciated that their workspace was provided to them by a company half-owned by the funds run by the country's biggest tax avoider, Barclays, courtesy of a blossoming market in PFI contracts.

The unlikely coupling arose through Barclays' private equity arm's ownership of a PFI investment fund called Infrastructure Investors, itself the holder of stakes in eighty-four operational PFI projects.[11] Among these was a 50% stake in the company with the HMRC/Treasury PFI contract, Exchequer Partnerships, which Infrastructure Investors had itself bought three years before from the property developer on the scheme, Stanhope plc. Thus, through a couple of unnoticed deals, the offices of Britain's finance ministry, or a half share in them at any rate, had silently passed into the hands of Britain's most prolific tax avoider.

Bulging with profits from state-guaranteed thirty-year income streams, PFI contracts made ideal financial products for buying and selling on what became a 'secondary market' in PFI companies. It was a market actively encouraged by a Treasury trying to squeeze as much investment as it could through the PFI sausage machine as quickly as possible, a process which would be accelerated if the builders and bankers initially behind each scheme could sell up and move on to the next project without delay.

The new market came with its own tax subsidy in one of a raft of tax breaks brought in for business in Gordon Brown's 2002 budget: exemption from capital gains tax for companies selling shares in trading companies, into which category most PFI companies, as 'composite traders', happily fell. Before long the big PFI construction companies were cashing in their stakes in the PFI companies they had set up with the bankers, converting what were in essence trading profits into tax-free windfalls. In its 2009 annual report, for example, builder Carillion was able to boast of its PFI business: 'Over the last six years, we have sold a total of 28 investments, generating proceeds of some £279.9m and a pre-tax profit of £105.6m.'[12]

Most of the big PFI constructors and service companies were in on the act. Carillion's twenty-eight sales were rivalled by John Laing plc's twenty-two, Interserve's fifteen and many others.[13] When the Public Accounts Committee took a look at the market in 2007 it noted Carillion's success even at that stage in having turned PFI investments costing £24m into £46m. But the Treasury, eager to feed the PFI beast and intensely relaxed in the face of fat returns for its backers, took a look at the market and decided that, unlike refinancing windfalls, these gains were 'outside the project' and it would not recoup any share of them.[14]

The market quickly hit the multibillion-pound level. A multitude of new investment funds emerged, using the private equity business model of the moment to snaffle up PFI contracts, re-engineer them, and sell them on. By the end of 2010, a study by PFI specialist Dexter Whitfield found, there had been 240 deals involving the sale of PFI companies, covering 1229 separate projects. There weren't even 1229 PFI projects in existence; only around 700 had been signed and the extra 500 was accounted for by PFI deals that, like kids' dog-eared trading cards, get passed among different owners several times. It can be very profitable: while Britain's public services are hawked around, the PFI companies have drunk in gains estimated at £4.4bn, almost entirely tax free.[15]

Far-from-home office

If the pension funds and insurance companies who were private equity's main investors could plant their snouts in the tax-free PFI trough, why shouldn't other stock market investors get in on the act? To do so they needed investment companies that could hold, buy and sell stakes in PFI companies just as investment trusts do with the shares of other companies, and there was an obvious place to set these up: offshore.

Britain's biggest international bank, HSBC, was the first to capitalize, in 2006 forming HSBC Infrastructure Company Ltd (HICL) in Guernsey – with shares listed on the London Stock Exchange – to take over stakes in fifteen PFI contracts from the bank's UK operations. By 2011 the offshore company's portfolio ran to thirty-three deals, including full ownership of some of the largest PFI contracts like the West Middlesex and Barnet hospitals and 90% ownership of the contract for Stoke Mandeville hospital. On a smaller scale, the Guernsey company could boast stakes in fifty-six schools from Kent to the Isle of Skye.

The attraction of the St Peter Port base is clear from HICL's 2011 results: profit £46m; tax £0. Since over half the company's income came in the form of interest paid tax-deductibly by British PFI companies controlled by HSBC – reducing their total tax bills to a piddling £0.9m in 2010/11 – the structure was highly tax effective.[16] Nowhere was it better exemplified than at the Home Office and its PFI contract with Annes Gate Property plc. The millions that this company was paying on loans carrying interest at 14.75% headed to its owner and funder, HICL in Guernsey.

The tax efficiency of PFI could sit gallingly alongside the real world consequences of the exorbitant initiative. When in 2011, for example, HICL bought a stake in the company running a 35-year PFI contract for the Pinderfields hospital in Wakefield, it acquired a loan that would pay over £1m a year ultimately to Guernsey.[17] There of course it would not incur any of the tax that might in some small way have compensated for the £20m deficit back at the hospital trust, which was caused by the PFI payments in the first place and by 2012 had led to job cuts and nurses having to clean the wards.[18]

For many companies owning interests in PFI companies the offshore flit was irresistible. A few months after HSBC's Guernsey move, the PFI investment arm of investment bank Babcock & Brown performed the same trick, taking with it ownership of such diverse public infrastructure as Strathclyde Police Training Centre and Tower Hamlets' twenty-five PFI schools. Others like John Laing, owner of a 26% stake in the Ministry of Defence's offices, joined the exodus. And in December 2010, a 25% shareholder in Exchequer Partnerships called Catalyst Lend Lease Ltd transferred its PFI interests to a new Jersey company. Which meant that only one of the four great departments of state now operated from offices not at least partly owned offshore. It was, oddly enough, the Foreign Office.

Not that much real business is done in St Helier or St Peter Port. Those calling the shots for the PFI investment companies continue to do so from London, working as 'investment advisers' while paying the usual Channel Island residents to host the board meetings that keep their companies tax resident offshore. HSBC's Guernsey company HICL, for example, may own a large PFI portfolio but this is run by its UK investment managers, InfraRed Capital Partners Ltd.

All told, by 2012 over 200 PFI companies were partly owned offshore, more than 100 of them majority-owned in tax havens and 70 of them running health service projects.[19] By my calculations

168 state schools – several of which are generally run under a single PFI contract – are at least partly owned offshore.[20] That so many public assets should be shunted into tax havens is a remarkable outcome, given the chastening experience of a more direct move several years ago. Back in 2003, after the Revenue had been criticized by parliament for selling its offices to a Bermudan company, the minister responsible, Dawn Primarolo, wrote to Whitehall's mandarins telling them not to do deals with tax havens. Alas the private finance initiative and the market in public assets that has grown from it have done it for them.

The following table shows a small selection of Britain's major public service assets that are now owned offshore:

Public Building	Private Owner	% Owned	Territory Of Ownership
HMRC, 600 tax offices	Mapeley Steps Ltd	100	Bermuda
HM Treasury and HMRC Head Office	Lend Lease PFI/PPP Infrastructure CIHL Holdings Ltd	25	Jersey
Home Office HQ	HICL Infrastructure Co Ltd	100	Guernsey
Stoke Mandeville Hospital	HICL Infrastructure Co Ltd	90	Guernsey
Colchester Garrison	HICL Infrastructure Co Ltd	55	Guernsey
Redcar Schools	3i Infrastructure	50	Jersey
Findlay House Care Home, Edinburgh	3i Infrastructure	50	Jersey
Norfolk Police HQ	International Public Partnerships	100	Guernsey

Hereford & Worcester Magistrates Court	International Public Partnerships	100	Guernsey
Tower Hamlets Schools	International Public Partnerships	100	Guernsey
Ministry of Defence Whitehall HQ	John Laing Infrastructure Fund Ltd	26	Guernsey
M40, junction 1A to 3	John Laing Infrastructure Fund Ltd	50	Guernsey
Kingston Hospital	John Laing Infrastructure Fund Ltd	60	Guernsey
Norfolk and Norwich hospital	3i Infrastructure	37	Jersey
Haverstock School, Camden	HICL Infrastructure Co Ltd	50	Guernsey

Sources: see footnote.[21]

Green taxes

The virtually tax-free status of the private finance initiative should never have surprised Treasury mandarins. Year after year the finance bill they put together was fattened by legislation closing down tax avoidance schemes dreamt up by the Big 4 accountancy firms. And these were the very accountants who were advising both sides of a PFI negotiation – public authority and private company – and thus effectively dictated the structure of PFI contracts. What's more, PFI finances were the stuff of a tax planner's dreams, allowing for huge debt and interest payments, flexible definitions of a company's trade, tax allowances that outpace income and plentiful opportunity to convert future taxable income into non-taxable gains.

At best PFI contracts were only ever going to produce taxable profits after many years, giving plenty of time to put in place the wheezes needed to ensure that before a tax bill arrived, the returns were whipped out tax free. When Barclays acquired Infrastructure Investors and its maturing PFI portfolio in 2009 using a £360m bond with interest at 8% that would eliminate a large chunk of its UK companies' profits, its accounts quietly noted a £243,000 bill for 'corporate tax and restructuring advice' from PwC,[22] simultaneously the country's largest PFI consultant and tax adviser.[23]

Yet, while the private finance initiative makes no meaningful tax payments, the Treasury assumes it does. In 2003, in either a wilful or especially stupid episode of unjoined-up government, the Treasury accepted the conclusion of tax adviser-cum-PFI consult-ant, KPMG, that when it came to assessing whether a particular PFI contract represented value for money compared with funding the infrastructure in question through conventional government borrowing, it should be assumed that the PFI company would pay tax on its profits. A flow chart produced by the accountants and incorporated in the Treasury's 'Green Book' procurement manual enabled those pushing through their PFI deals to claim likely future tax payments up to 10% of total PFI fees. This implies that up to 40% of PFI fees translate into taxable company profit (an outcome that would get any PFI tax adviser sacked on the spot) and is more than enough in most cases to swing the procurement decision in favour of using PFI. And while proffering this vision of PFI com-panies merrily paying large amounts of corporation tax, KPMG itself was simultaneously successfully advising PFI companies on engineering their way out of tax.

When the Public Accounts Committee finally looked at the point in 2011, it recorded with some incredulity: 'The Treasury could not tell us if PFI investors had paid tax in the UK on profits and on equity gains, or whether corporation taxes had been collected from PFI.'[24] The more likely truth was that officials would not provide the figures, or even estimates, as they would turn out to be vanishingly small.

A chancellor who in opposition had pilloried what he called 'Labour's discredited PFI model' might have been expected to correct the glaring tax flaw in the model. But George Osborne would soon be relying on PFI every bit as much as Gordon Brown did to bolster infrastructure investment without increasing official measures of debt.[25] The paradox first seen in 1997 persisted: parlous public finances and political calculation favoured a financing scheme that itself plundered those very finances. But PFI would still, officially at any rate, have to provide value for money. So when Osborne's junior minister was confronted with the lunacy of assuming tax income that would never appear, she still wouldn't budge: 'We are not going to rewrite the Green Book.'[26]

It was thus no surprise when the coalition's first major hospital PFI deal, to rebuild the Alder Hey children's hospital in Liverpool, was signed in 2013 with a joint venture between the Jersey-based Henderson group, which has a record of ensuring that income on PFI projects flows offshore, and the Cyprus-based Laing O'Rourke group.[27]

The British government remains content to feed the PFI industry contracts that will cost public service budgets over £250bn,[28] on the understanding that it would make a commensurate tax contribution. When it was shown that this simply doesn't happen, the government looked the other way. It accepted public services as tax avoidance schemes. The British state was fiscally eating itself.

10
Poor Show

How Britain's tax avoidance industry
entrenches poverty in the developing world

Tax avoidance is no great respecter of the needs of those it deprives. A pound taken off a multinational's payments to one of the world's poorest countries means the same to the markets as a pound kept from the richest. Both go to the bottom line. So some of Britain's biggest companies have no more qualms about taking the now relatively routine steps required to minimize their tax bills in the developing world than they do back home.

The looting of developing countries by corrupt elites has long captured the headlines. The more subtle and generally legal tax avoidance methods deployed by some of the biggest corporate players in these economies, by contrast, went largely overlooked until recent efforts by campaigners led by the Tax Justice Network and Christian Aid brought the issue right up the political agenda.[1] By 2010 the OECD recognized the importance of the matter and hosted a 'tax and development' conference at which the UK minister then responsible for tax, Labour's Stephen Timms, noted that 'research suggests that developing countries lose at least $50bn per year, and perhaps as much as $280bn in corporate profit sharing [i.e. avoidance] and evasion by individuals.'[2] As total worldwide annual aid to developing countries is around $100bn, tax dodging was hitting the world's poorest people very hard.

When the charity ActionAid and I teamed up to take a closer look at one of Britain's largest operators in the developing world, SABMiller, we discovered the shocking reality of tax avoidance there. The multinational behind such global brands as Grolsch and Peroni operates extensively across Asia and Africa, having grown out of the South African Breweries company that started life 115 years ago slaking the thirsts of the men mining the Witwatersrand goldfields. Piecing together a multinational's faraway tax affairs is not, however, a straightforward matter, so we focused on the group's operations in just one country, Ghana, where per capita daily income is less than £3.

Some essential facts about SABMiller's local business, Accra Breweries Ltd, were clear enough. It brewed and sold a range of beers locally and apparently successfully, but publicly available accounts showed that it was paying no tax, because it was making no profits on which to pay them. This certainly surprised some local people when ActionAid policy adviser Martin Hearson and I visited the country in September 2010. Among them was Marta, a local stallholder who was selling the company's beer at the food stall she ran for fourteen hours a day, making around £50 per week. From this modest income she had paid more income tax to the Ghanaian exchequer in the previous year than SABMiller (global profits around £2bn) had. What we needed to know was *why* the brewer with a one third share of the country's beer market wasn't making any taxable profit.[3]

Small beer

Our breakthrough came with a trip to Ghana's patents and trademarks registry where, after some negotiation, we sat in front of a computer of impressive vintage staring at a list of African beers and their corporate owners. One name flickered before us more than any other: SABMiller International BV. The suffix – '*besloten vennootschap*' – indicated that local rights to brands including Ghana's popular Stone Lager and Castle Milk Malt, South African favourite Castle Lager and even a southern African sorghum-based brew called Chibuku were owned by a Dutch limited company. But try ordering a Stone, Castle Milk or Chibuku in a bar in Amsterdam and you'll go thirsty. These were African beers, brewed in Africa from largely African ingredients, sold in Africa to Africans by local vendors like Marta. So why were their brands now owned thousands of miles away in the Netherlands?

The answer, of course, is tax. Between 2007 and 2010 Accra Breweries Ltd paid £1.33m, or 2.1% of its turnover, in tax-deductible royalties to SABMiller International BV for using the drinks' names and trademarks. These fees formed just a small part of the £50m annual turnover that the Dutch company derives from licensing names not just to Ghana but many countries around the world, over half of it from Africa.[4] When the royalties reach the Netherlands they are strictly taxable, but the winning Dutch rules that enticed the Johnnie Walker brand from Scotland (see chapter 5) were equally effective for African 'intellectual property' including brand names, logos, designs and, we discovered at the trademarks offices, even the slogan registered for Stone Lager, 'You've earned it!'

From its Rotterdam offices, SABMiller International BV, doesn't have to put in too many Stone lager-earning shifts for its £50m. Back in 2005 it simply bought a batch of trademarks from a sister Dutch company for over $200m, an amount that for tax purposes it can set against the income it then receives for licensing the trademarks to the companies that really use them, wherever they happen to be. The tax break is pretty flexible, to be taken whenever it suits SABMiller, enabling the company in 2009/10 to claim just enough of the cost of the trademarks to eliminate any Dutch corporate tax bill. Back in Ghana, meanwhile, Accra Breweries Ltd's taxable profits are reduced by the royalty payments. Although the company still pays a 'withholding tax' of 8% to the Ghanaian revenue when the payments leave the country, as local corporate tax is charged at 25%, SABMiller effectively saves 17% in tax.

Barely less distant than the Rotterdam trademark-owner, another SABMiller company extracts even more cash from Accra Breweries. Bevman Services AG, based in Zug, Switzerland, takes 4.6%, or almost £1m, of the company's turnover every year in 'management fees'. Just like the royalties, these reduce Ghanaian profits and again are not taxed any further when they arrive in the Alpine tax haven, where the going tax rate for management services of 7% is offset by a credit for the withholding tax (now at 8%) paid in Ghana. Once again, a 17% tax saving.

SABMiller has bought into all the standard tax-planning techniques. Only slightly closer to most of its African operations than the Dutch brand owners and Swiss managers, in 2008 it set up a Mauritius company called Mubex, through which it runs most of its African purchasing. Now when Accra Breweries Ltd buys maize from South Africa's farms, for example, the produce still gets shipped up Africa's Atlantic coast but the paperwork heads north-east to Mubex in the Indian Ocean tax haven. In legal terms, the maize is bought first by Mubex, which then sells it to Accra Breweries. Mubex can make a decent profit for acting as the middleman, taxed at just 3%, in the process siphoning profits out of countries such as Ghana. Which explains why, when we asked one of Accra Breweries' procurement managers what lay behind the Mauritian connection, he dismissed it as 'all tax planning'.

These quite rudimentary tax techniques leave Accra Breweries Ltd with barely any profit to speak of. In the four years we looked at, from its £63m turnover the company made just £0.5m operating profits after payments to tax haven-affiliated companies totalling nine times this amount. This was a derisory return by any standard and, at less than a 1% margin on its sales, especially poor for a member of a multinational group making a 16% return worldwide. Once it had paid its finance costs, Accra Breweries was left with a £3m loss. In three of the four years it thus paid no corporate income tax, and in the other sent a cheque to the Ghanaian government for just £0.2m.

The pattern appeared to be repeated for SABMiller's operations elsewhere in the developing world: profits of its Indian Skol Breweries operation were wiped out by management fees, this time paid to the Netherlands, while large proportions of Zambian and Tanzanian profits disappeared to Europe in royalties and management fees. Back in Britain, as we put together what we'd learned of SABMiller's tax arrangements in a report 'Calling Time: Why SABMiller should stop dodging taxes in Africa',[5] we were not surprised to learn that this was a multinational with fewer subsidiary companies in the whole of the African continent doing real business, sixty-four of them, than it had in the world's tax havens sucking up money. In these territories – fortuitously for the impact of the report, if not for Africa's economies – the total was sixty-five.[6]

The result is a serious dent in developing countries' revenues and their efforts to move out of aid dependency. Ghana takes 22% of its gross domestic product in taxation, far more than its neighbours but still a long way behind the 40% typically raised in the rich world when its citizens need public services every bit as much. Of this tax revenue, in 2009 14%, or around £280m, came from corporate income tax, most of it from the scores of multinationals operating in the country. While it is impossible to quantify the economic benefits that eradicating tax avoidance would have, if SABMiller is anything to go by it would be very significant. ActionAid and I estimated that, just through the offshore royalty and management fee payments, SABMiller's arrangements cost African economies around £20m annually – enough to educate a quarter of a million of their children.[7]

There was nothing exceptional about SABMiller. Reviewing half a dozen multinationals' operations in the developing world before we settled on the brewer as a case study, I'd come across repeated examples of taxable profits extracted in similar ways. Shell, for example, operates extensively in India through both a 'downstream' business selling oil products and, on a far larger scale, through a liquefied natural gas plant at Hazira. Neither makes taxable profits. Half of Hazira LNG Pte Ltd's near £1bn turnover is spent on raw materials supplied by companies in Bermuda and Singapore, leaving nothing for the Indian taxman to get his hands on.[8]

My attempts to analyse these arrangements in depth were immediately thwarted by the absence of data or accounts for the tax haven companies being used and the refusal, from every company I asked, for details beyond those already published in their glossy annual accounts. Equally uniform were the boasts, some maybe merited, of great local munificence and environmental care. Shell, it was impressed on me, has 'a vibrant social responsibility program in India'. It had recently 'won the National Award for our work with the disabled as an employer in 2008' and 'initiated the country's largest afforestation project having completed 1100 hectares of mangrove plantations ... the Shell Foundation has invested over USD 10 million across four programs that have a footprint across nine states in India and impact more than 700,000 households.' Like many others, Shell was happy to fill my inbox with claims of corporate social responsibility, but not hard facts and figures about tax arrangements. And I couldn't help feeling that, by paying no corporate tax but doing some good deeds, the world's second biggest company was saying politely but firmly: '*We'll* decide how we contribute to the societies we operate in, thank you very much, not their elected governments. And we'll make sure we squeeze the last drop of PR advantage out of every penny we do spend.'

Chain of command

The industry in restructuring major conglomerates in order to slash tax bills – which grew rapidly in the rich world in the 1990s – has now reached developing countries that have far weaker defences against the onslaught. To challenge the most basic cross-border tax planning requires detailed investigation that developing countries – funded from inadequate public revenues subject to intensely competing demands – simply aren't equipped to take on. So when the big tax avoidance advisers move in the ensuing fight is far from a fair one. And move in they certainly have.

For the right audience, the tax avoidance industry parades its wares as shamelessly as any arms company showcasing missile launchers at a weapons fair. At an International Fiscal Association conference in Delhi in 2008, for example, a partner from accountants Ernst & Young outlined exactly what the world's tax consultants could do for multinationals operating in a country with per capita income of around £2 a day. As in the rich world, 'tax efficient supply chain management' was the name of the game. The 'hubs' of international businesses, explained the E&Y man, should be 'located in low tax jurisdiction' where there would be 'centralization of management, control and business risks'. In countries that charge normal tax rates, 'operating entities', i.e. the companies making and selling things, should 'perform routine functions and bear subordinate risk'.[9]

The stark master-servant demarcation is explained by the rules of this particular game, dictating that any transaction between two related companies is priced commercially. So, for example, when a multinational puts managers and technicians in a company in a tax haven like Switzerland, the 'operating companies' such as Ghana's Accra Breweries pay fees at an 'arm's length price' for its expertise. Or, as with Diageo's Johnnie Walker business, the operating company acts simply as an agent for the hub company by manufacturing and selling goods locally not on its own account but on behalf of the remote tax haven-based company that retains ownership of goods, stock and orders and thus makes the real money. The E&Y tax specialist bluntly explained the relationship to his Indian audience: 'principal company located in low tax jurisdiction earns substantial profits; operating cos [sic] earn low and stable profits'.

Dependency culture

The consequences of these tax arrangements go beyond tax avoidance. If the fees that SABMiller pays to a Swiss company for various services are justified and its 'brand management' does take place in the Netherlands, the real business and technical expertise of a proudly African business must be located 3000 miles away in a low-tax Swiss canton. Tax planning, in other words, sends economic control over one of Ghana's more important local businesses out of the country and into one at least fifteen times wealthier.

Of course many companies operating in the developing world will be owned by multinationals controlling them from some distant headquarters in the rich north anyway, imposing a degree of external control. But 'tax-efficient supply chain management' strips out a further layer of local autonomy, entrepreneurship and innovation. 'Aggregation of entrepreneurial risks at a hub entity' – located in a faraway tax haven – is exactly what Ernst & Young recommends. The same accountants conscientiously advise companies to ensure that their 'transfer pricing' arrangements faithfully follow real business operations so as not to fall foul of any future tax investigation. Tax haven companies must be paid for what they really do and what they really own, not just what the paperwork says. 'Ensure alignment of transfer pricing and legal documentation with business substance' insists E&Y responsibly, standing by to advise on the practicalities – for an appropriate fee – should any assistance be required.

International tax planning thus becomes more than just a tax matter; it determines exactly how a multinational operates in a developing country. To meet its tax plan, its local 'operating company' must perform a routine job with minimal expertise and certainly no flair or innovation. Even if its task is technically complex, if it is to be paid the miserly amounts demanded by the tax strategy, the 'operating company' must be allowed access to the technology only as an indentured labourer. In the jargon of supply chain management, it is consigned to the less remunerative end of the value chain. In plain English, it gets the shitty end of the stick.

I began to sense something of this as we toured the brewery in Accra. First we had an illuminating discussion with one of the company's bright young technicians about the biochemistry of fermentation and the processes required to industrialize it. Then we chatted to an assured and equally youthful 'corporate affairs' manager about the Ghanaian drinks markets. But where do these people go from here? What if the scientist wanted to improve the efficiency of the plant? What if the manager had a smart idea for marketing his drinks, beyond the corny centrally imposed SABMiller advertising formula (a group of beaming twenty-somethings with perfect teeth sporting the national football shirt as they raise a bottle of the local brew)? If these questions are the preserve of technicians in Switzerland and brand managers in the Netherlands then local people's ideas and careers are constrained.

The tax planning now deployed almost uniformly by the large corporations controlling big chunks of developing countries' economies thus removes from them the assets, expertise and opportunity essential for development. It charges extortionately for the capital it invests in them and it sentences their major businesses – many of which may have local origins – to permanent servitude. And by introducing a huge tax subsidy to companies owned by foreign multinationals it also awards them a formidable competitive advantage and erects a barrier to domestic businesses whose growth, it is almost universally agreed, is essential for sustainable economic development.

Development economists would recognize in this argument shades of 'dependency theory', the proposition that economic relations between developed and developing countries perpetuate the latter's dependence on the former. The notion has been well documented in trade relations, mineral wealth exploration and other areas, yet never, so far as I can see, by reference to tax planning. As one economist recently remarked, 'at the core of the dependency relation between center and periphery lays the inability of the periphery to develop an autonomous and dynamic process of technological innovation'.[10] For the 'center' and 'periphery' read Ernst & Young's 'hub' and 'operating' companies and you see that, along with other gravitational pulls on expertise away from developing countries, tax structuring furthers economic subjugation. In fact, it *demands* it.

Compromising positions

A few months before we toured SABMiller's Accra brewery wondering what the managers in Zug were doing for their money, Ghana's parliament had given a significant boost to the company's tax planning by ratifying a 'double taxation agreement' with Switzerland. The idea, as with around two thousand other such bilateral agreements between countries, was to carve out the rights to tax income that is earned in one state by a resident of the other.

Governments have grappled with the problem for a century. And it's easy to see how different economies would want the cake cut differently. In crude terms, richer countries that are home to businesses earning large sums abroad want most of the tax bill to be allocated to the country of residence of the enterprise earning the money; the poorer countries in which they earn it want the tax bill largely awarded to the country in which it arises.

In principle the dilemma is easily resolved. The 'source' state, where the income crops up, levies a 'withholding tax' on the payment, such as a royalty, leaving its country. The business's home tax authority then taxes the income and gives credit for the withholding tax. If, for example, a business in country A pays £100 in royalties to a related one in country B, country A might levy a 15% withholding tax. Country B might then tax the income at 30%, giving credit for the £15 already paid and so charging just a net £15. A total tax charge of £30 would thus be shared equally between the two countries.

Such compromises are hammered out in the bilateral 'double taxation agreements' that countries sign (see chapter 5). In the above example, without any agreement between the two, a total of £45 tax might have been charged, far higher than the rate in either country. So these agreements, averting punitive tax levels, are crucial to investment and trade between countries. The tricky question is how to share out the cake: who merits the bigger slice, the 'source' or the 'residence' country?

The League of Nations set about addressing the matter after the First World War, but it was only at the end of the Second that the issue seriously commanded governments' attention. By then 'Capital exporters' from the rich north, led by the UK, preferred agreements that apportioned tax more to the country of residence of the tax-payers earning cross-border income; capital importers in the poorer south wanted tax bills to be awarded largely to the country in which the income had its source. By the late 1940s the League's grand idea had two variants: the London model favouring low or no withhold-ing taxes, and the Mexico model favouring source states through much higher withholding taxes.

This divergence persisted for most of the second half of the twentieth century. When the OECD produced its 1963 'model' agreement – favouring its rich, capital exporting members – devel-oping countries, most of them emerging from one empire or other, had to look elsewhere to protect their interests and by the late 1970s were drawing up their own model agreement through the League's successor, the United Nations. It, unsurprisingly, incorporated far higher levels of source state taxation.

These competing models now provide the parameters for negotiation when rich and poor companies sit down to agree a tax treaty. But the discussions never take place in isolation. By the time developing countries started to come to the table as emerging independent states in the 1970s and 1980s, aid and trading arrangements already had higher profiles than the arcane subject of double taxation. Under almost everybody's radar, the taxation agreements – often pawns in the wider negotiations, either explicitly or indirectly linked to agreements on aid and trade – were weighted towards the wealthier and more powerful negotiating partner's interests.

For decades the outcome has been the kind of agreement that Ghanaian finance minister Kwadwo Baah Wiredu unveiled in Accra in July 2008 as 'a boost to the President's vision of the "Golden Age of Business in Ghana"'. The new treaty with Switzerland, he pointed out, recognized not just the importance of Swiss business investment, but also the $40m – or $5m a year – that Switzerland had committed in aid to Ghana since 2002.[11] In return, the agreement surrendered large amounts of tax to the European country. Royalties leaving Ghana, previously taxed at 10%, are now taxed at 8%; management and technical service fees, previously taxed at 15%, also now incur just an 8% levy. This is how tax fits into the 'development assistance' picture: an impoverished country is fed some aid, on which it remains dependent in the short term. Then the trade ambassadors and tax negotiators come in and the developing country is powerless to resist demands to cede its rights to tax income arising within its borders.

Meanwhile, predatory nations such as Switzerland, the Netherlands and Luxembourg redesign their own tax systems to exploit the new terms. The 8% withholding tax rate on management and technical fees is strikingly near the corporate tax rate applied to profits on such income when received in Switzerland, with the result that there is no more tax to pay when they arrive in Europe. The same payments, as we have seen, reduce – or even eliminate – profits taxed at more normal rates in the developing countries. ActionAid and I estimated that management and royalty fee payments by Accra Breweries alone cost the Ghanaian exchequer over £200,000 a year (and that was under arrangements set up before the new tax agreement's greater incentives). If this is what is at stake with just one company, it poses serious questions over linking significant tax-reducing agreements with an aid programme raising just £5m annually.

The greater effect, though, may come in how the multinational businesses controlling swathes of developing countries' economies are encouraged to behave. As source state withholding taxes fall, it becomes ever more lucrative to send interest, royalties, and management and technical fees to the north's tax havens. Which means locating capital, brands, know-how, expertise and management there. When in 2010 accountants from PricewaterhouseCoopers pitched their plans to another brewer, Heineken, for a transformation of its supply chain to incorporate 'tax arbitrage', they made clear that the pain would be felt in operating companies locally. The fate of these firms, some in the world's poorest countries, was to be 'loss of influence, authority', 'loss of staff' and 'no big deals'.[12] Life at the bottom of the pile, in other words. The plan would be highly lucrative for the multinational, however, which was expected to gain at least £50m annually, and for the advisers who would implement it for fees put at £21m.

By signing taxation treaties that invite this kind of tax planning, developing countries are in effect replacing the 'tax holidays' for multinationals operating in their countries which have long been recognized as harmful. These explicit tax breaks, which became fashionable in the 1980s, merely led to an overall reduction in tax payments with no increase in investment since one country simply had to match its competing neighbour's generosity. Identikit networks of tax agreements that allow corporate taxes to be vastly reduced or eliminated now achieve much the same thing.

Haven sent

This trend would be serious enough without the encouragement of the British government. But the changes to laws governing the tax haven subsidiary companies of British multinationals, outlined in chapter 7, will make the avoidance of tax in developing countries far easier. The previous 'controlled foreign companies' laws, if properly policed, imposed a UK tax charge on profits diverted into tax havens from third countries like Ghana, and demand that the haven operations have real substance.

But the changes ushered in over 2011 and 2012, taking effect largely in 2013, create enormous opportunities. Straightforward schemes will include the tax haven finance subsidiary that will strip out profits in the form of interest payments from operations subject to normal tax rates, such as those in developing countries with tax rates between 25% and 30%. Previously, the tax haven company's profit would have been caught by the UK 'controlled foreign companies' laws but under the relaxations will be taxed at no more than 5.5%, presenting an instant 20%+ tax saving to the British multinational. In fact the new laws present more than an opportunity; many companies and their advisers will see such arrangements as their fiduciary responsibility. One partner from PwC summed up the tax industry's reaction: 'The ability to finance overseas operations in a tax efficient way that is mandated by government is a very welcome change.'[13]

Even more generously, under a beggar-my-neighbour, 'foreign-to-foreign' tax exemption, profits of foreign subsidiaries diverted to a tax haven company through transactions such as buying and selling goods or providing services will never be touched by the UK tax authorities. Even if the tax haven company earns money by vastly overpricing its goods to related companies in developing countries, or underpricing purchases from them (never actually touching the goods), the British taxman will look the other way.

The most abusive transfer pricing schemes – often known as 'invoice routing' – will be exempt from the rules. It will be left to under-resourced and inexpert tax authorities in developing countries to mount any kind of challenge to the schemes, and it's obvious who will win that battle.[14]

Despite the cost of these changes on developing countries, they had not even been discussed with the Department for International Development until ActionAid protested, using an admittedly crude estimate, that they could put £4bn a year tax at risk for developing countries.[15] [16] Since the Department for International Development was busily pursuing a private sector development agenda driven partly by the need to bolster poorer countries' tax receipts as a route out of aid dependency, this was quite an oversight.[17] The failure even to think about the impact of domestic tax policy on international development became a source of some official embarrassment. In August 2012 parliament's International Development Select Committee looked at the matter and concluded that the impact of the UK's new rules on developing countries should be assessed as a matter of urgency.

What tax help the British government does give to developing countries is provided through OECD initiatives to advise them on tax administration, including a welcome 'tax inspectors without borders' programme under which experienced tax investigators join developing countries' tax authorities. But, with the dice loaded hopelessly against these nations, this can make only the smallest difference in the great international tax avoidance game.

Transparently unfair

Campaigners' efforts at redressing the balance have focused on changing the international tax system. They want one that shares out tax revenues more fairly based on companies' real physical presence and operations, determined by factors such as the number of people working in each territory. So-called 'formulary apportionment' methods would be far less a plaything of the world's most creative tax accountants and lawyers. But they remain a pipe dream given how wedded the OECD countries as a bloc remain to the 'arm's length' principle that allocates large taxable profits to capital and assets including intellectual property and thus favours the rich club's members and facilitates their companies' transfer pricing schemes.

More realistic are attempts to force companies to report how much profit they make and how much tax they pay in each territory in which they operate, alongside data on assets and employees in those locations. 'Country-by-country' reporting, first proposed by accountant and tax justice campaigner Richard Murphy in 2003[18] and now receiving at least some interest at the OECD, would not change the rules on how profits are shared out but it would expose the results. At present, it is all but impossible to see what tax contributions, if any, a given multinational makes to developing economies. We could only analyse SABMiller's performance because its Ghanaian operations had minority shareholders outside the SABMiller group and thus had to publish accounts. Without these, details of its tax payments, royalties, management fees and all the rest would have remained secret. When I tried to analyse the tax affairs of several other companies most were impenetrable. Accounts for multinationals' local subsidiary companies are either entirely inaccessible or available only for local inspection. And of course all figures for their tax haven companies are strictly for insiders' eyes only.

Greater transparency is possible. A worldwide 'Extractive Industries Transparency Initiative' reveals payments that companies make for mining developing countries' mineral wealth. It is being adopted by scores of countries and has effectively been signed into US law for American companies.[19] The policy recognizes that companies should declare what they pay for access to poorer countries' mineral wealth, and it seems reasonable that what goes for resources below the ground should apply equally to those above it. Making profit in developing countries does, after all, amount to exploiting a country's markets and labour – ideally to mutual benefit – and the least that could be expected is some openness on what remote and far wealthier shareholders pay for the privilege.

Yet business groups vehemently object to transparency for their corporate profits and tax payments, claiming that the authorities can already access the information. These, they say, are the only people with a legitimate interest in it. 'Greater transparency for multinationals is a red herring,' according to Mike Devereux of the business-funded Oxford Centre for Business Taxation.[20] Publicizing details, runs the argument, would open companies to attack from campaigners who might not understand legitimate reasons for low tax payments. Exactly this argument was once advanced by opponents of publishing data on hospital safety performance, MPs' expenses and much other information that now informs public debate and improves standards.

Not all businessmen miss the point: former CBI director general Sir Digby Jones – no lefty activist – has noted the value of country-by-country reporting to shareholders, who might actually like to know where their profits are being made and where tax is paid.[21] For one thing, the information might identify whether the company is at risk of a potentially expensive tax audit. More importantly for society beyond the company's shareholders, multinationals would feel some pressure to report taxable profits that correspond in a broad sense to their presence in a country. This is the real value of country-by-country reporting for developing countries, as a countervailing influence on multinationals' tax planning. On the one hand, the biggest companies would still have strong financial incentives to divert profits into tax havens but, on the other, they would fear the consequences of doing so. A more reasonable allocation of taxable profits and the more economically valuable functions that go with them would almost certainly result.

Business as usual

Instead, established methods for slicing up of the international tax cake create incentives pointing all one way: tax avoidance. While OECD member governments dispense 'administrative assistance' and 'capacity building', they do so as the flip side of imposing the rules under which contrived techniques like 'tax-efficient supply chain mechanisms' must be respected by governments given no choice but to sign up to tax treaties that incorporate the OECD's methods. They were reinforced in 2010 when the OECD published its report, strongly supported by the British government, on 'The Transfer Pricing Aspects of Business Restructurings'.[22] Only in the most obscure and rare cases, it decided, can international tax schemes designed by the likes of Ernst & Young and PwC be overruled by governments. No amount of 'administrative assistance' will deal with the fundamental problem thus entrenched: that low source state taxes demanded by the OECD, coupled with rules that respect the parking of more valuable assets and activities in low-tax areas, present irresistible opportunities for tax avoidance which developing countries cannot fight.

The British government, meanwhile, bends to the will of the tax schemers by adapting its own laws to accommodate these tax avoidance possibilities. UK tax laws have been relaxed because the old ones, a 2011 Treasury briefing paper stated, 'require modernisation so that they have a better fit with the way in which [multinational enterprises] structure their commercial operations, for example with regional service centres and for general supply chain management'.[23] Anti-tax avoidance laws, in other words, had to be relaxed to accommodate companies' tax avoidance schemes.

British taxation policy really had been so comprehensively captured by the world's biggest corporations that screw-the-poor policies like these could be written into the statute book at their whim, without a pang of conscience being felt anywhere in Whitehall.

11
Called to
Account

Tax dodging moves centre stage, but what can we do about it?

By the autumn of 2010 the big economic question was how the two-year-old financial crisis was going to be paid for. Yet, while unprecedented public spending cuts were being lined up, the billions lost to tax avoidance remained some way down the political agenda. That would change at lunchtime on 27 October when a mobile phone shop on Oxford Street was shut down by a group of protesters.

A few days earlier a dozen Londoners had met for a drink in the Nag's Head in Islington and fulminated over the devastating spending cuts announced in George Osborne's first spending review that week. Half a million public sector jobs were to be lost and the less well off were going to be hit with £7bn of cuts from the welfare budget to pay for a crisis of others' making. And whilst the government's austerity programme might have come with the slogan 'we're all in it together',[1] the revelation a few weeks before of Vodafone's enormous offshore tax avoidance scheme and the manner of its settlement suggested some were far less in it than others. As the night wore on, determination to do something grew. 'Later in the evening,' confessed one of the group's founders, 'when we were all a bit tipsy, we decided to blockade a Vodafone store.'[2] As you do.

These fairly traditional roots for a protest movement immediately sprouted far more modern shoots. 'We started as an idea and a hashtag; they both went viral,' the group would recall on its first anniversary. Which meant putting the plan out on Twitter under the label 'UK Uncut' and seeing it spread like wildfire. The following Wednesday lunchtime seventy people arrived at Vodafone's Oxford Street store with banners denouncing the company's tax avoidance, sat down inside and closed it down. Three days later the campaign went national and on the Saturday afternoon thirty Vodafone stores, from Portsmouth to Edinburgh, were closed. The following week, a further twenty-three were targeted.

Within a few weeks other companies linked to escaping tax, notably Philip Green's Topshop, were subjected to increasingly innovative protests that vividly linked the recondite world of tax avoidance to the reality of cuts to public services. Banks and shops were transformed into impromptu libraries, crèches and classrooms, while a number of Boots branches became ersatz NHS hospitals complete with surgeons and fake blood. And since HMRC appeared not to be too interested in collecting tax from the wealthiest corporations, UK Uncut entered into the spirit of the day by declaring itself the 'Big Society Revenue and Customs'. Newspaper, television and radio profiles weren't far behind, and for a while in 2011 tax avoidance overtook bankers' pay as the totemic demonstration of the majority being forced to pay for the excesses of a rich minority.

The protesters could no longer be ignored by parliament. They were posing serious questions about one of its central purposes: raising revenue for government through the tax laws which it trusted HMRC to enforce. With at least some of the failures in one particular case now in the open, here was a chance for a long-overdue examination of how big-ticket tax avoidance was policed.

Or it should have been. Instead, parliamentary scrutiny was repeatedly frustrated by the selective deployment of laws governing 'taxpayer confidentiality'. At his first major parliamentary grilling – before the Treasury Select Committee in March 2011 – HMRC's Dave Hartnett came armed with legal advice that, he claimed, allowed him to rebut 'mistakes and misconceptions that are out there' about the Vodafone settlement but, conveniently, say very little else. The £6bn reported tax loss was 'absurd'. What was more, 'there were plenty of QCs lined up telling us and the media that we were not going to get a penny through litigation'. Pressed on the point by Labour's Andy Love, this became 'Half of them, Mr Love. Sorry.'[3] Which merely begged the question of why, with external legal opinion finely balanced, Hartnett had settled a multibillion-pound case without consulting his own specialists and lawyers on the law in dispute? In came an evasion destined to be repeated ad nauseam: 'our lawyers were involved throughout'.

The deal had also conflicted with HMRC's own stricture, under its 'litigation and settlements strategy', that cases should be settled either for all the tax – if necessary through the courts – or none of it, and not negotiated to some fudge in the middle. It wasn't that negotiating settlements would necessarily have been a bad thing if struck at the right value, but Hartnett insisted to Tory MP Jesse Norman this had not happened and 'we did not get a penny less from Vodafone than we thought we could'. When it came to any questions addressing the many ways in which the deal, whose essential terms Vodafone had publicly disclosed to the stock market, evidently fell well short of the full amount, down came the barrier marked 'STOP – Taxpayer Confidentiality'.

The same occurred a couple of months later when Chuka Umunna, the slick 32-year-old Labour MP fast-tracking through the committee on his way to bigger things, raised a £20m let-off that US investment bank Goldman Sachs had received at a meeting with Hartnett in November 2010.[4] At stake this time was an interest bill on a national insurance avoidance scheme for top earners at the American bank. This was far smaller than Vodafone's concession but the allegation was more clear-cut. The interest had been due but for some reason it had been waived, to the consternation of HMRC's own solicitors. Officials again stonewalled the MPs before writing to Umunna that they had 'concluded that they cannot give any information, for reasons of taxpayer confidentiality'.[5]

Relationship difficulties

By the time the Public Accounts Committee came to consider the Goldman Sachs settlement one afternoon in October 2011, dumb insolence was less of an option. A note of an internal HMRC meeting reporting that Hartnett has 'shaken hands' on the deal had been exposed by *Private Eye* and put up on the internet that morning. Alongside combative chairman Margaret Hodge MP sat committee stalwart Richard Bacon, a Conservative MP with a few government cock-up exposés under his belt, and his colleague Stephen Barclay, a no-nonsense northern Tory lawyer with a background in money laundering compliance and not much sympathy for the cavalier handling of such large amounts of money. Between them they soon established what a personal affair Goldman Sachs's settlement had been, just like the Vodafone deal.

The official version of events was that Hartnett had stepped into Goldman's tax affairs 'to assist my colleagues to deal with a very difficult relationship issue', flying in the head of the bank's worldwide tax affairs whom he knew from the international conference circuit. When it came to the bonus tax avoidance scheme, Hartnett and his HMRC colleagues had incorrectly thought that there was some 'legal impediment' to charging interest on the bill and let the bank off £20m. Again, this was without consulting their own lawyers on the point, even though it had been the subject of tortuous litigation for five years and was firmly in the hands of HMRC's legal department. Its director, Anthony Inglese, could seek only to mitigate the error with management-speak: 'Mr Hartnett and I have discussed as a learning point is [sic] that where there is litigation afoot and a settlement discussion takes place, it is always good practice to consult the litigating lawyers in case something is there.' Bacon almost burst. 'Yes! You have answered what to me is one of the most astonishing sentences.'[6] That HMRC's most senior officials should have need of this 'learning point' – consulting a lawyer on a multimillion-pound legal question – was indeed astonishing. But in truth it was where the Goldman Sachs and Vodafone cases came together to show the reality of tax administration for large businesses: relationship first, law a distant second.

Bacon and Barclay did well to get this far as, hearing after hearing, Hartnett and then Inglese stonewalled on the basis of legal advice that, they claimed, prevented them revealing anything to do with a taxpayer's affairs. In fact the legal advice, Barclay discovered, gave the department discretion to answer the questions of a parliamentary committee but it was discretion that, conveniently for the officials, was vested in one D. Hartnett – and he was not going to use it too liberally. Hodge became so frustrated that after an unproductive half hour trying to get some answers out of Inglese, the lawyer was – with high melodrama – put on oath, the first time a parliamentary witness had faced the indignity for a decade. Little did it achieve, however, as stock non-answers, notably the mantra that in the Vodafone case 'lawyers were involved throughout', continued to spew forth.

The watchdog that didn't bark

Parliament's scrutiny of HMRC's dubious settlements did at least get further than the National Audit Office had done when it had been asked to look at HMRC's large corporate tax settlements a year before, in light of early concerns about the Vodafone deal. Its findings – some quibbles over 'governance' and not much else – showed Britain's public spending watchdog at its toothless, gummy worst.

The auditors had been informed of all the gory Goldman details by a whistle-blower within HMRC, but managed merely to refer to it in passing as a 'financial error' as if an official had fat-fingered his calculator when working out a tax bill. They even appeared to endorse the process by which the Vodafone settlement had been reached by reporting that 'relevant technical and legal expertise remained available',[7] as if that was any use to the taxpayer ('OK, the hospital did get an office manager to perform the heart transplant,' it might as well have said, 'but cardiac surgeons remained available').

The cover-up had been no great surprise. NAO boss and Auditor and Comptroller General Amyas Morse, a former PricewaterhouseCoopers management consultant still awaiting the knighthood that comes after a respectable stint in the 150-year-old post, was not a man to rock boats. Sitting in the Public Accounts Committee hearing that had first discussed the Vodafone deal in November 2010, he had shot reassuring smiles at the then HMRC chief executive Dame Lesley Strathie before venturing the opinion that 'there might be a case for qualifying [HMRC's accounts] on grounds of irregularity if it was seen that a decision had been made unreasonably. I did warn that I thought that that wasn't very likely.'[8] His was an enquiry that from the outset was not going to find very much.

A year later, after MPs with far more limited powers had made some of the progress that Morse's auditors should have done, Hodge dispatched the NAO to have another try, this time with the help of retired tax judge (and one-time Rossminster adviser) Sir Andrew Park. The judge did confirm the major failings that the MPs had alleged. In the Vodafone case, lawyers and specialists had not been consulted on the settlement, the most crucial stage of the case. They had not therefore, as HMRC bosses had claimed, been 'involved throughout'. Hartnett's claim that HMRC 'did not collect a penny less than we thought we could' was also flatly contradicted. The deal, reported the NAO, was 'lower than the tax liability that would have been established if the department had won in litigation', while the interest-free five years to pay a chunk of the bill reflected the fact that Vodafone 'had reached the maximum figure that they were pre-pared to pay' and so might have walked away from the negotiating table if they had been pressed for it.[9] Margaret Hodge's complaint weeks before of 'potentially misleading answers given to us by senior departmental officials' was beginning to look spot on. But Sir Andrew Park's work – the details of which were to remain strictly confidential – was filtered through Morse, who concluded that the deals were still 'reasonable', precisely the word required to avoid the humiliation of having to reopen the tax authority's accounts and rescind the clean audit certificate he had already given them.

When it came to Goldman Sachs, this 'reasonable' conclusion required the most tortuous logic. There was no arguing that the interest let-off was wrong, so how could it be reasonable? Morse decided that because it was settled alongside other disputes, the let-off might have persuaded Goldman to concede the other points (even though such trade-offs themselves breached HMRC's poli-cies). And there was also the benefit of 'normalising the relationship between [Goldman Sachs] and the Department' (not something that generally counts for much when Joe Public settles his tax bill). So the deal was, obviously, 'reasonable'.

Exit stage right

Unlike Britain's official auditors, UK Uncut was not giving up. Towards the end of 2011 an offshoot, UK Uncut Legal Action, started judicial review proceedings against the Goldman Sachs settlement. Although a judge would eventually rule that, given HMRC's wide discretion, the deal was legal, the proceedings did reveal that in refusing to overturn the erroneous concession to Goldman Sachs once it had come to light, Dave Hartnett had been more concerned with reputations than the taxpayer's interests. 'The risks here are major embarrassment to CHX [Chancellor George Osborne], HMRC . . . and me', he emailed a colleague in justifying his decision to allow Goldman to keep its windfall. The saga, noted the judge, was 'not a glorious episode in the history of the Revenue'.[10]

At the same time, their comrades' stunts were growing more theatrical, no more so than when a dozen activists wangled their way into a tax conference in the City, featuring Barclays' and Tesco's tax directors speaking on 'managing tax optimisation expectations'. When Dave Hartnett took to the podium, up they went, affecting to be Vodafone and Goldman Sachs executives, armed with flowers and champagne as thanks for their deals. No sooner had the well-wishers been ushered out (to a chorus of 'For he's a jolly good fellow . . . and so say Goldman Sachs, and so say Goldman Sachs . . .') than the taxman appealed to the business audience. 'At the moment, I and my colleagues are bearing the brunt of [the protest]. I think a challenge for business and those that advise business, is what you want to do if you value the relationship, because we are bearing it on our own' (a view Vodafone and Topshop might not have shared).[11] Right on cue one businessman close to HMRC, General Electric's tax director Will Morris, fretted in the letters pages of the *Financial Times* that 'business is seriously concerned that the baby could get thrown out with the bathwater'.[12]

They were both hopelessly out of touch. The HMRC-big business relationship needed jettisoning. Even the president of the Chartered Institute of Taxation – not the bolshiest body of men and women – was calling for a return to 'that healthy tension between HMRC and the tax profession that existed 10 to 20 years ago: no special relationships, no cosy conferences, no favours, deals and understandings; no inside tracks and private access'.[13]

Campaigners and parliamentarians from all sides agreed. To protesters broadly on the left, it was clear that large companies should not receive favourable deals. To MPs on the right (where, in a poor reflection on the modern Labour Party, most of those taking an interest were to be found), if big business was going to receive special treatment in some greater national economic interest, then that needed to be explicit and open to parliamentary scrutiny. Neither would tolerate an unaccountable shadow tax system under which HMRC said one thing publicly – that the letter of the law was strictly followed – while officials were privately doing deals giving companies something better. As one MP told me, 'they [the Treasury] want it both ways: sticking by the rules outwardly, fudging behind the scenes'.

In December 2011 Dave Hartnett announced the retirement that not long before he promised he had no intention of taking. Perhaps the Public Accounts Committee's loss of confidence in his way of doing business sealed his fate. A few months later he would be given a consultancy position at Deloitte – the firm whose chairman, David Cruickshank, he had become close to on many big cases, notably Vodafone, and a place on a financial crime committee set up by HSBC in the wake of major money-laundering scandals at the bank.[14] Some ascribed his departure to the committee's publication a couple of days before of a detailed argument from the man who had originally blown the whistle on the Goldman Sachs case, an HMRC solicitor called Osita Mba, of how parliament had been misled by HMRC.

The outsider

Mba was a pivotal figure in exposing how the tax system worked for big business. HMRC had brushed off the Vodafone allegations as an 'urban myth' and hoped that this sound bite would stick in the public consciousness. With another clear-cut dodgy deal exposed, and internal papers showing unease at senior levels, it became impossible to claim with any credibility that large companies did not get special treatment.

So why did Mba take a stand when other insiders had either shrugged and moved on or aired grievances only inside the department to no meaningful effect (other than seeing themselves side-lined)? He was certainly brave and prepared to take significant personal risk; however justified, whistle-blowing is rarely a good career move. Indeed, HMRC's knee-jerk response was to announce that he was under investigation for possible breaches of confidentiality laws and could face prosecution. But, as a lawyer, Mba was also able to read the Public Interest Disclosure Act – no easy feat – and be confident that he was legally covered. As important as these personal and professional attributes, however, he was an outsider.

Mba had come to Britain from Nigeria as a qualified barrister, completing a master's degree in Oxford before joining HMRC's tax litigation team in 2007. Unlike his new colleagues, he was not steeped in the traditions of fudge and rule-bending to suit the whims of senior management and the big companies to which they were close. Like many a Nigerian lawyer, he was attuned to the possibilities of corruption and the reality of the abuse of public office. When he witnessed what he considered to be an example of this, speaking out was to him a professional obligation.

In voicing his objections, Mba was intruding on a private function. Nobody was supposed to peer through the windows of the exclusive tax avoidance club. But between them this whistle-blower, thousands of campaigners and eventually parliament had found a couple of gaps in the curtains through which they glimpsed the executives, their advisers, government officials and policymakers enjoying each other's company.

It was a scene that appalled everyone except its privileged membership and, with the Public Accounts Committee's damning views hitting the front pages days before Christmas 2011, the government's leaders made taxation one of their first policy initiatives of 2012. David Cameron promised that his government would be 'business-friendly to small businesses', whereas 'with the large companies, that have the fancy corporate lawyers and the rest of it, I think we need a tougher approach'.[15] Not to be outdone, his deputy Nick Clegg clearly had Vodafone and Goldman Sachs in mind when he promised to take on 'a wealthy elite of large businesses who can pay an army of tax accountants to get out of paying their fair share of tax, who basically treat paying tax as an optional extra where you can pick and choose the taxes you pay'.[16] Their interventions were part of a politically shrewd broadside against 'crony capitalism' that took in not just tax dodging but other scourges such as excessive boardroom pay. If their austerity programme was to carry public support, they needed to look like they were confronting greed at the top too.

When it comes to taxation, the need for fairness is especially acute. If individuals and small businesses sense that the privileged are not paying their fair share, compliance with tax laws can fall dramatically, with economically ruinous consequences. But what is a 'fair share' for the biggest companies? Cameron himself put his finger on it in fairly simple terms. Benefiting from the lowest corporate tax rates of any major economy, he pointed out, companies in Britain 'should pay that rate of tax rather than avoid it'.[17] Which was pretty much what the protesters who first sat down in Vodafone's Oxford Street store over a year before had been saying. The prime minister had finally caught up with UK Uncut.

To turn this rhetoric into reality, or more accurately to appear to be doing so, there was a convenient international initiative to latch onto. In the wake of mounting international tax avoidance scandals from 2010, notably those involving Google, Starbucks and Amazon, the OECD's 'Global Forum on Taxation' had been focusing increasingly on corporate tax avoidance across borders, or 'base erosion and profit shifting' (BEPS) in the jargon.

These efforts held great promise for the British government, mainly because they could be held up as the answer to corporate tax dodging at any number of international talking shops such as the G8 and G20 and Treasury ministers and officials could claim without much fear of contradiction to be 'leading' them. David Cameron could tell a Davos audience in January 2013 that it was time for corporate tax avoiders to 'wake up and smell the coffee' and claim the British government was on the case.

Measures proposed by the OECD, notably in a major report in 2013, did indeed address many of the critical problems such as the conjuring up of finance costs to wipe out tax bills and setting up structures to exploit major markets while keeping taxable operations within them to a minimum. There was even the crucial suggestion that countries' 'controlled foreign companies' (CFC) laws, which sweep up profits diverted into tax havens, should be strengthened.

This, however, was precisely the opposite of what the British government was doing by effectively trashing its own CFC laws (as OECD tax chief Pascal Saint-Amans would point out to a US congressional committee in June 2013). This exposes the limitations of the OECD's work. Most essential changes to the corporate tax system require domestic law changes and, however laudable the organisation's pronouncements, there is no sign that these will be forthcoming. With the UK leading the race to the bottom on corporate tax, our government comprehensively undermines the international effort against multinationals' tax avoidance.

As Cameron waxed lyrical and the OECD beavered away, down at the British tax avoidance club the Treasury and Britain's biggest tax avoiders were reshaping the law to frustrate their sentiments and intentions. With some straightforward offshore planning the biggest multinationals can now take their tax rates way below any headline rate the government announces. The club's members have rewritten the rule book so that they will no longer need tax avoidance as the government chooses to define it. They can shave billions of pounds off their tax bill without finding a loophole or even getting a cosy deal. They just follow the very laws they themselves drafted. If the British tax system is ever to be wrested from these vested interests and be made fair again, the scandals of recent years must therefore translate into some radical action.

Open sesame

Given the limitless likely supply of tax avoidance opportunity, the priority must be to kill demand for it. Potential tax avoiders need to be given strong reasons *not* to indulge in tax dodging, to counter the obvious motivations to do so. The best deterrent is far greater openness. Multinational corporations must publish what tax they pay in each country and territory in which they have any presence and make publicly available accounts for the subsidiary companies and branches they have there. Tax is a public obligation and corporations enjoying privileges such as limited liability, using capital derived from people's pensions savings (subsidized by other taxpayers) and exploiting taxpayer-funded infrastructure, should be expected to show how they are fulfilling it. With no sign that opportunities to divert profits into tax havens will end (quite the reverse), the attraction of doing so would at least be tempered by the knowledge that investors, campaigners, the media and the public could see the results. As society awakens to the value of tax contributions commensurate with real economic activity, the price of tax avoidance in loss of reputation – as the Starbucks episode demonstrated – would for many not be worth paying. Disclosure of tax payments would ideally form a worldwide corporate financial reporting standard, but could in the first place be imposed relatively straightforwardly on UK multinationals by the British government. Tax payments could then become as routine a part of a company's financial announcements as its sales and profit figures.

Sunlight would also be the best disinfectant when it comes to artificial tax avoidance schemes that have to be disclosed to the tax authorities. These should be placed on public record, whether executed by individuals or corporations. If you want to shirk your obligations by undertaking a tax avoidance scheme, your fellow citizen ought to be able to know you're doing so. The same should go for favourable personal tax status. If you claim non-domiciled or non-resident reliefs we want to hear about it. We don't need to know what you earn; that may be going too far in Britain and revive historic levels of animosity to taxation. But if we've enticed you and your unique talents into Britain with our tax breaks, let's celebrate them!

New world order

It is not enough, however, simply to demonstrate the outcome of tax avoidance; the laws themselves need to be made far fairer. When it comes to corporate taxation, action is required at both the international and domestic level to end the now standard practice for multinationals to shunt their income into the world's tax havens. The rules of this game, largely imposed by the Organization for Economic Cooperation and Development and controlled by the world's wealthier nations, should be amended to allow governments to tax profits based more on companies' real presence in their countries rather than those arrived at through transactions contrived for lower tax bills. In particular, tax authorities should be able to override internal reorganizations effected for tax purposes, such as moving capital and assets into special tax haven subsidiary companies.

These practices become especially pernicious when members of the international club, privileged by taxation agreements and free trade treaties, behave exactly as such tax havens when most people assume they are *not*. As the volume of tax avoidance routed through Luxembourg, Ireland and the Netherlands (and soon the UK) proves, the European Union now embraces some tax havens whose club membership makes them far more toxic than the traditional tropical island variety. Existing moves against the abuse of the freedoms afforded by club membership are feeble: a lumbering European Commission takes only the most ineffectual measures against member states that facilitate tax dodging, while European courts endorse the activity. European law requires amendment so that 'fundamental freedoms' do not extend to tax-motivated corporate structures, while meaningful sanctions need to be imposed on member states offering tax avoidance opportunities. With the European financial system in a state of flux, the opportunity exists for this key reform; what is required now is the political will.

When it comes to the secret tax havens hiding the world's untaxed trillions, a new standard for forcing them to provide information to the world's tax authorities is urgently needed. All countries and territories must be required automatically to hand over details of income, assets and financial structures such as trusts to the countries whose residents lie behind them. Progress being made in this direction through EU directives on savings and tax administration, mimicking the searching US Foreign Accounts Tax Compliance Act, should be reinforced. However, requiring countries and territories to exchange information is only of any use to the extent that authorities hold information. But one of the world's tax havens' longstanding selling-points is that they don't ask questions and therefore simply don't hold such crucial information regarding who is behind the shell companies and trusts within their borders that hide income and wealth. A worldwide push on opening up opaque financial arrangements is thus essential; it needs to go far beyond the tepid proposals agreed at the June 2013 G20 meeting at Lough Erne and it needs to impose fully public registries of the beneficial ownership of companies, trusts and other structures. In 2014 the UK's coalition government appeared to lead the way in announcing a public register of companies' beneficial ownership, but woeful policing of company registers in Britain will limit its effectiveness. The country is home to tens of thousands of dubious shell companies and fraudulent accounts are routinely filed with impunity. And the coalition's decision to allow the UK's tax havens to decide for themselves on whether they have open registers – with no prizes for guessing how that will turn out – undermines the move entirely. Action against territories that refuse to implement such standards (or are unable to for whatever reason, including lack of resources) should be firm and direct. Britain could isolate and if necessary close down the tax havens within its direct sphere of influence and through domestic tax law make it far harder to get money into other recalcitrant tax havens in the first place. It could also prevent financial services involving such havens from being marketed in the UK. Internationally, when the limited effect of exchange of information becomes obvious in the not too distant future, tough economic sanctions must be agreed against tax havens. To compensate for the losses to these territories' economies, their 'mother' countries will have to provide economic assistance but it will prove far cheaper in the long run, compared to lost tax revenue.

The home front

Over the last few years the British government has ripped the guts out of laws that protect the country's corporate tax base. It has adopted a 'worst of all worlds' system that exempts British multinationals' foreign profits but allows tax relief for the costs of funding them. In doing so it has turned Britain into a corporate tax haven, inviting multinationals to shelter income offshore and encouraging them to place real business overseas. These developments need to be reversed at the first opportunity in order to restore some integrity to the UK corporate tax system. If they remain, not only will tax losses be huge, but a disincentive for investment in real business in Britain, and in favour of using the UK as a platform for worldwide tax avoidance, will become entrenched. For similar reasons, Britain must end its tax haven status for wealthy individuals, which means scrapping archaic non-domicile status and reverting to a tax system based on residence alone.

For both individuals and corporations there is also a strong case for minimum tax payments in order to limit the scope for reducing taxable income by artificially generated reliefs and shifting income into more lightly taxed forms such as capital gains or investment income. For an individual the minimum payment would be based on income and capital gains above a certain threshold, on the model of the 'alternative minimum tax' levied in the United States. A decent step in this direction was made in 2012 when the coalition government limited personal tax reliefs (excluding charitable donations) to 25% of income. In the case of companies, it could be based on dividends paid to shareholders along the lines of the 'advance corporation tax', credited against final tax bills, which was scrapped by the last government in 1999. If a company's shareholders wanted to get their hands on their money, they would at least have to pay some tax. To the extent that the profits were earned overseas, credit would be given against the 'minimum tax' bill for foreign taxes paid. The effect would be to limit the possible value of corporate tax avoidance while not penalizing companies that make profits in normally taxed countries (as opposed to tax havens).

Tax avoidance needs to become a two-way bet in which the avoider can lose as well as gain. Most carefully planned schemes involve neither the fraud nor negligence required to trigger penalties (and where they do the authorities generally turn a blind eye), so tax avoidance goes unpenalized and there is no deterrent to avoiding tax. This imbalance needs to be redressed. Where any arrangements established with tax savings in mind – such as artificial tax avoidance schemes or international corporate restructurings – prove not to have complied with the laws, penalties at a meaningful level should automatically apply to the profits under-declared. The levying of these penalties should also be public, adding to the reputational incentive not to seek to avoid tax in the first place.

That's the end of the schmooze . . .

These changes are relatively straightforward in principle but are a long way from being achieved in practice, largely because the institutions that shape the tax system have been captured by the tax industry and corporate interests. Policy is determined through committees and consultation processes in which the tax avoidance industry's representatives dominate, before being nodded through by parliament without proper debate. This cosy cartel urgently needs dismantling. Significant tax policy developments should be debated publicly among experts and civil society with equal access given to all sides of the argument. Individuals, companies and tax advisers contributing to the process should be required to make declarations of the likely impact of the changes on their own tax affairs and those of their clients.

When it comes to tax administration, there are two crucial tasks. One is to disengage the corporate elite and HMRC's upper echelons from the warm embrace in which they have been locked for too long. The notion of taxing wealthier individuals and companies based on 'relationships' must be replaced by a clear focus on the objective application of the law in which even (or especially) the largest taxpayers are kept at arm's length. This means no more schmoozing and no special relationships with favoured advisers. It also means seeing the bigger tax avoiders face more serious and more public consequences. Tax avoidance needs to be exposed in court more often – not always smoothed over behind closed doors – in the interests of objective interpretation of the law and public confidence in the system. The first step in reaching this harder-nosed, less partial model should be a thorough, independent, review of tax administration for the largest corporations and wealthiest individuals undertaken by a group including interested civil society groups. The second task is to reverse the jobs cull of recent years. In April 2005 HMRC employed 105,000 people; five years later this was 68,000 – a fall of 35% with more cuts to come. The budget for chasing up tax avoidance and evasion has almost halved, from £3.6bn to £1.9bn, in five years.[18] Some sticking plasters have been applied to these repeated axe-blows. Scandals and protests against tax dodging are met with temporary commitments to increase investigation budgets by fractions of the annual cuts and no commitment to build a permanent capability against tax dodging.[19] Yet this is among the most economically productive activity in the country. With qualified tax inspectors recovering many times their costs (the multiple for someone dealing with the biggest cases running into three figures), a major recruitment and training drive would pay for itself several times over in the short run. In the long run it is essential for the future of tax collection – where potential avoiders and evaders fear the consequences – that the tax authority becomes a credible force.

Taxation needs to be reclaimed from the vested interests by public and parliament. That MPs were unable to scrutinize major tax avoidance scandals involving Vodafone and Goldman Sachs was itself scandalous. There is no reason why laws governing taxpayer confidentiality should stretch to frustrating the process by which Britain's tax administration ought to be held to account. At a minimum, settlements of tax disputes must be fully open to questioning by the National Audit Office and parliament. In what quickly becomes a closed, stale world if not regularly ventilated, it is essential that there is a powerful incentive to the authorities to apply their laws firmly and objectively and not to give special deals. Parliamentary scrutineers and the taxpayers they represent also need to discover when things are going wrong in the first place, to which end recent history proves the importance of whistle-blowing. Laws imposing blanket 'taxpayer confidentiality' need a rethink. Criminal sanctions against divulging tax information – more absolute even than official secrets legislation governing national security – should be tempered by a public interest justification. Public auditors then need to show they will act properly on information received from whistle-blowers.

Tax belongs to us and, although it is often complicated, we have to get to grips with it. Campaigners need to educate themselves and take on those who would abuse the system and remain unaccountable. Non-governmental organizations need to step up their impressive work to date, acquiring more expertise with which to confront tax avoidance. One effective practical initiative would be to monitor systematically multinationals' tax payments and action (or inaction) against tax avoidance, as far as they can be identified: 'TaxWatch', perhaps. Most of my recommendations demand action from institutions captured by the tax avoidance industry and are consequently optimistic, to say the least. Even in the face of the loudest ever demands for action against tax dodging, national and international political responses have fallen far short of what is required. This final suggestion – the Big Society Revenue & Customs made real – is entirely realistic. The work of holding tax avoidance to account has started. It can go on.

Notes

Prologue

1 PAC, 12 October 2011, q. 1.

1. Welcome To Tax Dodge City

1 www.charityfacts.org/resources/for_the_media/charity_costs/

2 www.oxfam.org.uk/resources/downloads/reports/report_accounts09_10.pdf
Figure includes support costs (9%), governance (approx. 0.5%) and other (approx. 1%).

3 See Commonwealth Fund study 2011; and 'Comparing the USA, UK and 17 Western countries' efficiency and effectiveness in reducing mortality', Colin Pritchard and Mark Wallace, reported by Randeep Ramesh, *Guardian* 7 August 2011 http://www.guardian.co.uk/society/2011/aug/07/nhs-among-most-efficient-health-services

4 See 'Measuring Tax Gaps 2010' available at www.hmrc.gov.uk/stats/measuring-tax-gaps-2010.htm.pdf Direct tax evasion is not separately estimated but amalgamated with non-fraudulent errors. However, the paper suggests that of the total Tax Gap, 'evasion' accounts for 17.5% and 'hidden economy' 7.5%. Treating both of these as evasion and applying the ratio to a total direct Tax Gap of £22bn produces an estimate for direct tax evasion of £5.5bn.

5 See 'Tax Justice and Jobs: the business case for investing in staff at HMRC', by Richard Murphy, March 2010, available at www.taxresearch.org.uk/Documents/PCSTaxGap.pdf and Tax Research blog, January 2010, http://www.taxresearch.org.uk/Blog/2010/01/17/why-wont-hm-revenue-customs-admit-the-scale-of-tax-evasion/ The competing figures from Richard Murphy and HMRC are assessed by HMRC in its response to a Treasury Select Committee report on closing the Tax Gap, 18 May 2012, and a series of Murphy's blog posts of the same date, http://www.taxresearch.org.uk/Blog/ On income tax evasion, HMRC dismisses Murphy's estimate on the grounds that a large proportion of undeclared trading income is paid out to employees under deduction of PAYE and tax is thus eventually paid on the money. Yet much undeclared income is not paid out to employees and any that is will rarely go through the books. HMRC's estimate extrapolates from evasion identified from tax returns examined and almost by definition misses a large

amount of undeclared income. On income tax evasion, although he has probably overestimated the size of the black economy, Murphy is likely to be nearer the mark.

6 Figures for direct and indirect tax prosecutions obtained by the author under freedom of information laws from Crown Prosecution Service, July 2011. Direct tax prosecutions: 30 in 2009/10; indirect 358, of which excise duties fraud 263.

7 From HMRC's 'Child and Working Tax Credit Fraud and Error statistics, 2009/10', published June 2011.

8 Reported in *Being Bold – a radical approach to raising revenue and defeating the deficit*, by the Association of Revenue Customs, published September 2010.

9 This distinction appeared in a 1906 select committee report, and is reported in B.E.V. Sabine's landmark *A History of Income Tax* (London: Allen & Unwin, 1966), as the first usage of the phrase.

10 The chancellor was Sir John Simon. See B.E.V. Sabine, *A History of Tax Avoidance*.

11 Lord Templeman in Commissioner of Inland Revenue v. Challenge Corporation Ltd [1987] AC 155.

12 Evidence of Dave Hartnett, permanent secretary for tax at HMRC, before Treasury Select Committee, 11 March 2011.

13 See HMRC v. Philippa D'Arcy [2007] EWHC 163 (Ch), available at www.bailii.org/cgi-bin/markup.cgi?doc=/ew/cases/EWHC/Ch/2007/163.html&query=d%20arcy&method=boolean

14 Prudential plc v. HMRC [2009] EWCA Civ 622, available at www.bailii.org/cgi-bin/markup.cgi?doc=/ew/cases/EWCA/Civ/2009/622.html&query=prudential&method=boolean

15 Taken from calculations in 'Measuring Tax Gaps 2010'; tax estimated to be recovered on avoidance schemes v. total tax at risk on them.

16 See 'Measuring Tax Gaps 2010'.

17 *Hansard*, 22 July 1914.

18 Sabine, *A History of Tax Avoidance*.

19 http://www.guardian.co.uk/business/2008/may/17/tesco.supermarkets

20 2011 budget speech, 24 March 2011.

21 1. *Retail Week* conference, March 2003, reported in *Retail Week*, 7 March 2003; 2. *Daily Telegraph* report, 24 October 2003; 3. *Evening Standard*, 12 July 2004; 4. *Mail on Sunday*, 5 September 2004, reporting Dorothy Perkins annual meeting; 5. Interview, *Guardian*, 23 October 2004; 6. *Daily Mail*, 27 October 2006.

22 See Alliance Boots' 2010/11 accounts at media.allianceboots.com/App_Media/AllianceBoots/Financial%20information/AllianceBootsAnnualReport2010–11.pdf

23 This was one of several tax avoidance schemes reported by the *Guardian* in its Tax Gap series in February 2009, to which the author contributed. For the Diageo story see www.guardian.co.uk/business/2009/feb/02/tax-gap-diageo-johnnie-walker

24 See Treasury Select Committee press notice covering its report on Mapeley, 12 February 2003: www.parliament.uk/business/committees/committees-archive/treasury-committee/tc120203-18/

25 Survey conducted for BBC by ComRes. Other questions revealed that 60% of people thought tax avoidance should be cracked down on 'even if it causes unemployment, or some companies to leave the UK' – both in fact unlikely consequences of a crackdown. Forty-nine percent of people agreed that 'if

companies can reduce the amount of tax they pay then they should do so because their first duty is to maximize returns to their shareholders'. But this statement does not mention using tax avoidance to achieve this reduction. www.comres. co.uk/bbcradio4decisiontimejun11.aspx

26 See 'Measuring Tax Gaps'; this figure is the sum of £2.9bn avoided by companies dealt with by the Large Business Service and £0.9bn avoided by companies in the (confusingly) 'large and complex' band. There appears to be no avoidance measured for small and medium-sized companies.

27 'The Missing Billions – The UK Tax Gap, 2008', written for the TUC by Richard Murphy. These figures are vigorously disputed by the government and may include some legitimate tax reliefs. But just like the official Tax Gap figures, they effectively leave out much tax-motivated offshore structuring that amounts to real world tax avoidance. They look at the difference between a multinational's effective tax rate and the headline UK rate, when a large group's overall rate should reflect the fact that many make a large proportion of their profits in countries where tax rates are much higher, e.g. the US. Overall they are likely to be nearer the mark than the government's figures. Available at www.tuc.org.uk/touchstone/Missin gbillions/1missingbillions.pdf

28 FoI response to author, 20 June 2011.

29 Estimate based on breakdown provided to author under freedom of information laws, September 2011, now at http://www.hmrc.gov.uk/freedom/type-of-risk. htm

30 From 'HM Treasury Spending Review, October 2010', Table A.2, cdn.hm-treasury. gov.uk/sr2010_completereport.pdf

31 'Corporate Tax Reform: delivering a more competitive system', November 2010; www.hm-treasury.gov.uk/d/corporate_tax_reform_complete_document.pdf

32 See *Private Eye* issue 1231, February 2009.

33 See for example; www.dailymail.co.uk/news/article-459766/City-fat-cats-paying-tax-cleaners.html This gratuitous tax giveaway has been half-heartedly reversed, but at 28% capital gains are still taxed much more lightly than income for high earners, and the tax avoidance opening remains.

34 Interview with author, 2011.

35 Corporation tax payments taken from HMRC statistics; www.hmrc.gov.uk/ stats/tax_receipts/tax-receipts-and-taxpayers.pdf; corporate profitability figures from Office for National Statistics, series CBGY. While these figures have to be treated with some caution – the corporate profitability figures used are for British corporations excluding foreign companies operating and paying tax here – the trend is a marked diversion between profits growth and tax receipts growth.

36 Ibid.

37 'The Missing Billions – The UK tax gap', published by the TUC, 2008.

38 There is no official breakdown of private sector profits according to size of company, but in 2000 'small and medium-sized enterprises' were estimated to employ 54% of the private sector workforce; in 2011 the figure was 59% (source: DTI; BIS), implying a small increase in smaller companies' share of the economy.

39 Based on HMRC CT statistics, table 11.1A. 'Small company' is defined as one not required to make quarterly corporation tax instalment payments, the threshold for which is annual profits of £1.5m.

40 'Responding to the global financial and economic crisis: the tax dimension. 2nd Meeting of the SEE Working Group on Tax Policy Analysis', 16–19 June 2009, Dubrovnik. W. Steven Clark, CTPA, OECD, Christian Valenduc, Belgian Ministry of Finance, see http://www.oecd.org/dataoecd/9/38/43215230.pdf

41 Deloitte tax directors' academy, 23 November 2010.

42 Dave Hartnett, speaking at International Tax Conference, Mumbai, December 2010, reported in *Private Eye* issue 1277.

43 Quoted in Nick Shaxson, *Treasure Islands* (London: Random House, 2011).

44 See, for example, www.hm-treasury.gov.uk/d/corporate_tax_reform_part3b_foreign_branch_taxation.pdf

45 Sabine, *A History of Income Tax.* Leader of the Whigs was J.C. Hobhouse. The landed Tory was Sir John Sinclair MP.

46 Exchequer secretary David Gauke admitted as much when responding to a BBC Radio 4 interviewer asking about offshore tax concessions. He told *The Report*, 30 December 2011: 'Obviously a company that relocates outside the UK [if the tax breaks aren't given] isn't going to be paying any tax here at all.' This completely missed the point that it is only head offices that move and companies' UK businesses pay tax in the UK in exactly the same way as before. Reported in *Private Eye*, issue 1279.

47 Calculated from ONS GDP figures, series PUBL published June 2012; HMRC statistics for tax rates.

48 *False Assumptions*, Institute of Public Policy Research, 21 May 2012.

49 For details of funding see http://www.sbs.ox.ac.uk/centres/tax/about/Pages/Funding.aspx

50 See W. Arulampalam, M.P. Devereux and G. Maffini, 'The direct incidence of corporate income tax on wages', Centre for Business Taxation Working Paper CBTWP07/07, 2007, and, countering this view, the Institute on Taxation and Economic Policy www.itepnet.org/pdf/guide6.pdf

51 For a compelling defence of the case for corporation tax, see the following article by Nick Shaxson, 15 March 2011; www.guardian.co.uk/commentisfree/2011/mar/15/tax-corporations-treasury-large-companies

52 HMRC website, 'Tax on UK Dividends'; http://www.hmrc.gov.uk/taxon/uk.htm#3

53 Speech by David Gauke to Deloitte Tax Directors' Academy, 23 November 2010; www.hm-treasury.gov.uk/speech_xst_231110.htm

54 Ibid.

2. An Unwelcome Guest

1 Quoted in Sabine, *A History of Income Tax*, p. 31.

2 Ibid., p. 18.

3 Board of Inland Revenue report, 1872.

4 1914 Finance Bill debate, *Hansard*, column 679. By 1914/15 direct taxes were estimated to account for 59.5% of government revenues.

5 Sabine, p. 183, quoting a report of a 1920 Select Committee of MPs.

6 The episode is vividly recounted by author Nick Shaxson in *Treasure Islands*.

7 ONS and Companies House info.

8 Nigel Tutt, *The History of Tax Avoidance* (London: Wisdene Ltd, 1989).

9 Letter forwarded by Tony Benn MP to Denis Healey, 3 June 1975, quoted in *Treasure Islands.*

10 Judgment in Griffiths (Inspector of Taxes) v. J.P. Harrison (Watford) Ltd, March 1962.

11 Ayrshire Pullman Motor Services v. Inland Revenue [1929] 14 Tax Case 754, at 763, 764.

12 IRC v. Duke of Westminster [1936] 19 TC 490.

13 Michael Gillard, *In the Name of Charity: the Rossminster Affair* (London: Chatto & Windus, 1987).

14 Obituary of Edmund Vestey, *Daily Telegraph* 29 November 2007.

15 Nigel Tutt, *The History of Tax Avoidance*, (London: Wisdene Ltd, 1989).

16 Nigel Tutt, *The Tax Raiders* (London: Financial Publications Ltd, 1985) is a comprehensive and occasionally sympathetic insider account, while Gillard, *In the Name of Charity*, is an excoriating exposé.

17 The full version, not for the easily offended, is reproduced in Tutt's *The Tax Raiders*.

18 Quoted by Gillard in *In the Name of Charity*, p. 191, from interview with *World in Action*, 1980.

19 Ibid.

20 The case is reported as W.T. Ramsay Ltd v. Inland Revenue Commissioners [1981] UKHL 1 (12 March 1981).

21 Gillard, *In the Name of Charity*, p. 259.

22 Comments made to *Observer* newspaper, 4 November 1979, quoted by Gillard, p. 232.

23 Ensign Tankers Ltd v. Stokes (HM Inspector of Taxes), House of Lords 12 March 1992.

24 The partnership is Ingenious Film Partners LLP. In 2012 HMRC concluded its enquiries into the scheme, the prelude to a tax tribunal hearing. Reported in *Financial Times*, 21 September 2012; http://www.ft.com/cms/s/0/8eab614c-0408-11e2-b91b-00144feabdc0.html#axzz27i1NBayq

25 For a useful analysis of this period of British economic history and its role in creating the unsustainable pre-financial crisis economy of 2007, see Larry Elliott and Dan Atkinson, *Fantasy Island* (London: Constable and Robinson, 2007).

3. Opportunity Knocks

1 Prudential Plc v. Revenue and Customs [2007] UKSPC SPC00636 (11 September 2007).

2 Dave Hartnett evidence to Lords Economic Affairs Select Committee, 27 April 2004, Q76, see http://www.publications.parliament.uk/pa/ld200304/ldselect/ldeconaf/109/4042702.htm

3 First reported as A PLC, Re an Application by the Commissioners for her Majesty's Revenue and Customs to serve a Section 20(3) TMA 1970 Notice [2007] UKSPC SPC00647 (16 November 2007). The decision was upheld in the High Court and the Court of Appeal and was to be heard by the Supreme Court in November 2012.

NOTES

4 Prudential plc Annual Report 2002; see p. 46 and note 16 for more detail on tax charge. Operating profit after tax and related minority interests before amortization of goodwill, used for earnings per share calculation, was £314m in 2002.

5 Over the second half of the 1990s the market in bespoke 'over the counter' derivatives that the Ernst & Young scheme would draw on for its tax-efficient off-market swaps had doubled in scale. See Bank for International Settlements quarterly reviews, at www.bis.org/publ/qtrpdf

6 *Daily Telegraph* report 27 May 2003; see http://www.telegraph.co.uk/finance/personalfinance/2853092/Taxman-makes-accountants-see-red.html

7 See, for example, PA Holdings Ltd & Anor v. Revenue and Customs [2009] UKFTT 95 (TC) (7 May 2009).

8 Statement by Mark Everson 29 August 2005; see http://www.irs.gov/newsroom/article/0,,id=146998,00.html

9 Trevor Smallwood Trust v. Revenue and Customs [2008] UKSPC SPC00669.

10 Drummond v. Revenue & Customs [2007] UKSPC SPC00617 (05 July 2007).

11 Astall & Anor v. Revenue and Customs Rev 1 [2007] UKSPC SPC00628.

12 Interview with *Accountancy Age*, 20 October 2005; see http://www.accountancyage.com/aa/analysis/1783630/the-taxman-tough

13 http://www.hmrc.gov.uk/stats/tax_receipts/1_2_v2_dec05.pdf

14 HMRC v. Debenhams Retail plc, Court of Appeal, 2005; http://www.bailii.org/cgi-bin/markup.cgi?doc=/ew/cases/EWCA/Civ/2005/892.html&query=debenhams+and+vat&method=boolean

15 Based on tax returns up to 2002/03 as judged by Inland Revenue case directors, information obtained in freedom of information request by author, reported in *Private Eye* issue 1222, November 2009.

16 Reported by *Guardian* 1 July 2002.

17 D. Hartnett, evidence to Lords Economic Affairs committee, 23 May 2011.

18 Written ministerial statement, 2 December 2004, *Hansard*, column 45WS; see http://www.publications.parliament.uk/pa/cm200405/cmhansrd/vo041202/wmstext/41202m02.htm#41202m02.html_spmin0

19 Interview with *Daily Telegraph*, 31 January 2005, see http://www.telegraph.co.uk/finance/personalfinance/2904681/Backdated-tax-would-trap-unwary-workers.html

20 Written ministerial statement, 20 January 2006, and Hartnett's evidence to committee 27 May 2006.

21 Freedom of information request by author, available on HMRC website under FoI disclosures.

22 HMRC disclosure statistics; http://www.hmrc.gov.uk/avoidance/statsmarch12.pdf Stamp duty land tax schemes are ignored as these are individual schemes not marketed, are generally small and distort the figures.

23 Interview with Alex Hawkes, *Accountancy Age*, 6 October 2005; see http://www.accountancyage.com/aa/news/1756561/death-knell-sounds-avoidance

24 Interview with author, 2011.

25 House of Lords decision [2004] UKHL 51; previously in Court of Appeal as [2002] EWCA 1853.

26 'Fundamental review of major cases', internal HMRC report, 2004, provided to the author.

27 Bank of England 'Financial Stability Report', December 2011, chart 5.6.

28 *Wall Street Journal*, 30 June 2006.

29 See, for example, *Daily Mail*, 19 January 2007, 'How shamed athlete's brother is sprinting to £75m'; http://www.dailymail.co.uk/news/article-429861/How-shamed-athletes-brother-sprinting-75m.html

30 Evidence submitted by HMRC to Treasury Select Committee, June 2011; see http://www.publications.parliament.uk/pa/cm201011/cmselect/cmtreasy/writev/hmrc/m36.htm

31 Information gleaned from accounts of Barclays Assurance (Dublin) Ltd and Barclays Insurance (Dublin) Ltd available at Irish companies register. Reported in *Mail on Sunday*, 21 October 2007, and interviews with author.

32 A number of researchers have counted these. Discussed at Treasury Select Committee, 11 January 2011.

33 For a brief outline of each case, see http://www.guardian.co.uk/business/2009/mar/20/barclays-tax-documents-guardian Further details seen by the author.

34 *Guardian* 19 March 2009; see http://www.guardian.co.uk/business/2009/mar/19/new-barclays-tax-whistleblower-claims

35 See *Guardian* report 11 February 2009, at http://www.guardian.co.uk/business/2009/feb/11/tax-gap-lloyds

36 Treasury Select Committee, 11 February 2009; http://www.publications.parliament.uk/pa/cm200809/cmselect/cmtreasy/144/144i.pdf

37 Treasury Select Committee, 11 January 2011; http://www.publications.parliament.uk/pa/cm201011/cmselect/cmtreasy/uc612-vi/uc61201.htm

38 http://www.guardian.co.uk/media/2011/feb/18/guardian-barclays-tax-secrets

39 Information provided by HMRC to Jesse Norman MP as part of 2011 Treasury Select Committee enquiry into the administration of HMRC.

4. Foreign Adventures

1 'Implementing a Treasury Center in Switzerland', Ernst & Young; http://www2.eycom.ch/publications/items/tax_fs_treasury/en.pdf

2 Among several cases before the European Court of Justice at the time were Lankhorst-Hohorts (C-234/00), challenging German tax laws that limited tax deductions for interest payments to foreign holding companies and Hoescht (C-410/98) and Metallgesellschaft (C-397/98), challenging UK tax laws that charged 'advance corporation tax' on dividends paid to non-resident companies but not on those to British companies. These claims were successful during 2001 (Hoescht and Metallgesellschaft) and 2002 (Lankhorst). But they did not herald the end of national governments' defences against cross-border tax avoidance within the EU as some companies hoped. Within a few years further challenges to domestic anti-tax avoidance laws would be less successful, and the early 2000s would be seen as the high-water mark for the encroachment of European law on domestic tax laws.

3 De Beers, 5TC213.

4 This figure emerges in one of the many court cases concerning the scheme, [2006] EWCA Civ 1132, judgment paragraph 9.

5 See Vodafone group accounts for year ended 31 March 2001, notes 14 and 15. Total loans for the group were £14.2bn, equivalent to €22bn.

NOTES

6 Accounts of Vodafone Investments Luxembourg sarl are available from the Luxembourg companies register, www.rcsl.lu

7 Cadbury Schweppes and Cadbury Schweppes Overseas, Judgment of European Court, 12 September 2006 case C-196/04; http://curia.europa.eu/juris/showPdf.jsf?text=&docid=63874&pageIndex=0&doclang=en&mode=doc&dir=&occ=first&part=1&cid=656006

8 All accounts available from rcsl.lu.

9 Information provided in parliamentary answer to Rt Hon. David Davis MP, *Hansard*, 28 April 2011, col 517W.

10 Vodafone's results announcement on 23 July 2010 reported: 'On 22 July 2010 Vodafone reached agreement with the UK tax authorities with respect to the CFC tax case. Vodafone will pay £1.25bn to settle all outstanding CFC issues from 2001 to date and has also reached agreement that no further UK CFC tax liabilities will arise in the near future under current legislation. Longer term, no CFC liabilities are expected to arise as a consequence of the likely reforms of the UK CFC regime due to the facts established in this agreement. The settlement comprises £800m in the current financial year with the balance to be paid in instalments over the following five years.'

11 Bloomberg survey, reported in *Guardian*, 30 November 2010.

12 Vodafone investor presentation, 23 July 2010; recorded by Thomson Street Events.

13 Progressive Tax Blog, 13 February 2011; since removed from web but available on Nick Shaxson's Treasure Islands website at http://treasureislands.org/progressive-tax-blog-reloaded/

14 Vodafone earnings call, 14 November 2006.

15 http://www.linkedin.com/in/foleykevin; http://www.linkedin.com/pub/sean-cosgrove/9/a89/3ba

16 *Private Eye*, issue 1270, 2 September 2010.

17 Vodafone Luxembourg 5 sarl accounts available from Luxembourg companies register. This scheme was reported in *Private Eye* issue 1305, January 2012.

18 Alex Brummer, *Daily Mail*, 20 October 2011.

19 Stephen Barclay MP, speaking at the Public Accounts Committee, 6 November 2011, 'We are looking at potentially £8bn of tax lost.'

20 Interviews with author, 2011.

21 Dave Hartnett, Treasury Select Committee, 16 March 2011.

22 David Gauke speech to Deloitte tax directors' academy, 23 November 2010; http://www.hm-treasury.gov.uk/speech_xst_231110.htm

23 Vodafone results announcements, 23 July 2010.

24 Treasury press notice announcing working groups, 29 November 2010; http://www.hm-treasury.gov.uk/consult_cfc_reform.htm

25 The documents would form the basis of a France 2 documentary, *Les Petits Secrets des Grandes Enterprises*, produced by Premières Lignes, broadcast May 2012.

26 Survey can be found on ActionAid's Tax Justice Campaign website; http://www.actionaid.org.uk/103031/ftse_100_tax_haven_tracker.html

27 'Why Luxembourg? A Unique Location to Expand your Business', by PwC and the American Chamber of Commerce in Luxembourg; http://www.setupineurope.com/setupineurope/docs/pwc-why-luxembourg.pdf

28 IMF World Economic Outlook, 2010 for GDP per capita; on EU deficits see, for example, http://www.europolitics.info/ireland-and-greece-top-eu-list-art269835-28.html Luxembourg deficit in 2009 was 0.7% of GDP (the UK's was 11.5%) and its debt as a proportion of GDP 14.7%.

29 Treasury press release, 30 June 2011, announcing 5.75% tax rate for offshore financing profits.

30 For an analysis of Tesco's tax bills, showing average 'tax paid' of 22.6%, see a blog by Richard Murphy, Tax Research LLP; http://www.taxresearch.org.uk/Blog/2008/05/19/tescos-tax-weve-got-a-right-to-talk-about-it/

31 From accounts of Cheshunt Overseas LLP, available from Companies House website.

32 See Financial Secretary Jane Kennedy's speech to the Finance Bill committee, 3 June 2008; http://www.publications.parliament.uk/pa/cm200708/cmpublic/finance/080603/am/80603s01.htm

33 The cases are reported in full in *Private Eye* issues 1211 and 1212, May 2008.

34 Hearing on Tesco Stores Ltd v. Guardian News & Media Ltd & Alan Rusbridger, attended by author, July 2008.

35 Reported in A. Rusbridger, 'A Chill on the Guardian', *New York Review of Books*, 15 January 2009.

36 See Judith Freedman, Geoffrey Loomer and John Vella, 'Moving Beyond Avoidance?', Oxford University Centre for Business Taxation, Saïd Business School, June 2007.

5. Breaking Up Isn't Hard to Do

1 Allison Christians, 'Networks, Norms and National Tax Policy', University of Wisconsin, 2010, citing League of Nations, Econ. & Fin. Comm'n, Report on Double Taxation Submitted to the Financial Comm., by Profs Bruins, Einaudi, Seligman and Sir Josiah Stamp, League of Nations Doc. E.F.S.73 F. 19 (1923).

2 The Carroll Report to the League of Nations identified the problem and recommended the solution.

3 Set up as the Organization for European Economic Cooperation, a body of seventeen European countries. Became the OECD in 1961, extending membership beyond Europe, notably to US and Japan.

4 Figures taken from Diageo plc's 2010 annual report. Tax paid as per cash flow statement; profits are pre-tax profits as per consolidated profit and loss account. Note 7 gives details of UK tax credits and charges; http://www.diageo.com/Lists/Resources/Attachments/640/Diageo_AR10_full_report.pdf

5 Diageo plc annual report, year ended 30 June 2009.

6 *Guardian*, 5 February 2009, 'How to save a packet'; http://www.guardian.co.uk/business/2009/feb/05/tax-gap-walkers

7 Widely reported. See for example *Independent*, 24 February 2010; http://www.independent.co.uk/news/business/news/astrazeneca-agrees-to-pay-163505m-to-settle-15year-tax-battle-1908490.html

8 The precise details of the case are, like all investigations that don't make it to court, confidential. This information is gleaned from limited press reports based

on Glaxo's financial announcements and interviews with people close to the case. Only in Canada did the transfer pricing issues associated with Zantac reach a court (GlaxoSmithkline Inc v. The Queen, of which there is a useful summary at http://moorestephensresources.com.au/articles/386/1/GlaxoSmithKline-Inc-v-The-Queen/Page1.html)

9 See GlaxoSmithKline annual report 2010, available at http://www.gsk.com/content/dam/gsk/globals/documents/pdf/GSK-Annual-Report-2010.pdf, tax position explained at note 14. £4.5bn was before restructuring costs. Profit after these was £3.16bn.

10 Details emerged in litigation in Delaware, June 2010, concerning patent infringement. Patent for underlying drug Rosuvastatin earned by a Japanese company, licensed to IPR Parmaceuticals Inc then on-licensed as Crestor. Accessed at http://www.scribd.com/doc/33834634/In-re-Rosuvastatin-Calcium-Patent-Litig-C-A-No-08-1949-JJF-LPS-D-Del-June-29-2010-Farnan-J

11 The company now shaves several hundred million dollars off its annual tax bill by using such territories. See, for example, AstraZeneca annual report 2011, note 4. The savings from lower overseas tax rates are $340m. As this is a net figure incorporating higher tax bills in, for example, the US, the saving from using low tax territories is even higher.

12 From KPMG's Swiss website; http://www.kpmg.com/ch/en/whatwedo/tax/international-corporate-tax/services/pages/tescm.aspx, picked up by Richard Murphy and decoded by him on http://www.taxresearch.org.uk/Blog/2011/06/09/tax-efficient-supply-chain-management-or-how-kpmg-sell-tax-haven-services-to-capture-tax-revenues-for-private-gain/

13 £2.7m in 2009 and a repayment from the Exchequer to the company of £1.8m in 2010; company accounts available from Companies House.

14 All accounts available from Companies House and the Dutch Trade Register; www.kvk.nl/english/traderegister/default.asp

15 Tom Bergin, 'How Starbucks Avoids UK Taxes', Reuters, 15 October 2012; http://uk.reuters.com/article/2012/10/15/us-britain-starbucks-tax-idUKBRE89E0EX20121015

16 From Microsoft Ltd accounts for year ended 31 December 2010, available at Companies House.

17 Figures reported by John Collins in *Irish Times*, 20 April 2011; http://www.irishtimes.com/newspaper/finance/2011/0420/1224295068643.html

18 Microsoft Corporation Annual Report 2010, available at http://www.microsoft.com/investor/reports/ar10/index.html

19 Exposed and very well explained by Jesse Drucker at Bloomberg, online at http://www.bloomberg.com/news/2010-10-21/google-2-4-rate-shows-how-60-billion-u-s-revenue-lost-to-tax-loopholes.html

20 Accenture UK Ltd accounts for year ended 31 August 2011 and information provided to Edouard Perrin on PwC-advised schemes run through Luxembourg (see chapter 4).

21 Alliance Boots plc accounts for year ended 31 March 2007; Boots Company accounts for year ended 31 March 2000.

22 Alliance Boots accounts, available at http://www.allianceboots.com/financial-information/annual-report.aspx

23 Accounts available from Companies House. See for example Alliance Boots Unichem Flex LLP.

24 Analysed in Robert Peston, *Who Runs Britain?* (London: Hodder & Stoughton, 2008), in a section of the book headed 'We are all subsidizing private equity'.

25 Reported by Corporate Watch, 17 March 2012; http://www.corporatewatch.org/?lid=4251

26 According to 2011 figures from UK Trade and Investments, the government investment promotion body; see http://www.ukti.gov.uk/fr_fr/uktihome/home/item/print/172480.html

27 In 2010 Kraft bought Cadbury. In less than a year the UK vehicle it used, Chromium Acquisitions Ltd, paid £172m in interest to offshore companies in the group. Since this was available for set-off against other companies' profits, for that year the main company Cadbury UK Ltd showed a net tax credit and no tax payment. See accounts for Chromium Acquisition Ltd and Cadbury UK Ltd, year ended 31 December 2010, available from Companies House.

28 Treasury Select Committee report, 30 July 2007; http://www.publications.parliament.uk/pa/cm200607/cmselect/cmtreasy/567/56709.htm

29 Mirlees Review, conducted by Professor James Mirlees with Institute of Fiscal Studies, reported 13 September 2011; see http://www.ifs.org.uk/mirrleesReview

30 Speech to Policy Exchange think-tank, 22 March 2010.

31 For an overview of the market, see http://www.thecityuk.com/assets/Uploads/Hedge-funds-2011.pdf, downloaded from Wikipedia entry on hedge funds.

32 *AIMA Journal*, April 2003.

33 Based on an investigation by the Bureau of Investigative Journalism, using data from 2005 to February 2011, available at http://www.thebureauinvestigates.com/2011/02/08/the-data-top-ten-city-financiers-of-the-tory-party/

34 Information from accounts for y/e 31/12/2010 for CQS (UK) LLP and CQS Management Ltd.

35 ISAM (UK) Ltd accounts, year ended 30 June 2011.

36 Quoted in *Wall Street Journal*, 19 September 2006.

37 Research by the author in 2009, reported on *Guardian* blog.

38 See HMRC's 'regulatory impact assessment', http://customs.hmrc.gov.uk/channelsPortalWebApp/channelsPortalWebApp.portal?_nfpb=true&_pageLabel=pageLibrary_ShowContent&id=HMCE_PROD1_026219&propertyType=document

6. A Rich Man's Kingdom

1 The turning point was the 'Bosman ruling' of 1995. Some limitations, beyond the scope of this book, have been reimposed for younger players.

2 Finance Bill debate, 23 July 1914, *Hansard*, vol. 65, column 681.

3 Ibid.

4 Freedom of information response from HM Treasury, 2007, reported by *Sunday Times* 22 July 2007.

NOTES

5 From Special Commissioners for Income Tax Case SC3114-16/99, Sports Club, Evelyn and Jocelyn v. HM Inspector of Taxes, available at http://www.taxbar.com/documents/sports_club_sp.pdf

6 Ibid.

7 The names appear to have been inspired by Evelyn Waugh's satire on the press, *Scoop!*

8 Conal Walsh, Denis Campbell and Anthony Barnett, *Observer*, 6 June 2004; http://www.guardian.co.uk/media/2004/jun/06/football.advertising

9 Reported by Laura Williamson, *Daily Mail*, 21 January 2010; http://www.dailymail.co.uk/sport/football/article-1244847/Sol-Campbell-sues-troubled-Portsmouth-money-owed-Arsenal-defender.html

10 Robert Watts, Maurice Chittenden, Cal Flyn, *Sunday Times* 16 January 2011, http://www.thesundaytimes.co.uk/sto/news/uk_news/National/article511761.ece?lightbox=false

11 Judgment of Lord Justice Thorpe in Parlour v. Parlour, Court of Appeal, 7 July 2004; http://www.bailii.org/cgi-bin/markup.cgi?doc=/ew/cases/EWCA/Civ/2004/872.html&query=arsenal+and+parlour&method=boolean

12 Robert Winnet and David Robertson, *Sunday Times*, 13 August 2003.

13 MacDonald (HMIT) v. Dextra Accessories Ltd & Others, see http://www.hmrc.gov.uk/practitioners/macdonald-v-dextra.htm

14 From official Premier League history; http://www.premierleague.com/page/History/0,,12306,00.html

15 McFarlane v. McFarlane [2009] EWHC 891 (Fam).

16 Murray Wardrop, *Daily Telegraph*, 10 June 2011; http://www.telegraph.co.uk/news/uknews/theroyalfamily/8567222/Duke-and-Duchess-of-Cambridge-in-first-public-event-as-married-couple.html

17 Ibid.

18 From 2009 and 2010 accounts of EIM (United Kingdom) Ltd, available at Companies House.

19 See EIM website, http://www.eimgroup.com/en/home.php

20 Partner from Simmons and Simmons, quoted in House of Commons library research paper SN/BT/4604 'Taxation of Non-Domiciles', 7 May 2008.

21 The 700 comes from http://www.thecityuk.com/assets/Uploads/Hedge-funds-2011.pdf

22 Will Hutton, 'As We Suffer, City Speculators are Moving in for the Kill', *Observer*, 29 June 2008.

23 According to economist Ha Joon Chang, 'it is estimated that the stock of financial assets to world output rose from 1.2 to 4.0 between 1980 and 2007 ... the ratio of financial assets to GDP in the UK reached 700 percent in 2007'. From *23 Things They Don't Tell You About Capitalism* (London: Penguin, 2010), citing Gabriel Palma, *Cambridge Journal of Economics*, 2009, vol. 33, no.4.

24 'Institutional Investment in the UK: a Review', Paul Myners, 6 March 2001, fig 12.2; http://archive.treasury.gov.uk/pdf/2001/myners_report.pdf

25 Ibid., fig 12.2.

26 Ibid., para 12.3.

27 Robert Peston, *Who Runs Britain?*

28 Treasury Select Committee report on private equity, 24 July 2007, paragraph 9.

29 Reported in *Daily Mail*, 5 June 2007.

30 Treasury Select Committee report on private equity, 24 July 2007, paragraph 85.

31 Robert Peston, *Who Runs Britain?*

32 *Observer*, 17 June 2007; http://www.guardian.co.uk/business/2007/jun/17/executivepay

33 See "Key dealmakers facing questions", *Daily Telegraph* 21 Jun 2007.

34 *Daily Telegraph*, 24 June 2007; http://www.telegraph.co.uk/finance/migration temp/2811018/Just-one-KKR-partner-pays-tax-in-Britain.html

35 *Daily Mail*, 13 March 2009; http://www.dailymail.co.uk/news/article-1161642/As-France-rejoins-NATO-humorous-reminder-missed-them.html

36 *Private Eye*, issue 1231, March 2009.

37 See DMGT plc annual report 2010, p. 59 for details of beneficial shareholding and p. 151 for dividends per share; http://www.dmgt.co.uk/uploads/files/6423-DMGT-AR-2010-5JAN2011-FINAL-Linked.pdf

38 This tale was fully recounted in *Private Eye*, issue 1231, February 2009.

39 Available on YouTube; http://www.youtube.com/watch?v=JGwuf2ZQ7RA&feature=related

40 Details of the Barclay Brothers' tax arrangements emerged in a High Court case in 2012, see [2012] EWHC 2343 (Ch).

41 Labour Party conference speech, 1996.

42 Widely reported during coverage of a scandal concerning Tory donor Lord Ashcoft's tax status in March 2010, see for example www.guardian.co.uk/politics/2010/mar/09/lord-paul-non-dom-status

43 Financial Secretary Jane Kennedy MP said in parliament:'Resident non-domiciled people remain a relatively small group who are liable to pay UK tax on their earnings in the UK. Indeed, the Exchequer benefits to the tune of £3 billion.' *Hansard* debates, 12 July 2007, column 1605.

44 HM Treasury/HMRC, 'Reviewing the residence and domicile rules as they affect the taxation of individuals: a background paper'. See paragraph 2.14; two thirds of non-domiciled residents estimated to work in banking and financial services: http://www.hm-treasury.gov.uk./budget/bud_bud03/associated_documents/bud_bud03_adres.cfm

45 Parliamentary answer 4 February 2011, c556W.

46 Blog entry, 9 September 2007 http://www.taxresearch.org.uk/Blog/2007/09/09/the-domicile-rule-costs-£43-billion/

47 *Sunday Times* Rich List 2012. The exceptions appear to be Philip Green, whose wealth is held in trusts for the benefit of his Monaco-resident wife anyway; Richard Branson, whose personal tax affairs remain a closed book even though he controls his business empire through British Virgin Islands trusts; the Duke of Westminster; Earl Cadogan and Sir Anthony Bamford.

48 Jim Cousins MP, *Hansard*, 12 July 2007.

49 http://www.telegraph.co.uk/finance/economics/2785187/CBI-blasts-non-dom-plans-as-criticism-mounts.html

50 http://www.ft.com/cms/s/0/08e4c3d4-6458-11df-8cba-00144feab49a.html#axzz1XpkSlwgn

51 Home Office press release, 'Government rolls out the red carpet for entrepreneurs and investors', 11 March 2011.

52 United Trust, Russia private clients conference, Zurich, 29 February 2012.

53 See ArcelorMittal annual report 2011, map of global presence.

54 Mike Truman, writing in *Taxation* magazine, February 2008, quoted in House of Commons library note SN/BT/4604 written by Antony Seely, 7 May 2008; http://www.parliament.uk/briefing-papers/SN04604

7. Sell-Out

1 Based on personal recollection and believed to be a reasonable paraphrase.

2 'Review of Links with Business', Inland Revenue, November 2001.

3 Nick Davies, *Guardian*, 23 and 24 July 2002.

4 HMRC departmental board meeting 13 August 2007; http://www.hmrc.gov. uk/about/minutes-aug07.htm

5 'Review of Information Security', Kieron Poynter, June 2008.

6 CBI press release, 4 November 2005.

7 CBI Annual Conference, 28 November 2005.

8 Make-up and remit explained in Large Corporates presentation 18 May 2006; http://www.hmrc.gov.uk/lbo/review-of-links.pdf

9 Whistle-blower letter to *Private Eye*, July 2012.

10 Interview with author.

11 'UK business tax: a compelling case for change', CBI, November 2006; http:// www.cbi.org.uk/media/999090/cbi_tax_report_text.pdf

12 *Financial Times* comment piece, 'Why the Chancellor is Missing the Point', 15 July 1999.

13 Freedom of information response to author, October 2008; http://www.hmrc. gov.uk/freedom/board-hospitality.pdf

14 A review by the Bureau of Investigative Journalism, June 2010, found Hartnett had received hospitality on 107 occasions between April 2007 and September 2009, which was in fact a lower rate than for previous periods; http://www. thebureauinvestigates.com/2010/06/17/bureau-publishes-comprehensive-civil-service-hospitality-database/

15 Discussion with author, September 2009.

16 Reported in trade magazine the *Post*, 9 September 2009; http://www.postonline. co.uk/post/news/1532892/rsa-launches-reinsurer-scrapping-tax

17 Email from HMRC press office to author, 23 September 2009.

18 See, for example, Public Accounts Committee hearing 12 October 2011; http:// www.publications.parliament.uk/pa/cm201012/cmselect/cmpubacc/uc1531-i/ uc153101.htm

19 BT 2006/07 third quarter results announcement, transcript at http://www. btplc.com/Sharesandperformance/Quarterlyresults/Financialpresentations/ q307transcript.pdf

20 See, for example, evidence of Judith Freedman to Treasury Select Committee, 29 June 2011; http://www.publications.parliament.uk/pa/cm201012/cmselect/ cmtreasy/uc731-v/uc73101.htm

21 Information provided to author and reported in *Private Eye*, May 2008, issue 1211.

NOTES

22 Interview with *Guardian* Tax Gap reporting team, reported in *Guardian*, 6 February 2009; http://www.guardian.co.uk/business/2009/feb/06/tax-gap-gamekeeper-inland-revenue

23 National Audit Office report on HMRC annual accounts 2010/11 shows 'value of open issues for Large Business Service Companies' falling from £35.1bn in 2007 to £25.5bn in 2011. See figure 4; www.hmrc.gov.uk/about/annual-report-accounts-1011.pdf

24 Provided to author under freedom of information; available at http://www.hmrc.gov.uk/freedom/type-of-risk.htm

25 Freedom of information response to author, December 2011.

26 Interview with author, 2012.

27 Penalties given in freedom of information request to author, available at http://www.hmrc.gov.uk/freedom/penalties-lbs.htm. Yield from LBS enquiries was £3.9bn in 2006/07 and £5.7bn in 2010/11; see HMRC evidence to Treasury Select Committee, June 2011, http://www.parliament.uk/business/committees/committees-a-z/commons-select/treasury-committee/publications/

28 Public Accounts Committee report on 'Management of Large Business Corporation Tax', 2 June 2008; http://www.publications.parliament.uk/pa/cm200708/cmselect/cmpubacc/302/302.pdf

29 Evidence to Public Accounts Committee, 7 November 2011; http://www.publications.parliament.uk/pa/cm201012/cmselect/cmpubacc/uc1531-ii/uc153101.htm

30 John Kay, *Financial Times*, 16 November 2011.

31 National Audit Office report on HMRC annual accounts 2010/11, part 2, 'The Resolution of Tax Disputes'.

32 Evidence submitted by Association of Revenue and Customs to Treasury Select Committee, March 2011; http://www.publications.parliament.uk/pa/cm201012/cmselect/cmtreasy/731/731.pdf

33 Figures given on HMRC internal website, reported by whistle-blower to *Private Eye* July 2012.

34 List of corporation tax tribunal decisions provided to Jesse Norman MP in course of Treasury Select Committee enquiry, seen by author. No avoidance transactions considered by the tribunals or courts took place after 2003. In evidence to the committee, HMRC said that in the previous five years it had litigated seventy-three 'corporate avoidance' cases; http://www.publications.parliament.uk/pa/cm201012/cmselect/cmtreasy/731/731.pdf Of these, FoI response to author revealed, twenty-nine related to corporation tax, the remaining will have been VAT or other duties, but none of the transactions took place after 2003.

35 Reported to author by journalist attending the conference, December 2010.

36 David Gauke speaking at *Tax Journal* conference, 9 November 2011.

37 Answering questions at this conference, reported by attendee from UK Uncut.

38 Parliamentary answer from David Gauke, 9 March 2011; http://www.publications.parliament.uk/pa/cm201011/cmhansrd/cm110309/text/110309w0004.htm#11031010001625

39 Information provided under freedom of information laws to the author and private discussions with author. See also report by Rupert Neate, *Daily Telegraph*;

http://www.telegraph.co.uk/finance/budget/8394227/Budget-2011-George-Osborne-tries-to-woo-WPP-back-to-Britain-with-promise-of-tax-cuts.html

40 Internal Treasury email 16 March 2011, provided to author under FoI.

41 Progressive Tax Blog, 24 March 2011, 'Don't be fooled by WPP's announcement on returning to the UK'.

42 Bill Dodwell, Deloitte, *Tax Journal* web seminar, November 2011.

43 Evidence to Lords Economic Affairs Select Committee, Finance Bill Sub-Committee, 23 May 2011.

44 The tax debate prompted one tax professional to write an extremely important Progressive Tax Blog for a few months in 2011. Tax campaigner Nick Shaxson has cached the blog at http://treasureislands.org/progressive-tax-blog-reloaded/

45 'Finance Company Regime', KPMG, February 2012; http://www.kpmg.com/UK/en/WhatWeDo/Tax/Documents/finance-company-regime.pdf

46 Interview with author, 2011.

47 ARC response to GAAR proposal, 5 April 2012; http://www.fda.org.uk/Media/Union-questions-Government-stance-on-tax-avoidance.aspx

48 Webcast available at: http://www.aei.org/events/2012/09/27/uk-tax-reform-a-road-map-for-the-us/

49 Speaking at Policy Exchange seminar, 8 December 2011.

50 Adam Smith, *An Inquiry into the Nature and Causes of the Wealth of Nations* (London: 1776), Book I, Chapter XI.

51 FoI response to author, 19 April 2011.

52 The service is outlined in E&Y's website description of its tax policy development service; http://www.ey.com/UK/en/Services/Tax/Business-Tax/Tax-Policy-and-Controversy/Tax-Policy-Development

53 Finance Bill (no. 2), 1984 debate, April 1984 *Hansard*, vol. 58, columns 248–88.

54 Aon filing with Securities Exchange Commission, 13 January 2012.

55 Reported in *Private Eye*, issue 1349, September 2013.

56 Pfizer Inc directors' conference call with analysts 29 April 2014.

57 Podcast by Bill Dodwell, Deloitte, September 2011; http://www.lexisauditorium.com/theatre.aspx?c=1225&fwd=1

8. Hear No Evil, See No Evil

1 Tribunal case reported as Financial Institution v. Revenue and Customs [2006] UKSPC (16 February 2006); http://www.bailii.org/cgi-bin/markup.cgi?doc=/uk/cases/UKSPC/2006/SPC00536.html&query=fishing+and+expedition+and+bank+and+account&method=boolean The figure of £75,000 is the Revenue's estimated £1.5bn divided by the average £20,000 it found on each account it had looked at.

2 Tax Gap, 6 November 2006 update.

3 See Richard Murphy, 'The Direct Cost of Tax Havens to the UK', February 2009, which puts the figure at £8.5bn.

4 BBC News, 25 June 2007; http://news.bbc.co.uk/1/hi/business/6238918.stm.

NOTES

5 Freedom of information response to author, 28 June 2011.

6 *Panorama*, 2 February 2009; summary at http://news.bbc.co.uk/panorama/low/front_page/newsid_7856000/7856445.stm

7 The message appears to have been removed from YouTube. I accessed it from accountingweb on 17 September 2011 at http://www.accountingweb.co.uk/topic/tax/dave-hartnett-youtube

8 Joint HMRC-Liechtenstein agreement, 22 April 2009; http://www.hmrc.gov.uk/international/joint-declaration-lich.pdf

9 Tax Justice Network, 21 October 2011; http://www.taxjustice.net/cms/upload/pdf/TJN_1110_UK-Swiss_master.pdf

10 Public Accounts Committee hearing with HMRC, 28 October 2013.

11 UK-Swiss Confederation Tax Cooperation Agreeement, see http://www.hmrc.gov.uk/taxtreaties/ukswiss.htm and http://www.hmrc.gov.uk/taxtreaties/letter-hmrc.pdf

12 Treasury Select Committee, 12 September 2011.

13 US Department of Justice press release, 21 August 2009; http://www.justice.gov/opa/pr/2009/August/09-tax-831.html

14 FoI response to author from Crown Prosecution Service, 22 July 2011.

15 HMRC press release, 17 July 2012, 'Offshore tax dodger to pay back over £800k', http://hmrc.presscentre.com/Press-Releases/Offshore-tax-dodger-to-pay-back-over-800k-67d32.aspx

16 HMRC press release, 16 August 2011.

17 Full speech to Congress, 4 March 2009, reproduced at http://www.guardian.co.uk/world/2009/mar/04/gordon-brown-speech-to-congress

18 'A progress report on the jurisdictions surveyed by the OECD global forum in implementing the internationally agreed tax standard', 14 September 2011; http://www.oecd.org/dataoecd/50/0/43606256.pdf

19 FoI response to author, 15 February 2011.

20 Business Tax Forum, international sub-group, 4 February 2010; http://www.hmrc.gov.uk/businesses/inter-sub-minutes040210.pdf

21 'The Era of Bank Secrecy is Over', OECD, 26 October 2011.

22 Press notice accompanying Christian Aid and Tax Justice Network Financial Secrecy Index, 4 October 2011; http://www.christianaid.org.uk/pressoffice/pressreleases/october-2011/tax-haven-secrecy-worsening-index-reveals-0410.aspx

23 Niels Johannesen, 'The End of Bank Secrecy? An Evaluation of the G20 Tax Haven Crackdown', University of Copenhagen, Gabriel Zucman, Paris School of Economics 31 January 2012.

9. On Her Majesty's Offshore Service

1 House of Commons research paper 01/117, December 2001; http://www.parliament.uk/documents/commons/lib/research/rp2001/rp01-117.pdf, and pre-budget report November 2005, table B25.

2 Kemble Water Holdings Ltd's accounts for year ended 31 March 2011.

3 All figures from annual report for Annington Holdings plc, year ended 31 March 2011; http://annington.co.uk/uploads/assets/Annington_2011(1).pdf

NOTES

4   Peter Mandelson and Roger Liddle, *The Blair Revolution: Can New Labour Deliver*, (London: Faber & Faber, 1996).

5   Reported in *Private Eye*, issue 1102, March 2004, 'Special Report by Paul Foot, PFEye – An Idiot's Guide to the Private Finance Initiative'.

6   Octagon Healthcare Group Ltd accounts, year ended 31 December 2010.

7   Annes Gate Property plc accounts, year ended 31 December 2010.

8   Figures available from accounts of Annes Gate plc and its immediate holding company AGP Holdings (1) Ltd.

9   Accounts of Exchequer Partnership Holdings Ltd.

10 'The Refinancing of the Norfolk and Norwich PFI Hospital', Public Accounts Committee, 27 March 2006. Edward Leigh's comments on the unacceptable face of capitalism reprised Edward Heath's 1973 remarks on controversial businessman Tiny Rowland.

11 http://www.altassets.com/private-equity-knowledge-bank/industry-focus/transportationandlogistics/article/nz15009.html

12 Carillion annual report, 2009.

13 Dexter Whitfield, 'The £10bn sale of shares in PPP Companies: New source of Profits for Builders and Banks', European Services Strategy Unit, January 2011.

14 Update on PFI debt refinancing and the PFI equity market, published 15 May 2007.

15 Dexter Whitfield, 'The £10bn sale of shares in PPP Companies'.

16 HICL Infrastructure Company Ltd, annual report for year ended 31 March 2011; http://hicl.com/assets/downloads/AnnualReportandConsolidated FinancialStatementsto31Mar2011.pdf

17 Accounts for Consort Healthcare (Mid-Yorkshire) Holdings Ltd, year ended 31 December 2011.

18 'Nurses wash wards as cover for cleaners at cash-strapped hospital', *Guardian*, 30 July 2012.

19 Kathryn Cooper, 'Finance Firms Get Tax Bypass on NHS', *Sunday Times*, 2 September 2012. Confirmed by Dexter Whitfield.

20 Sum of number of schools in each PFI contract in which stake disclosed by investment fund, eliminating cases where more than one has stake.

21 PFI signed projects list published, HMT Treasury website; company websites: www.hicl.com, www.jlif.com/index.php/group_investment_portfolio/asset_breakdown/, www.3i-infrastructure.com/, www.internationalpublicpartnerships.com/assets.html

22 BIIF Holdco Ltd accounts, year ended 31 December 2009.

23 See: http://www.unison.org.uk/acrobat/b681.pdf

24 Public Accounts Committee report, 'Lessons from PFI and other Projects', September 2011; http://www.publications.parliament.uk/pa/cm201012/cmselect/cmpubacc/1201/120104.htm

25 See infrastructure plans announced in July 2012. Public schemes to be run through PFI. Treasury press notice 18 July 2012; http://www.hm-treasury.gov.uk/press_62_12.htm

26 Justine Greening, then economic secretary to the Treasury, *Hansard*, 23 June 2011, column 192WH.

27 Reported in *Private Eye*, issue no. 1362, March 2014.

28 Budget 2012 figures show £240bn on completed projects up to 2049/50, around £230bn of it in the next twenty years. Others signed but not open will take the total well over £250bn; http://www.hm-treasury.gov.uk/d/summary_document_pfi_data_march_2012.pdf

10. Poor Show

1 See, for example, 'Death and Taxes: the true toll of tax dodging', a report from Christian Aid, May 2008.

2 Speech to OECD Tax and Development Conference, 27 January 2010; http://webarchive.nationalarchives.gov.uk/20100407010852/http://www.hm-treasury.gov.uk/speech_fst_270110.htm. Timms probably meant 'profit *shifting*', not 'profit sharing'.

3 The figures and reports cited in this section are all contained in the report 'Calling Time: why SABMiller should stop dodging taxes in Africa', written by Martin Hearson and Richard Brooks, published by ActionAid, November 2010. Available online at www.actionaid.org.uk

4 Ibid.

5 Action Aid, November 2010, updated April 2012; http://www.actionaid.org.uk/doc_lib/calling_time_on_tax_avoidance.pdf

6 SABMiller annual return 2010.

7 Ibid.

8 The Singapore company is Shell Eastern Trading Pte Ltd; the Bermudan company is Shell International Trading Middle East Ltd. Hazira's turnover in the year ended 31 March 2009 was R62bn, its payment to these two companies R25bn and R6bn respectively. Data from Hazira LNG Private Limited's 2009 accounts.

9 'Tax Efficient Supply Chain Management and Transfer Pricing', presentation by Srinivasa Rao, partner, Ernst & Young, International Fiscal Association conference, 13 December 2008.

10 Matias Vernango, 'Technology, Finance and Dependency: Latin American Radical Political Economy in Retrospect', 2004, available at http://www.econ.utah.edu/activities/papers/2004_06.pdf

11 Speech by Ghanaian finance minister 23 July 2008, available at http://www.mofep.gov.gh/documents/speech230708.pdf

12 'Proposal to work with Heineken on the design and implementation of a new group purchasing company', September 2010, PricewaterhouseCoopers LLP. Downloaded from https://docs.google.com/viewer?a=v&pid=explorer&chrome=true&srcid=0B-YK4zVc_KuCODFjZjk2NDAtM2IzNy00NGE4LThmOGUtNGIzMjRmNzM1NmFj&hl=en on 23 October 2011.

13 PwC tax partner Andrew Boucher speaking on a *Tax Journal* podcast, 14 November 2011; http://www.taxjournal.com/tj/webcasts

14 The tax changes are outlined in HM Treasury's 'Corporate Tax Roadmap', published 29 November 2010; http://www.hm-treasury.gov.uk/d/corporate_tax_reform_part1a_roadmap.pdf

15 Freedom of information request by author; response 19 April 2011.

16 ActionAid submission to HM Treasury, February 2011, reported in *Financial Times*, 22 February 2011; http://www.ft.com/cms/s/0/a8e0dfbc-3dfb-11e0-99ac-00144feabdc0.html#axzz1bcoaQQtr

17 See, for example, DfID's May 2011 paper: The engine of development: the private sector and prosperity for poor people; http://www.dfid.gov.uk/Documents/publications1/Private-sector-approach-paper-May2011.pdf

18 Richard Murphy, 'A Proposed international Accounting Standard, Reporting Turnover and Tax by Location', on behalf of the Association for Accountancy and Business Affairs, 2003; see http://visar.csustan.edu/aaba/ProposedAccstd.pdf

19 Cardin-Lugar amendment to the Dodd-Frank Wall Street Reform and Consumer Protection Act, 2010.

20 'Transparency in reporting financial data by multinational corporations', a presentation at the CBT Summer Conference, July 2011. Devereux chairs a group appointed by the OECD, comprising NGOs and business, to look at country-by-country reporting. The remark appears in slides headed 'A personal view'; http://www.sbs.ox.ac.uk/centres/tax/conferences/Documents/Conf2011/Devereux%20OECD%20report%20presentation%20CBT%20Conference%20July%2011.pdf

21 Comments made on BBC Radio 4, *Decision Time*, 8 June 2011.

22 OECD, 'Report on the Transfer Pricing Aspects of Business Restructurings', 22 July 2010.

23 Obtained by author under freedom of information, 19 April 2011.

11. Called to Account

1 First used by George Osborne in his speech to the 2009 Conservative Party conference, 6 October 2009. Repeated by David Cameron in his speech on the economy, 7 June 2010.

2 The story was published in *Private Eye* in September 2010 and brought to the meeting by one of the group. The comments quoted were reported by Terry Messenger, *Islington Tribune*, 29 December 2010.

3 Treasury Select Committee, 11 March 2011, questions 159 and 176.

4 First reported in *Private Eye*, issue 1287, April 2011.

5 'Administration and Effectiveness of HMRC', Treasury Select Committee report session 2010–12, supplementary evidence submitted by HMRC June 2011.

6 Public accounts committee hearing, 7 November 2011, Qs 393,394.

7 Report by Comptroller and Auditor General on HMRC 2010/11 Annual Accounts, Part II.

8 PAC hearing, 16 November 2010; author observed Morse from press seats directly opposite the Auditor General.

9 Treasury Select Committee, 11 March 2011.

10 Case reported in *Private Eye*, issue 1341, May 2013.

11 Hartnett's comments reported by Jaimie Kaffash, *Accountancy Age*, 10 November 2011.

NOTES

12 Vanessa Houlder, *Financial Times*, 13 November 2011; http://www.ft.com/
    cms/s/0/1bd64d14-0c95-11e1-88c6-00144feabdc0.html#axzz1jc3rvSYR
13 CIOT President Anthony Thomas, speaking at CIOT AGM 17 May 2011.
14 http://www.theguardian.com/commentisfree/2013/may/28/dave-hartnett-one-
    sweetheart-deal-too-many
15 David Cameron was speaking to an audience of small businessmen and women
    in Maidenhead on 5 January 2012.
16 Nick Clegg speaking on BBC Radio 4 *Today* programme, 5 January 2012.
17 David Cameron, Maidenhead speech, 5 January 2012.
18 Figures cited in 'Being Bold', a publication from the Association of Revenue and
    Customs, September 2010, based on HMRC annual reports.
19 Chancellor George Osborne's response to high profile tax scandals in 2012 was to
    announce an additional £77m for tax investigations up to 2014/15 inclusive.

Acknowledgements

This book began with the idea that, as tax dodging hit the headlines towards the end of 2010, it would be timely to tell the story of how it became so endemic. I'm grateful for the encouragement and thoughts I received in shaping the idea from author Nick Shaxson and my *Private Eye* colleague Solomon Hughes.

In researching the book I was fortunate to have the views of some of the best tax experts around, both past HMRC staff and those from "the other side" of the tax profession. I am especially grateful for the wisdom and generosity of Tony Attwood and Simon Davis and for enlightening discussions with John Neighbour, Richard Thomas, Mike Waters, Martin Brooks (no relation), Richard Parry and Martin Hearson. Others must receive their thanks anonymously. None necessarily shares my views and certainly takes no responsibility for any mistakes, which are mine alone.

Those who have helped me on specific tax avoidance tales generally have to remain in the shadows but I can publicly thank two hacks who helped unravel Tesco's offshore schemes and thus played a vital role in getting corporate tax avoidance into the mainstream press: scourge of FIFA, Andrew Jennings, and his Swiss friend and colleague Jean-Francois Tanda.

I was privileged to chew over the history of tax avoidance with journalist Michael Gillard, whose book on the Rossminster affair I relied on heavily for my account of the episode. Again, any errors

283

ACKNOWLEDGEMENTS

that have crept into the re-telling are mine. For the earlier history of income tax, the late tax inspector Basil Sabine's 1965 "A History of Income Tax" proved equally indispensable. British Library staff were a tremendous help in unearthing nineteenth century tax reports.

My thanks go, too, to Karolina Sutton, to Mike Harpley at OneWorld for sometimes ruthless but invaluable editing and to Sean Costello for expert copyediting.

Above all, I am profoundly grateful for the support of my family, without whose forbearance the whole project would never have come to fruition.

Index

Tables are indicted by *t*, illustrations are in italics.

AA *see* Automobile Association
Aaronson, Graham 192, 193
AB Acquisitions Ltd 140
Abacus 2007–AC1: 205
Abrahams, Iain 87, 89
Abramovich, Roman 167
Absolute Returns for Kids (ARK) 155, 157
Accenture 138, 139
accountants 43, 49–50, 52, 61, 75, 144; *see also* Arthur Andersen; Deloitte; Ernst & Young; KPMG; PricewaterhouseCoopers
Accra Breweries Ltd 224, 225, 226, 229, 231, 232, 234
ActionAid 118, 224, 227, 234, 237
Addington, Henry 35
advance corporation tax (ACT) 73, 256
Africa 155, 224–7, 230
aid 10, 155, 223–4, 227, 234–5, 237; *see also* ActionAid
alcohol duty 13
Alliance Boots 139, 140, 161
amnesties 199–201, 205
Anderson, David 103

Annes Gate Property plc 213, 217
Annington Homes Ltd 211
annuities 46, 47
anti-tax avoidance measures 72, 80–1, 116, 120, 180–1, 240
    and non-domiciles 168–9
    and Vodafone 97–8, 102–3, 105
    see also general anti-avoidance rule
anti-tax lobby 30
Aon 196
Apple 138
Arcadia 18, 19, 23, 33
ARK *see* Absolute Returns for Kids
Arsenal FC 148, 150–4
Arthur Andersen 48, 49, 69, 74
Ashcroft, Michael, Lord 25, 50, 168
Asquith, Herbert 38, 39
Associated Newspapers 163
Association of Revenue and Customs 187
Association of Tax-Surveying Officers 39
AstraZeneca 131, 132, 135, 175, 179
Attlee, Clement 42
Automobile Association (AA) 140, 159

INDEX

Baah Wiredu, Kwadwo 234
Babcock & Brown 218
Bacon, Richard 244, 245
Bahamas, the 44
Bank of England 44, 45
Bank of International Settlements 208
Bank of Ireland 92
banking 65, 86, 90, 166–7, 168, 197–8
    Swiss 201–5
    and tax breaks 61
    see also Barclays Bank; HSBC; Lloyds
        TSB; Royal Bank of Scotland
Barclay brothers 165
Barclay, Stephen 244
Barclays Bank 154, 183, 197–8, 248
    and private finance initiative 214,
        215, 221
    and tax avoidance 82, 83*t*, 84–5, 86,
        87–9, 90–1
Baring, Francis 35
Barlow, Ian 187
Barnett, Joel 55–6
Barr, Robbie 99
Barry, Gareth 152
beer 224–5, 227
benefits fraud 12, 13
Benyon, Tom 52
Bergkamp, Dennis 148, 150, 151
Bermuda 44, 138, 164, 207, 228
    and Inland Revenue 20, 173, 219
Bevman Services AG 226
bilateral taxation 126, 232–3
black economy 12, 47
Blair, Tony 209
bonuses 27, 73, 75, 76–7, 78, 80
    and Barclays Bank 87
    and football 153, 154
    and Goldman Sachs 7
    and Mannesmann 95
Boots 26, 33, 79, 139–40, 141, 159, 170
    and interest payments 22
    and protests 242
    takeover of 19, 20
    see also Alliance Boots

Bord Gáis 82, 84
borrowing 41, 114, 191, 210, 212,
        214
BP 176, 178, 193
brand names 124, 126, 195, 225
Brit Insurance 189
British Empire 44, 149
British Venture Capital Association 159
British Virgin Islands 44, 207
Brown, Gordon 25, 79, 144, 154, 172,
        175, 209
    and budget deficits 78
    and capital gains tax 23, 158, 216
    and offshore accounts 165, 166, 206
    and private equity 159–60
    and private finance initiative 74,
        210, 222
    and tax avoidance 72, 85
    and Vodafone 97–8
BT 173, 182, 211
budget deficits 78, 120, 177
Busson, Arpad 'Arki' 155, 156

Cable, Vince 90, 162, 192
Cable & Wireless 175
Cadbury 141, 162, 176, 179
Cadbury Schweppes 102–3, 108–9,
        119, 175
Cameron, David 17, 25, 201, 250, 251
Campbell, Sol 152
capital allowances 60–2
capital gains tax 20, 30–1, 158, 160,
        161, 255
    avoidance of 77–8
    creation of 46, 50
    exemptions 216
    and international trade 128
    reduction of 23
Carillion 216
Carr, Jimmy 17, 41
Carter-Ruck 123
cash-in-hand 12, 47
Cayman Islands 44, 76, 89, 140, 205
    and hedge funds 143, 146

INDEX

CBI, *see* Confederation of British Industry

CFC, *see* controlled foreign companies law

Chamberlain, Austen 40

Channel Islands 40, 44, 165, 197; *see also* Guernsey; Jersey

charities 11, 49, 155–6, 157; *see also* aid

Charles I, King 36

Chartered Institute of Taxation 248

Cheshunt Overseas LLP 121

child benefits 174

China 71

Christian Aid 208, 223

Christie, Julie 43

Churchill, Winston 17

Citibank 182

City, the 63, 65, 77, 78, 160

Clarke, Kenneth 66, 144, 178

Clegg, Nick 250

Clinton, Bill 86

Clyde, James, Lord 45–6, 47

Coca-Cola 124–5

Code of Conduct (Business Taxation) Group 119

Cohen, Sir Ronald 25, 142, 159–60, 165, 166

commodity carry schemes 55, 80–1

Confederation of British Industry (CBI) 31, 168, 175, 177, 239

confidentiality laws 8, 257–8

Connors, John 105, 112, 175, 193

Conservative Party 25, 54, 144, 168

controlled foreign companies law (CFC) 65, 110–11, 120, 127, 177–8, 195–6, 236

and Boots 140

and George Osborne 189, 190

and holding companies 96, 97

and Tesco 121–2

and Vodafone 98, 103, 107–8, 112

and Walkers Crisps 131

Cook Islands 207

Corn Laws 35

corporation tax 21, 24–5, 26*t*, 30–1, 46, 123, 255

and Accenture 138

and Arcadia 18

avoidance of 78, 81, 88, 188, 251

cuts 190, 191–2

and developing world 226, 227, 228

and dividends 72–3

and football 151

and GlaxoSmithKline 134–5

and large business 32–3, 177–8

and Luxembourg 118

and private equity 159

and private finance initiative 213

and Prudential 71

and Rossminster 59

and takeovers 139–42

and Tesco 121

and Thames Water 211

and Vodafone 105

see also advance corporation tax

Court of Appeal 76, 102–3, 108, 109

court proceedings 69, 70, 82, 91–2, 122–3, 154

and Rossminster 59–60

and tax avoidance 45, 46, 50, 76

and Vodafone 103

see also tribunals; prosecution

CPC Business Services sarl 116–17

CQS 144, 146

credit card schemes 79

Credit Suisse 89

Cripps, Sir Stafford 42

Cromwell, Oliver 36

cross-border deals 95–6, 97, 98–9, 119, 228–9, 233

Cruickshank, David 106, 107, 130

Curacoa 150

currency regulation 15, 63, 64, 67–9, 71; *see also* controlled foreign currency law

Customs and Excise 13, 34, 36, 173

INDEX

Daily Mail 23, 110, 162, 163, 165, 176, 182

Dalton, Hugh 40, 109

D'Arcy, Philippa 15

Darling, Alistair 160, 161, 166

Dawes, Melanie 107, 108

De Beers 99

Debenhams 79, 140, 159

debt 41–2, 65, 192, 205, 210–11, 222
  and Boots 19, 26, 170
  and exemptions 50–1, 59–60
  and interest 139, 140–1, 213–14, 220
  and Nike 136
  and Pearson 116
  and private finance initiative 213
  and Prudential 67–8, 71
  and Rossminster 53
  and tax avoidance 27, 85, 86
  and Vodafone 97, 100, 103, 111

deficit reduction programme 21

Deloitte 76, 77, 80, 144, 146, 191, 196
  and Diageo 130
  and football 153, 154
  and Vodafone 27, 106, 112

Denning, Alfred 'Tom', Lord 45

Department for International Development 11, 237

dependency theory 231–2

derivatives 15, 66, 71–2

Deutsche Bank 76

developing world 223–40

Devereux, Prof Mike 178, 194, 239

Diageo 20, 21, 127–30, 134, 176, 229

Diamond, Bob 87, 91

direct tax 12, 13, 36, 38

Disraeli, Benjamin 35, 36

dividends 23, 31–2, 86, 177, 178–9
  and corporation tax 72–3, 107, 255
  and football 153
  and Luxembourg 94
  and Prudential 70
  stripping 45, 46, 48, 81

Dixons 25

DMGT 163, 164

Dodd, Ken 13

Dodwell, Bill 191, 196

Dorothy Perkins 18

double dip tax relief 89

double taxation agreements 232–3, 234

drugs companies 131–3, 134–5

Drummond, Jason 77

Dublin 137, 138, 181, 189
  and Barclays Bank 88, 176, 183
  and Cadbury Schweppes 102–3, 108

Duke Street Capital 161

Eady, Justice 122

economic downturns 26, 54; *see also* financial crisis

economic growth 29*t*, 30

education 10, 31

Edwards, Graham 78

EIM (United Kingdom) Ltd 156

EMAP 118

Embankment Finance Ltd (EFL) 114–5

emergency tax 41

employee benefit trust (EBT) 153

employees 30, 31, 32, 75

Enron 49, 73, 173, 212

entertainment industry 43–4

Equitable Life 73

Ernst & Young 74, 76, 77, 78–9, 87, 195
  and developing world 229, 230, 232, 240
  and Prudential 67, 68, 69–70, 71
  and Switzerland 94

European Court of Justice 102–3, 108, 119

European Economic Community (EEC) 93, 98

European Union (EU) 93, 96, 103, 114, 119, 128, 253–4
  and tax relief 141

Ewart, David 103

excess profits tax 41–2

Exchequer Partnership plc 213, 215, 218

exempt debt scheme 50–1, 59, 60

Extractive Industries Transparency Initiative 238–9

Facebook 138

Ferguson, Nicholas 160

film industry 61–2

Finance Bills 122, 193

finance branches 94–5, 96, 98

finance leasing 61, 62–3

financial crisis 26–7, 86, 158, 208, 241

financial instruments 68, 69

Financial Times 64, 111, 114, 186, 248, 249

Fink, Stanley 146–7

First World War 39, 40, 124, 233

FirstGroup 77

Foley, John 69

football 148–55

Foreign Office 27, 44, 218

formulary apportionment 238

France 162, 163, 164, 165

fraud 12, 58, 95, 173, 184, 254, 256

Frito-Lay GmbH 130–1

Frost, David 43–4, 54

FTSE100: 30, 119, 189

G20: 32, 33, 206, 207, 208

Gaitskell, Hugh 42

Gap 136–7

Gauke, David 22, 27, 33, 107, 142, *203*

and HMRC 112, 188

and offshore accounts 189–90, 193, 194

GDP, *see* gross domestic product

general anti-avoidance rule (GAAR) 192, 193

General Electric 31, 176, 194, 248

General Trust plc 163, 176, 182

Gent, Sir Christopher 95

Germany 95–6, 97, 111, 118, 120, 202

Ghana 224–6, 227, 230–2, 234–5, 236, 238

Gibraltar 70, 139, 161

Gillard, Michael 47, 49

Gladstone, William 35, 37

GlaxoSmithKline (GSK) 31, 117–18, 131–3, 134–5, 176, 178

Goldman Sachs 69, 72, 76–7, 186, 205, 250

and tax avoidance 7–8, 243–5, 246, 247–8, 257

Goldsmith, Zac 168

Google 138

government securities ('gilts') 15, 52

government, the 27, 28, 32–3, 74, 195, 237

and tax avoidance 21, 22–4, 25, 44–5

see also parliament

Grant Thornton 167

Green Book 221, 222

Green, Damian 169

Green, Philip 18, 19, 20–1, 242

Green, Stephen, Lord 204

Green, Tina 18, 179

gross domestic product (GDP) 29*t*, 120, 209, 227

Guardian 17, 121, 122–3, 127, 165, 172

and Barclays Bank 88–9, 90, 91

Guernsey 176, 211, 213, 217–18

Hague, William 25

Haji-Ioannou, Sir Stelios 18

Halford, Andy 106, 107–8

Hanson 176, 182

Harles, Guy 99

Harmsworth, Jonathan, *see* Rothermere, Jonathan Harmsworth, 4th Lord

Hartnett, Dave 81, 164, 185, 186, 188, 249

and Barclays Bank 88, 176–7

and Goldman Sachs 7, 8, 243, 244, 245

and protestors 248

and tax avoidance 74–5, 78, 79, 82, 172, 175, 190

and tax evasion 200, 201, 202, *203*, 204

and Vodafone 105, 106–7, 108, 110–11, 247

Haste, Andy 181

HBOS 92, 176, 198

Healey, Denis 45, 58, 80

and tax avoidance 54, 55–6, 57, 72

healthcare 10, 11, 31, 140; *see also* National Health Service; Norfolk and Norwich hospital

Hearson, Martin 224

hedge funds 67–8, 142–7, 156–7, 158, 159, 170

Heineken 235

Her Majesty's Revenue and Customs (HMRC) 11, 14, 171–4, 175–7, 180, 190, 256–7

and annuities 46

and AstraZeneca 132

and big business 248–9, 250

and bonuses 76

and BT 182

and corporation tax 21, 73, 245–6

and court proceedings 91–2

and Diageo 130

and dividends 31–2, 45

and expertise 185–8

and football 152, 153

and GlaxoSmithKline 133

and hedge funds 146–7

Industry Business Tax Forum 194

Large Business Service 21, 102, 171, 183, 184

and legal matters 70, 242–5, 246–7

and Lord Rothermere 164

and offshore accounts 64, 97–8

and partnerships 122

and private finance initiative 215, 219

and Prudential 69

and Public Accounts Committee 8–9

and RSA 181

and tax avoidance 15, 16, 19, 92, 181–2

and tax evasion 12, 13, 199–201, 202, 204–5

and undeclared income 198–9

and Vodafone 102, 103, 105–7, 108, 109, 110–12

High Court 51, 90, 122

Hill Samuel 92

Hintze, Michael 144

HMRC, *see* Her Majesty's Revenue and Customs

Hodge, Margaret 7, 8–9, 244, 245, 246, 247

Hodkinson, Phil 176

Hoffmann, Leonard, Lord 84, 192, 193

holding companies 94, 96–7, 99, 139, 140, 161–2, 211

Home and Overseas Voluntary Aid Services 49

Home Office 169, 213, 217, 219

House of Lords 45, 59

HSBC 175, 176, 179, 193, 198, 204–5, 207, 213

HSBC Infrastructure Company Ltd (HICL) 217–18

Hungary 121

hybrid entities 26, 86–7

image 150, 151–2, 153

IMF, *see* International Monetary Fund

immigration 169

income tax 14, 18, 119, 151, 232–3, 255

avoidance of 12, 13, 37–8

and bonuses 78, 80

introduction of 28, 34–40

and private equity 160, 161

rates of 46–7, 54

undeclared 198

India 227–8, 229

indirect tax 12, 36, 38

industry 28, 190

Industry Business Tax Forum 194, 207

inequality 25, 30, 251

inflation 64, 65

Information Commissioner 14

InfraRed Capital Partners Ltd 218

Infrastructure Investors 215, 221

Inglese, Anthony 185, 244–5

inheritance tax 163

Inland Revenue, *see* Her Majesty's Revenue and Customs

Innisfree 214

Institute for Economic Affairs 63

Institute of Directors 31

intangible assets 124, 126, 127, 150

intellectual property 127, 128, 131, 190, 225

interest 52–3, 54–5, 64, 65, 68, 133, 195

and Goldman Sachs 243–4, 247

tax-deductible 139, 140, 191, 211–12, 213

and Vodafone 109–11, 247

Internal Revenue Service (IRS) 77, 131, 133, 203, 204

International Development Select Committee 237

International Fiscal Association 229

International Monetary Fund (IMF) 54, 209

International Standard Asset Management (ISAM) 146

Interserve 216

investment management exemption 143

Ireland 121, 137–8, 253

Isle of Man 44, 84, 197

Jack, Sir David 132

Jenkins, Roger 87, 91

Jersey 40, 41, 45, 65, 76, 77, 218

and football 153

and hedge funds 144

and Pearson 64

John Laing plc 214, 216, 218, 220

Johnnie Walker 20, 127–30, 225, 229

Johnson, Joe 249

Jones, Sir Digby 239

Kilshaw, David 168

Kimble & Jones 43, 48

King's Bench 37

KKR 161, 162

Knott, Sir John 52

Kohl, Marius 113, 114, 117, 120

KPMG 77–8, 168–9, 175, 179–80, 187, 221

and corporation tax 135, 191

Kraft 141, 162, 193

Labour Party 23, 142, 159, 165–6

Lalani, Hanif 182

Lambert, Richard 168, 177

Lamont, Norman 66, 165

land tax 36, 38, 39

large businesses 33, 183–4, 190, 192, 248–9, 251

Lawson, Nigel 65, 165, 178

League of Nations 125, 126, 233

leaks 112, 113, 120, 183

Leander Productions 44

legislation 28, 40, 51, 55–6, 66, 84, 98

lending 41, 114, 116, 117–18, 133, 190

LIBOR-rigging scandal 87, 91

licensing 126–7, 132, 225

Liechtenstein 200–1, 203

Linklaters 95–6

Lloyd George, David 16, 17, 39, 40, 41, 149

Lloyds TSB 90, 92, 176, 182, 198

London model 233–4

London Underground 74

loopholes 39, 81, 160

and offshore accounts 65, 77, 96, 98, 121–2, 169

and tax avoidance 14, 16, 72, 80

INDEX

Love, Andy 243

Luxembourg 64, 70, 93–5, 113–20, 133, 138, 196
  and Africa 234
  and Barclays Bank 89
  and hedge funds 157
  and tax evasion 203, 253
  and Tesco 122
  and Vodafone 95–6, 97, 98, 99–105, 108–12, 193

McCafferty, Ian 175
McFarlane, Kenneth 154
McKinsey 173–5
Macquarie group 211
Man Capital 146
management fees 226, 227, 234, 235, 238
Manchester United FC 142, 152
Mandaric, Milan 13
Mandelson, Peter 166, 209, 211
Mannesmann 95, 97, 98, 100–2, 104, 105, 111
Mapeley Steps Ltd 20, 219
Marks & Spencer 61, 79
Marshall Plan 126
Mauritius 77, 226
Maynard, Nikki 69
Mba, Osita 249–50
media, the 57, 122–3, 151, 168, 242
Mexico model 233–4
Microsoft 137–8
Midland Bank 61
Mills, Hayley 43
Mittal, Lakshmi 165, 166, 167, 170
Monaco 13, 18–19, 64, 165, 179
monetarism 63, 65
Montserrat 207
Morgan Stanley 92
Morris, Will 194, 248
Morritt, Sir Andrew 103
Morse, Amyas 246, 247
mortgages 54, 154, 175
Moses, Sir Alan 76

Mubex 226
multinationals 80, 175–7, 188, 193, 196, 253, 255
  British 96–7, 99, 113, 127, 177–8, 182–3, 189–91
  and developing world 224, 226–30, 231, 235–6, 238, 239
  and offshore accounts 69, 71, 93–5, 125–7, 131
Murphy, Dominic 161–2
Murphy, Richard 21, 167, 238
Myners, Paul, Lord 159

National Audit Office (NAO) 187, 245–6, 247, 248, 257
National Car Parks 57
national debt 41
National Grid 176, 182
National Health Service (NHS) 11, 141
national insurance 76, 78, 80, 151, 243
Nationwide 92
Nauru 207
Netherlands, the 64, 127–8, 130, 131, 135–8, 196, 253
  and Africa 224, 227, 234
New Disclosure Opportunity 200
Nike 136
Niue 207
non-deposit schemes 53
non-domiciles 149, 151, 153–4, 156–8, 161–70, 253, 255
Norfolk and Norwich hospital 212, 214, 220
Norman, Jesse 202, 243
Northern Rock 175

O'Donnell, Sir Gus 173
OECD, *see* Organization for Economic Cooperation and Development
off-market rates 68
offshore accounts 12, 17, 22–5, 32, 44–5, 190–1, 253–4
  and Barclays 89

INDEX

and bonuses 76
and capital gains tax 77–8
and football 150, 153, 154
and Goldman Sachs 7
history of 37–8, 40
and information 206–8
and intangible assets 127
and large business 28
and Luxembourg 93–5
and non-domiciles 169
and private finance initiative
    217–20
and Rossminster 58
and RSA 181
and tax avoidance 14–15, 20, 21, 26,
    63–5, 165, 193–5
and tax evasion 204–5
and Tesco 121
undeclared 197–201
and Vodafone 8
and WPP plc 190
see also developing world; individual
    destinations
Oliver, Stephen 69, 70
openness 252–3, 254
Operation Wimbledon 58
Oracle 138
Organization for Economic
    Cooperation and Development
    (OECD) 26–7, 29*t*, 126, 206,
    208, 253
and developing world 223, 233,
    237, 238, 240
Osbourne, George 166, 189, 190, 193,
    196, 222, 241, 254
and tax avoidance 18
and tax evasion 201
outward domestication 128, 130
Oxfam 11
Oxford Centre for Business Taxation
    30, 178, 182, 194, 239

PA Consulting 76
Page, Adrienne 122

Park, Sir Andrew 51, 246, 247
parliament 8, 122, 168, 180, 242–3, 257
and banking 90–1
and income tax 34–5, 36
and tax avoidance 18, 20, 39–40
Parliamentary Select Committees 20
Parlour, Ray 152, 154, 155
patents 124, 126–7, 131, 132, 134, 224
Paul, Swaraj, Lord 165
PAYE 151
payment protection insurance (PPI) 25,
    88, 176
Pearson plc 64, 114–17, 118
Peel, Robert 35
penalties 255–6
pensions 10, 32, 39, 71, 72, 74, 159
PepsiCo 130
Perrin, Edouard 113, 114, 116, 133
Pessina, Stefano 139
Peston, Robert 140, 160, 161
PFI, *see* private finance initiative
Pfizer 138
Pitt, William, the Younger 28, 34–5, 36
Platt, David 150–1
Plummer, Ron 48–9, 50–2, 55, 56, 57,
    58, 60
poor, the 13, 38–9; *see also* developing
    world
PPI, *see* payment protection insurance
Premier League 148, 150, 154
Price, Sir Norman 54
PricewaterhouseCoopers (PwC) 70,
    74, 75, 81, 193
and Barclays Bank 89, 221
and bonuses 76, 77
and developing world 235, 236, 240
and Luxembourg 113, 114, 117–18,
    120
and Vodafone 95–6, 97, 99
Primarolo, Dawn 80, 81, 219
private equity 23, 26, 139–40, 141–2,
    147, 158–62, 170
and Barclays Bank 215
Private Eye 47, 106, 110, 122, 164, 244

private finance intiative (PFI) 74, 210,
211, 212–22
privatization 210–11
profits 31, 32, 41–2, 124, 157, 178–9
and corporation tax 73, 107
and developing world 224, 226–8,
229, 234, 236, 238–9
and international trading 125, 127,
128, 134–5
and Luxembourg 94, 97, 114,
117–18
and offshore accounts 65, 116, 184,
189, 190, 195
and partnerships 121, 122
and private finance initiative 221–2
and tax avoidance 23, 24, 39–40
project schemes 88–90
prosecution 12, 13, 204
protest movements 19, 110, 112, 165,
181, 241–2, 248
Prudential 15, 67–71, 74, 92, 176
Public Accounts Committee 110, 184,
214, 250
and Goldman Sachs 7, 9, 244, 246,
249
and private finance initiative 216,
221–2
public services 30, 31, 209, 210,
211–13, 215–20, 241–2
and tax avoidance 222
Puerto Rico 134, 135
PwC, *see* PricewaterhouseCoopers

Railtrack 74, 173
Ramsay, William 59, 70, 84, 188
Rapidwave 99, 100, 101*t*, 102
RBS, *see* Royal Bank of Scotland
Reckitt Beckinser 176
Redknapp, Harry 13
Reed Elsevier 193
Rees, Peter 57, 195
refinancing 214, 216
retrospective legislation 80–1
Reuters 137

Revenue, *see* Her Majesty's Revenue
and Customs
rich, the 13, 22–3, 25, 27, 166–7
and offshore accounts 40, 77–8
and tax cuts 28, 30
Robinson, Geoffrey 210, 212
Rolls-Royce 178
Rooker, Jeff 57
Rooney, Wayne 62, 151–2
Rossminster 48, 52–60, 62, 64, 70,
73–4, 80–2, 85, 195, 246
Rothermere, Harold Harmsworth, 1st
Lord 23
Rothermere, Jonathan Harmsworth,
4th Lord 162–4, 167, 168
Roy Tucker & Co 50
Royal Bank of Scotland (RBS) 68, 69,
72, 90, 176, 198
royalties 126–7, 195, 225, 227, 234,
235, 238
RSA 176, 180–1, 193
Rusbridger, Alan 122, 123
Russia 169

SABMiller 224, 225–7, 230, 231, 232,
238
Saga 140
Saïd Business School 30
Sainsbury 79
sanctions 254, 258
Sanger, Chris 144, 146, 195
Santander 204
Scholes, Paul 151
Second World War 41, 126
Serco 214
Sevco 153
shareholders 30–1, 85–6, 179, 239, 255
shares 31, 75, 76, 80–1, 97
Shell 176, 227–8
Simmonds & Simmonds 178
Singapore 132, 133, 134–5, 228
SIS, *see* Special Investigations Section
Sky 148
Slater, Jim 49, 51

Slater Walker 49, 50, 52
Slaughter & May 87, 89
small businesses 25, 26, 32–3, 251
Smallwood, Trevor 77
Smith, Adam 194
social welfare 10, 38–9
Sorrell, Sir Martin 189
sovereign debt crisis 65
Spain 204
Special Investigations Section (SIS)
    56–60, 62–3, 64
Spire 140
stamp duty 121
Stanhope plc 215
Starbucks 137, 184, 251–2, 254
stock market 14, 57, 71, 107–8, 217–8, 243
Strathie, Dame Leslie 246
Sullivan, John 47
Sunday Times 57, 151, 167
Supreme Court 103
sustainable investment rule 209
Swiss Re 182
Switzerland 64, 94–5, 96, 97, 138, 196
    and Africa 226, 230, 232, 234
    and Boots 139, 140, 161–2
    and hedge funds 143, 146, 156
    and tax evasion 201–5, 207, 254
    and Tesco 121, 122
    and Vodafone 98, 100–2, 104–5,
        108, 110, 193
    and Walkers Crisps 130
    and Zantac 132, 133

Tanzania 227
tax administration 36–7
tax avoidance 14–20, 25–6, 57, 80,
    182–3, 196, 242
    aggressive 74–5
    and arbitrage 85–7, 135, 235
    artificial 21–2, 48–56, 59, 77–8,
        81–2, 192, 252, 255
    and banking 43, 92
    and Barclays 82, 83t, 84–5, 86, 87–9,
        90–1

and bonuses 76–7
and the City 65–6
and corporation tax 78, 81, 188
and developing world 223–9, 240
and dividend stripping 45
and the economy 26–7
and film industry 62
and football 149–55
and government 22–5
and hedge funds 143–7, 156–7
history of 37–8, 39–40
and international trading 127–9,
    130–1, 134–8
and KPMG 179–80
and large business 28, 33, 251–2
and legislation 51, 55–6
and Luxembourg 94–5, 97, 98–100,
    99, 113–20
and non-domiciles 157–8, 163, 164,
    165, 166–70
and offshore accounts 40–1, 42,
    43–5, 253–4
and Pearson plc 114–17
and penalties 255–6, 257
and privatization 210–11
and Prudential 68–71
reviews on 172–3, 175, 176
and takeovers 139–42
and tax law 46–7
and Tesco 121–3
and Vodafone 98, 99–102, 103–13,
    241–2
    see also anti-tax avoidance measures;
        general anti-avoidance rule
tax breaks 15–16, 20, 23, 26, 48, 60–2, 177
    and big business 189, 195
    and capital gains tax 216
    and debt 192
    and interest 52–3, 54–5, 114, 116,
        118
    international 85–7, 118, 194
    and non-domiciles 161–2, 169
    and private equity 159–60
    and shares 75, 76

tax credits 12, 72

tax efficient off-market swaps (TOMS) 68, 72, 74, 80

tax efficient supply chain management 135–6, 137, 183–4, 229, 230–1, 240

tax evasion 11–14, 37, 38, 197, 198–205, 257

tax exemptions 23, 190, 236–7

Tax Gap 14, 21, 199

tax havens, *see* offshore accounts

tax information exchange agreements (TIEAs) 206, 207, 208

tax inspectors 36, 37, 39, 112, 172, 184, 198

  and developing world 237

  and HMRC 175, 176–7, 257

  and Rossminster 56–9, 74

Tax Justice Network 202, 208, 223

tax law 22, 68, 195, 252, 253, 254–5, 257–8

  anti-tax avoidance 54

  and Barclays Bank 91

  employment 75

  history of 39

  international 85–7, 65, 111, 178–9, 196

  and large business 28

  outdated 66

  and the rich 27

  and tax avoidance 14–19, 41, 46–7, 59

  and Vodafone 243, 245

  see also controlled foreign currency law

tax planning 230–2, 235, 239

tax rates 10–11, 29t, 30, 43, 46–7, 54, 251

  and dividends 32

  international 125–6, 127, 128, 130, 132–3

  and private equity 161

  and profit 159

tax relief 62–3, 69, 141, 154, 255

  corporate 54–5

  and interest 116

  and offshore accounts 165

  see also double dip tax relief

Taylor, Peter 161

Telereal Trillium 78

television 57, 242

Templeman, Sydney, Lord 15, 22

Tesco 17, 30, 176, 182, 193, 248

  and offshore accounts 25, 28, 121–3, 127

  and VAT 79

Thames Water 211

Thatcher, Margaret 57, 63, 65, 165, 210, 211

thin capitalization 140–1

Thomas, Mark 164

TIEAs, *see* tax information exchange agreements

Timms, Stephen 178, 223

tobacco duty 12, 13

Tomlin, Thomas, Lord 46, 47

TOMS, *see* tax efficient off-market swaps

Topshop 18, 242, 248

trademarks 124, 126–8, 132, 134, 190, 224, 225

Trades Union Congress (TUC) 21

transfer pricing 42, 63–4, 88, 125–6, 183–4

  and developing world 230, 237, 238

  and GlaxoSmithKline 132, 133, 134

Treasury Select Committee 7, 110, 141, 160, 243

Treasury, the 30, 78, 81, 82, 112, 178

  and large business 27–8, 190, 192

  and offshore accounts 23, 98, 169, 193

  and private finance initiative 214–15, 216, 220, 221–2

Treaty of Rome (1957) 98

Treaty of Versailles (1919) 125

tribunals 69, 70, 77–8, 92, 150, 198

INDEX

Troup, Edward 178, 186–7, 191
trust-based schemes 40–1, 43
Tucker, Roy 48, 49–54, 55, 56, 57–8, 59, 60, 89
Twitter 17, 242

UBS 76, 203
UK Uncut 19, 110, 112, 181, 242, 247–8, 251
Umunna, Chuka 243, 244
underpricing 42
unemployment 26, 141, 174, 195
United Nations Millennium Development Goals 156
United States of America 78, 85–6, 113, 114, 118, 255
  and drugs companies 131–2, 133
  and tax breaks 191
  and transfer pricing 126
  and UK trading 137–8, 194
  see also Internal Revenue Service

Value Added Tax (VAT) 12, 25, 78–9, 173
Varley, John 90
Varney, David 173, 175, 176, 180
Verwaayen, Ben 182
Vestey brothers 40–1, 42, 47, 153
Virtual Internet 77
Vodafone 27, 30, 95, 175, 193, 249, 250
  and Hartnett, Dave 182, 186, 188, 243, 245, 246–7

and offshore accounts 8, 28, 96, 97–13, 118, 120
and parliament 257
and protests 181, 241–2

Walker, Peter 49
Walkers Crisps Ltd 130–1
war finances 34–5, 36, 38, 41–2; see also First World War; Second World War
welfare state 13, 41
Westminster, Hugh Grosvenor, 2nd Duke of 46
Weston family 167
W.H. Smith 79
Whitfield, Dexter 216
Whiting, John 75, 81
Wilberforce, Richard, Lord 59, 70
William, Prince, Duke of Cambridge 155–6
Wilshere, Jack 152
Wilson, Harold 46, 47
Wimpey 57
window tax 36–7
Witty, Andrew 31
WPP plc 176, 189–90

Yes Men 31

Zambia 227
Zantac 132–3